DATE			

ry

. 1-94

INTERNATIONAL POLITICAL ECONOMY SERIES

General Editor: Timothy M. Shaw, Professor of Political Science and International
Development Studies, Dalhousie University, Nova Scotia, Canada

Titles include:

Robert Boardman
PESTICIDES IN WORLD AGRICULTURE

Inga Brandell (*editor*)
WORKERS IN THIRD-WORLD INDUSTRIALIZATION

Richard P. C. Brown
PUBLIC DEBT AND PRIVATE WEALTH

Bonnie K. Campbell (*editor*)
POLITICAL DIMENSIONS OF THE INTERNATIONAL DEBT CRISIS

Bonnie K. Campbell and John Loxley (*editors*)
STRUCTURAL ADJUSTMENT IN AFRICA

Jerker Carlsson and Timothy M. Shaw (*editors*)
NEWLY INDUSTRIALIZING COUNTRIES AND THE POLITICAL
ECONOMY OF SOUTH–SOUTH RELATIONS

David P. Forsythe (*editor*)
HUMAN RIGHTS AND DEVELOPMENT
THE UNITED NATIONS IN THE WORLD POLITICAL ECONOMY

David Glover and Ken Kusterer
SMALL FARMERS, BIG BUSINESS

William D. Graf (*editor*)
THE INTERNATIONALIZATION OF THE GERMAN POLITICAL
ECONOMY

Betty J. Harris
THE POLITICAL ECONOMY OF THE SOUTHERN AFRICAN PERIPHERY

Steven Kendall Holloway
THE ALUMINIUM MULTINATIONALS AND THE BAUXITE CARTEL

Bahgat Korany, Paul Noble and Rex Brynen (*editors*)
THE MANY FACES OF NATIONAL SECURITY IN THE ARAB WORLD

The Political Economy of the Southern African Periphery

Cottage Industries, Factories and Female Wage Labour in Swaziland Compared

Betty J. Harris

Assistant Professor of Anthropology and Women's Studies
University of Oklahoma

St. Martin's Press

First published in Great Britain 1993 by
THE MACMILLAN PRESS LTD
Houndmills, Basingstoke, Hampshire RG21 2XS
and London
Companies and representatives
throughout the world

A catalogue record for this book is available from the British Library.

ISBN 0–333–54806–X

Printed in Great Britain by
Ipswich Book Co Ltd
Ipswich, Suffolk

First published in the United States of America 1993 by
Scholarly and Reference Division,
ST. MARTIN'S PRESS, INC.,
175 Fifth Avenue,
New York, N.Y. 10010

ISBN 0–312–08471–4

Library of Congress Cataloging-in-Publication Data
Harris, Betty J., 1953–
The political economy of the southern African periphery: cottage
industries, factories, and female wage labour in Swaziland compared
/ Betty J. Harris.
p.   cm.
Includes bibliographical references and index.
ISBN 0–312–08471–4
1. Swaziland—Economic conditions.   2. Migrant labour—Swaziland.
3. Women—Employment—Swaziland.   4. Cottage industries—Swaziland.
5. Lesotho—Economic conditions—1966–   6. Migrant labour—Lesotho.
7. Women—Employment—Lesotho.   8. Cottage industries—Lesotho.
I. Title.
HC925.H38   1993
338.96887—dc20   92–12784
                                                           CIP

For my grandmother, father, mother and Ed

Contents

List of Tables and Figures

Tables

Figures

Acknowledgements

This book could not have been written without the kind and willing assistance of a number of individuals in the United States and Swaziland at various stages in the process. Dr Curtis Huff of the United States Information Service and Ms Linda Rhoad of the Council for International Exchange of Scholars were instrumental in securing my Fulbright Fellowship to Swaziland.

Mr J. Brooks Spector, as Public Affairs Officer to the US Information Service, helped me to get settled and launch my research in Swaziland. While there, I interviewed many individuals including employers, governmental officials and trade unionists and secured the permission of employers to conduct a survey of their employees. I welcomed the co-operation, input and encouragement. I also had a collegial department at the University of Swaziland at Kwaluseni enjoying the support of Ms Mamane Nxumalo and Messrs John Kabagambe, Appollo Rwomire and Raynauld Russon, Professor C. K. Brown of the Social Science Research Unit and Dr Antoni Szubarga of the Department of Statistics and Demography. Four graduating seniors did an able job of assisting me in conducting the above-mentioned country-wide survey including Ms Phindile Nkambule, Mr Dumsani Mthembu, Mr Musa Dlamini and Ms Espar Magongo. Mr Jaime Villasainta conducted a mini-survey of Matsapha Industrial Estate.

For documentary research, I received assistance from Ms Kholekele Mthethwe of the National Archives, Mr Samkele Hlope and Ms Ntombi Dlamini of the Ministry of Agriculture and Ms Lungile Simelane of the Central Statistics Library.

In the United States, I have relied heavily on the resources and services of Ms Gretchen Walsh of the African Studies Library at Boston University. At the University of Oklahoma, I have appreciated the encouragement and support of my colleague Professor Joseph Whitecotton. Having had to rely heavily on interlibrary loan in the final stages of writing the book, I was fortunate to be assisted by Mmes Shelley Arlen and Carolyn Mahin at Bizzell Library. In the typing of the final version of the manuscript, I have worked closely with the Information Processing Center in a collective effort that included Mmes Mary McClain, Donna Epperson, Susan Houck,

Teresa Greer, Carol Roberts, Linda Baker, Kim Davenport and Carmen Murray.

The editor of the Macmillan International Political Economy Series, Professor Timothy Shaw, has been demanding and patient in helping me bring the book to completion. Furthermore, the comments made by Professor Gwendolen Mikell of Georgetown University, Professor Elliott Skinner of Columbia University, and an anonymous reviewer were greatly appreciated. Professors Lina Fruzzetti, Lucile Newman and Robert Jay, all of Brown University, have provided continuing inspiration and support.

Finally, I would like to thank Edward Sankowski for his patience and support throughout the whole process.

BETTY J. HARRIS

List of Abbreviations

ANC	African National Congress
BAC	Basutoland African Congress
BCP	Basutoland Congress Party
BLS	Botswana, Lesotho, Swaziland
BNP	Basutoland National Party
CDC	Commonwealth Development Corporation
CFTU	Cape Federation of Trade Unions
CONSAS	Constellation of Southern African States
COSATU	Congress of South African Trade Unions
EC	European Community
FAO	Food and Agriculture Organisation
FSE	Federation of Swaziland Employers
GDP	Gross Domestic Product
GWU	Garment Workers' Union
IBRD	International Bank for Reconstruction and Development
IDC	Industrial Development Corporation
ILO	International Labour Organisation
IMF	International Monetary Fund
INM	Imbokodvo National Movement
LCU	Labour-intensive construction unit
LDC	Less developed country
LHM	Lesotho Handspun Mohair
LLA	Lesotho Liberation Army
LNDC	Lesotho National Development Corporation
MFA	Multi-fibre arrangement
MFP	Marematlou Freedom Party
MITC	Manzini Industrial Training Centre
NATEX	National Textile Corporation
NIC	Newly industrialising country
NIDC	National Industrial Development Corporation
NIDL	New international division of labour
NNLP	Ngwane National Liberatory Party
NRC	Native Recruiting Corporation
OAU	Organisation of African Unity
PAC	Pan-Africanist Congress
PPP	People's Participation Project

PPU	Primary production unit
PTA	Preferential Trade Area (for Eastern & Southern Africa)
RDA	Rural development area
RDAP	Rural development areas programme
SACP	South African Communist Party
SACU	Southern African Customs Union (formerly South African Customs Union)
SADCC	Southern African Development Coordination Conference
SALC	Southern African Labour Commission
SAMA	South African Manufacturers' Association
SAP	Structural adjustment programme
SATUCC	Southern African Trade Union Coordination Council
SDP	Swaziland Democratic Party
SEDCO	Swaziland Enterprise Development Corporation
SMAWU	Swaziland Manufacturing and Allied Workers Union
SNAT	Swaziland National Association of Teachers
SNC	Swazi National Council
SNL	Swazi Nation Land
SPA	Swaziland Progressive Association
SPP	Swaziland Progressive Party
TEBA	The Employment Bureau of Africa
TNC	Transnational corporation
TWIU	Textile Workers' Industrial Union
UN	United Nations
UNIDO	United Nations Industrial Development Organisation
US	United States
WID	Women in Development

1 Introduction

Women in Swaziland are experiencing unprecedented opportunities for industrial employment. Whereas previously women had been employed as casual labourers in the agricultural sector, during the 1980s, they began to participate in the rapidly-growing manufacturing sector – particularly in the textile and clothing industries. However, Swazi women approach the industrialisation process from a position of marginality. For the most part they are paid low salaries and have few fringe benefits or opportunities for upward mobility. This typifies the situation of women workers on the periphery of the world-system.

Labour migration has been an important trend in the industrialisation process in southern Africa. Since the turn of the century, Swazi men and others from throughout the region have migrated to the South African gold mines and, more recently, women have begun to move to industrial areas within the country. These two gender-related migratory trends have had an adverse effect on family structure.

South African government policy and the enactment of economic sanctions against South Africa by various Western nations and international bodies have precipitated the increased mobility of South African manufacturing industries into the southern African periphery. The textile and clothing industries have been particularly mobile. In the recipient countries, all of which are members of the Southern African Development Coordination Conference (SADCC), the labour force is not only predominantly female but also single and relatively well-educated. This book focuses on the factors motivating international mobility of South African capital, on the one hand, and the impact of textile industrialisation on the political economy of Swaziland and other SADCC states, on the other. The bulk of the research that serves as the basis for the book was collected between September 1988 and August 1989. I received funding from the Fulbright Programme and was affiliated with the Department of Sociology at the University of Swaziland.

I have concentrated my research on peripheral areas of southern Africa having previously done field research in Lesotho in 1979–80. That research focused on the migratory labour system and its impact on Lesotho's underdevelopment. While there, I had some exposure to

1

a textile-related project sponsored by an international donor agency. On a subsequent research trip to Lesotho in July 1986, I visited a number of mohair-weaving cottage industries and co-operatives, and a clothing factory. My observations at those sites provide good comparative data for the Swaziland case.

I arrived in Swaziland in a period of relative peace. During the four-year interregnum between King Sobhuza's death and the coronation of King Mswati III there had been considerable political instability, with rival factions of the royal family vying for control of the monarchy. Many of the leaders of Liqoqo, the King's traditional council, were tried and imprisoned. However, towards the end of my research, a plot was revealed which indicated that the leader of the group, Prince Mfanasibili, planned to assassinate the King.

These issues did not impede my research in the least, however. I found Swaziland to be a very open and hospitable research environment. People were happy to co-operate with me in doing participant-observation, conducting interviews, collecting documentary data and doing a nationwide survey of the textile industry. Of course, co-operation was extended with the expectation that my research would be relevant to Swaziland's development imperatives.

While conducting field research in Swaziland, I interviewed the management of textile factories and cottage industries, met civil servants who were co-ordinating handicraft projects, visited agricultural project sites that were textile-related, and toured processing plants. To gain the perspectives of textile workers, I conducted a survey of textile industries throughout the country. I included two factories in the sample that seemed representative of the textile industry. One was the only cotton-spinning factory and the other, the largest clothing factory. I did survey all known cottage industries in the country, however. Later, I had a survey conducted of all manufacturing industries in Matsapha Industrial Estate, the principal industrial estate for investment in the country. My main objective there was to determine male and female employment levels and wage differentials. Often, in research of this kind, men are neglected in the analysis, thereby leaving important questions unanswered about women workers' relative status.

Conducting field research in southern Africa for the third time within a decade, I have become even more aware of the interdisciplinary pressures facing anthropology. Previous generations of anthropologists simply embraced the structural/functional paradigm and assumed that what they observed during the period of their field research was representative of what had taken place in the past and what would recur in the future. However, for anthropologists conducting research in the post-independence period in Africa and Asia, one has to address the issue of historicism. This is not simply an acknowledgement of Third-World demands. In the context of the First World, the Third World has ceased to be the research monopoly of anthropologists and has subsequently become the domain of the historian, the sociologist, the political scientist and the economist, who may also be an indigenous scholar. This has set the tone for much theoretical and methodological debate in African studies. In response, there has been a shift in the interdisciplinary basis of anthropology from the holistic analysis of small-scale societies to an emphasis on the synthesis of specialised data gathered by members of other disciplines to establish a context for more macrocosmic social anthropological analysis.

In so far as history is concerned, we have had to recognise that a given collectivity has a history that began before the founding of the nation-state. In fact, we have to view our empirical experiences at any given time as either a continuation or a culmination of certain historical processes. For the anthropologist, a year or two in the field provides some degree of longitudinality. It behoves us to be cognisant of this and to represent it in our analysis.

There has been an increasing interest in political economy that is not confined to political science and sociology but also includes history, and, to some extent, anthropology. Thus the study of political economy may lead to more interdisciplinarity. I would argue that for anthropologists, despite our great emphasis on empiricism, aspects of core/periphery relationships have both empirical and conceptual manifestations. In this book, the political economy of textile industrialisation in Swaziland will be dealt with on conceptual and empirical levels as well as locally, regionally and globally in the context of the world-system.

In conceptualising the southern African context *vis-à-vis* cores, peripheries and semi-peripheries, some interesting relationships emerge. South Africa itself is the core of the regional economy. The economies of the independent countries of the region form peripheries to that core. However, when viewed from the international perspective, especially in relation to Europe and North America, South Africa becomes a semi-peripheral country whose economy is intermediate between that of international core countries and the peripheral countries of the region. When viewed domestically, Johannesburg is the core of the South African economy. This holds true to a more limited extent in peripheral countries, depending upon the type and variety of their economic ties to South Africa.

Swaziland is a peripheral country which in the post-independence period has maintained economic relations with South Africa and with Europe and North America. Thus it has primary periphery–semi-periphery relations with the former through the South African Customs Union (SACU) and secondary periphery–core relations with the latter. Its periphery–periphery relations are minimal, with the Southern African Development Coordination Conference functioning as a vehicle for regional integration excluding South Africa. Even as a periphery, Swaziland has its own core areas – areas of capital concentration.

Swaziland's political economy is articulated into the South African political economy because it sends a sizeable contingent of men to the South African gold mines. However, its economy has a strong monocultural tendency towards sugar production. Rapid growth in the manufacturing sector is a very recent phenomenon that taps into Swaziland's peripheral female labour pool.

Historically, South African industrialisation was quite divergent from the general pattern of European industrialisation as reflected in its emergent semi-peripheral status. In Europe, the Industrial Revolution was precipitated by textile production, followed by mining production. In the South African case, industrialisation began over a century later, and mining production there preceded textile production by nearly three decades. In the context of the southern African periphery, cottage industries were being set up as early as the late 1940s but only began to gain impetus in the 1970s and 1980s. Thus textile factories with varying degrees of mechanisation 'leap-frogged' over existing cottage industries to set up shop there.

Gold mining production for peripheral male migrants to South Africa from the southern African periphery, and textile production for peripheral females illustrates the compatibility between the international division of labour and the gender division of labour in the region. Gold mining requires fixed points of production. However, in textile production and other forms of manufacturing, the production process can be performed in a number of different settings and circumstances. Moreover, the production process in one textile industry can be fragmented and farmed out to workers in broadly-dispersed locations. Containerisation has reduced shipping time and costs. Of course, production costs are lower if factories are located in close proximity to raw materials, capital goods, labour and adequate infrastructure. South African manufacturing industries have demonstrated considerable mobility in seeking out peripheral female labour reserves. In other words, industrial development is abandoning women in the core to exploit women in the periphery.

South Africa, as the core of regional political economy, is the major arbiter of conflict both within its borders and outside them. The country's Industrial Decentralisation Policy was formulated in the early 1960s in response to the centralisation of the manufacturing industry in the Witwatersrand area, the centre of gold mining production. Since the 1880s, this area has served as a magnet for urban migration. However, with the potential for uprisings in the area's black townships, the function of decentralisation was the redirection of labour flows towards the homelands and their immediate environs. Nevertheless, it was only recently that manufacturers began to relocate in significant numbers. The urban townships of the Rand remain as burgeoning labour reserves.

Duncan Innes argues that the Anglo American Corporation, South Africa's largest mining house, has gained increasing control over the South African economy since the post-Sharpeville period in the 1960s[1]. It has not only diversified its investments in its home country, but has also made substantial investments abroad. In so far as domestic investments are concerned, Innes suggests that the pattern of investment is contributing to the rationalisation of the South African economy. This was precipitated by the mechanisation of the gold mines in the mid-1970s. Other industries followed suit, including the textile and clothing industry.

Despite the advantages to capital of having a migratory labour force, the National Union of Mineworkers has made considerable strides in organising and representing the interests of the regional labour force of black miners. Since the mines cannot change location, they can only change their recruiting patterns to eliminate those most active in union activity, and to increase mechanisation in certain aspects of the production process. The gold mining industry is attempting to absorb the black male labour surplus on the Rand by recruiting and training skilled and semi-skilled workers there. However, because the current labour force is skilled and experienced, the mining industry is gradually phasing in its new recruiting pattern. When and if this pattern of recruitment is realised, there may be devastating effects for the economies of the southern African periphery. Whereas earlier strikes focused primarily on higher pay, some of the most recent ones have focused on mine safety in conjunction with a living wage.

Prior to the implementation of limited economic sanctions against South Africa, the South African government had decided to remove protective tariffs from the textile imports thereby allowing foreign competition, especially from the Far East. In addition to the other 'push factors' for relocation, the industry was forced to face one of two alternatives – to become more capital-intensive or to relocate in peripheral areas of southern Africa, including the homelands and the 'BLS' countries (Botswana, Lesotho and Swaziland). This was coming hard on the heels of incipient trade unionism, in which workers were demanding higher wages and better working conditions. An added dimension is that the textile industry has been a predominantly female employer.

Some textile industries had already begun to relocate to the BLS countries before economic sanctions were imposed on South Africa. Because the Industrial Decentralisation Policy offers a number of attractive incentives to investors, BLS governments have found that they also have to offer incentives, although not of the same dimension as homeland incentives. However, they find themselves competing with each other to provide long tax holidays, adequate infrastructure and a low minimum wage. Homeland governments have exhibited more adamant resistance to trade union activity whereas the BLS countries, as members of the International Labour Organisation, have had to exhibit more toleration. Thus, with the imposition of sanctions, textile industrialists have had to weigh a number of factors in deciding whether to move over international borders and, if deciding favourably, which borders. A number of industries have relocated more than once since leaving South Africa.

As has been made clear from the above, there are a number of factors that contributed to the mobility of textile industries, including the following:

1. South Africa's Industrial Decentralisation Policy;
2. Pressures for mechanisation of the labour process;
3. The lifting of protective tariffs on foreign textiles;
4. Increasing trade union activity among textile workers; and
5. International economic sanctions against South Africa.

In the meantime, mining capital has invested in some of the major textile firms and is acting as a stabilising force in the industry.

Textile industrialisation in southern Africa tends to be 'sub-imperial'; that is, within the South African sphere of influence.[2] Shaw defines sub-imperialism as the organisation of a number of countries into a regional economic grouping as a result of pre-existing colonial articulation. Such a peripheral grouping may be dominated by a more privileged state with greater mineral resources, consumer markets and/or militaries. In this particular case, it is South Africa's sub-imperial relationship with its neighbours – particularly the BLS countries – that facilitates capital migration from the former to the latter.

The actors involved in capital migration are not only South African textile manufacturers but also those from the core and from other semi-peripheral and peripheral nations who invested in South Africa originally because of cheap labour, high profits and access to international markets, but who are now finding it a less attractive environment. Due to the tenor of world opinion against the apartheid regime, one would speculate that South African textile manufacturers do not have the same trajectory of investment as has been the case with core manufacturers. Furthermore, semi-peripheral and peripheral manufacturers investing in South Africa – particularly the homelands – are being forced out of their home economies by competition from core manufacturers. They would have the capital and the diplomatic access to invest in peripheral and semi-peripheral economies only.

There are generations of women exhibiting varying degrees of proletarianisation in the southern African periphery. In 1963, legislation was enacted, prohibiting women from the British Protectorates (BLS countries) from entering South Africa to work. By that time, subsistence agriculture had declined to sub-subsistence level in most areas of southern Africa. Wives of gold miners were dependent on their husbands' remittances for subsistence while other women without that access had to migrate to towns to find employment. Formal wage employment was limited to the better-educated women. Informal employment included domestic service, trading and, in some instances, prostitution.

In anthropology, a considerable literature emerged in the early- to mid-1980s on runaway shops that emanated from core countries and made subsequent relocations in peripheral countries.[3] Another facet of the literature on runaway shops is an attempt to assess the impact of multinational textile industries investing in indigenous industries of peripheral countries.[4] Moreover, it has dealt with the characteristics of the labour force and working conditions. The literature focuses on such areas as the Caribbean basin, Mexico and Brazil as well as the Philippines, and parts of South-east Asia. Parts of Mediterranean Africa have experienced increasing investment by textile manufacturers in the European Community (EC).

By discussing aspects of South African political economy as they relate to the mobility of the textile industry, I do not intend to overwhelm the analysis of the periphery by focusing on the core of the regional economy. On the one hand, to focus on Swaziland exclusively would give its economy an autonomy that it does not have in reality. On the other hand, to accord South Africa too much economic power obscures the leverage that Swaziland does have. Also, SADCC is a potential force to modify power relationships among member countries and between member countries and South Africa.

As compared to other countries in the region, Swaziland contributes a small percentage of workers to South Africa's gold mining industry. However, since Swaziland has the smallest population of the countries in the region, the fifteen to twenty thousand workers it sends to the mines annually represent thirty-six per cent of Swaziland's able-bodied male labour force and about four per cent of the total mining labour force in South Africa for the year 1986.[5]

In many peripheral countries of southern Africa, gold mining remittances have provided substantial supplements to household economies. I had thought earlier that miners' wives were the bulk of the peripheral labour reserves tapped by cottage industries and factories. However, on further enquiry, I discovered that those women and children with access to migrant remittances from husbands, fathers and brothers were among the most privileged in rural areas. Nevertheless, recent studies indicate two significant trends emerging in the last decade in mining employment that have some bearing on peripheral wage redistribution:

1. Fewer men are being employed in the mines due to increased mechanisation and different recruiting strategies; and
2. Only five per cent of males recruited in any given year are novices.

The above factors have profound implications for peripheral areas of the region. Thus it is predominantly women without access to other sources of income who are being employed by the textile industries.

Turning to Swaziland's domestic political economy, one certainly has to consider male labour in order to discuss female labour. The country's plantation economy was started around the turn of the century. However, mining production began during the 1940s. Whereas men were the principal workers in the plantation economy at its inception, women began to replace men as workers as the latter were being recruited to work in the South African gold mines during the 1920s, 1930s and 1940s.[6] However, men continued to maintain the more skilled positions in plantation agriculture. The *mining industry* developed around asbestos, coal and pig iron production; *plantation agriculture* around sugar, citrus and pineapple production.

Swaziland's recently-developed manufacturing industry has been given impetus by the international implementation of sanctions against South Africa. The manufacturing industry in Matsapha Industrial Estate has a labour force that is about seventy per cent female. Unlike the agricultural sector, in which many women are seasonal workers, women employed in the manufacturing industry are relatively more permanent workers of the industrial labour force.

H. Braverman delineates the reserve army of labour, which includes the *floating* labour reserve, where workers move from job to job in urban industrial areas; the *latent* labour reserve, in which peasants are forced to migrate to urban areas because of sub-subsistence agricultural production; and the *stagnant* labour reserve in which proletarians have no recourse to migration and have access only to casual labour.[7] Thus, *vis-à-vis* the reserve army of labour in Swaziland, seasonal labourers who remain in rural areas are members of the stagnant labour reserve; plantation migrants are members of the latent labour reserve; and factory workers are members of the floating labour reserve. The above is modified and reflects the sexual segmentation of the labour force which P. Thompson argues that Braverman has ignored.[8] The former insists that women should be viewed as members of a segmented reserve army with different dynamics from its male counterpart.

Swaziland is now faced with the problem of high youth unemployment. In a society with such a strong patriarchal bias, this has been more pronounced among males. Random visits to the offices of The Employment Bureau for Africa (TEBA), the gold mine recruiting agency, revealed scores of young men waiting to be called to work in the mines. Gangs of young men have organised themselves in the Manzini–Matsapha area for the purpose of engaging in housebreaking and car theft. Yet textile and clothing industries are moving to Swaziland in large numbers to employ women. To address apparent employment inequalities between males and females, I would argue that domestic job generation and mine labour recruitment have failed to keep pace with the high rate of population increase in Swaziland. The Fourth National Development Plan (Government of Swaziland, 1984) projected, on the basis of 1976 census figures, that by mid-1982 the ratio of unemployed persons to employed persons would be 4:1.[9] Unfortunately, no gender-based projections were indicated. In 1988–89, it appeared that women were being employed at a higher rate than male members of their cohort.

Illuminating the Swaziland case in comparison to South Africa provides a way of determining the significance of this conjuncture. Representing a cog in a sub-imperial economic system, what happens with that one cog has implications for all the rest. That makes SADCC's plans and policies of even more significance as a counter-point to South African politico-economic designs; these will be considered later, in Chapter 7. Clearly, the southern African region is characterised by a hierarchy of urban industrial cores and labour reserves. The labour reserves are being differentially exploited by gender. This has profound implications for family structure in the region and the development of future labour reserves. In the case of Swaziland, men have the possibility of employment in South Africa or within Swaziland. However, female employment options are confined to Swaziland. Nevertheless, there are vast areas of the country that are totally devoid of industry in which grassroots job creation or migration are the only options available to able-bodied adults of either sex.

It is important to illuminate the comparative dimension of my research. At the time of my original work in Lesotho, there were no South African textile factories there – only development projects orientated towards women and privately-owned weaving establishments. There was little domestic employment for men or women. Moreover, in relative terms, women were grossly underemployed or unemployed. Development organisations were viewed as the prime movers of female labour within the country. As a consequence, one finds a situation of dual dependency. On the one hand, Lesotho is heavily dependent on the migratory labour system for male employment. On the other, it is heavily dependent on donor aid. This highlights Lesotho's peripheral position *vis-à-vis* Western core areas as well as the South African semi-periphery.

Swaziland presents a different research experience from Lesotho, because of both time and circumstance. The former's economy is more dependently developed than Lesotho is because of its strong direct ties to South African capital. Throughout its existence, there has been a pronounced settler presence including Europeans and white South Africans. Until recently, settlers owned half of the land; most of the big agricultural estates are still owned by whites. Furthermore, with the emphasis on free enterprise, many expatriates have come to Swaziland to start businesses. To a considerable extent, this has stifled Swazi entrepreneurial initiative.

Furthermore, Swaziland is divergent from Lesotho politically. During the years in which Lesotho was confrontational with South Africa, Swaziland was non-confrontational. Since the military coup of 1986, Lesotho has been quieted in its opposition to apartheid. In fact, most African National Congress (ANC) refugees have been removed from the country while refugees have remained in Swaziland.

In Swaziland, I would argue, because of its traditional non-confrontational stance with respect to South Africa, there was substantial ANC activity there prior to the suspension of the armed struggle in July 1990. Furthermore, a corridor existed from Mozambique for ANC guerrillas. Granted, there were concerted efforts to squash this activity by South African security forces. Interestingly, as was not the case in Lesotho, a number of Swazi nationals were involved in ANC activity. Yet in Swaziland itself, people are discouraged from any political involvement whatsoever. I think that the ANC became more entrenched in Swaziland than it did in Lesotho. However, with the suspension of the armed struggle, provisions were made for amnesty for some political exiles.

Unlike Lesotho, where there are attempts at decentralised industrial development, most of Swaziland's development is centred on Matsapha Industrial Estate in the middleveld; only the sugar and cotton industry are located in lowveld areas (see page 83). Thus, Swazi males participate in the international migratory labour system in the gold mines of South Africa as well as in a domestic migratory labour system. Efforts towards industrial decentralisation are only just beginning. Even so, women are increasingly becoming labour migrants.

In discerning significant shifts in southern African political economy, one cannot ignore the role of donor aid allocations in the periphery. In that context, donor aid serves to foster economic and manpower development to the point where it can be exploited by capital. The most accessible capital, of course, is South African. What impact does it have on national autonomy and the economic empowerment of the population – especially women?

Southern Africa may be entering into a conjuncture in which profound social change will occur. At a 1989 conference on SADCC held in Gaberone, Botswana, much discussion centred on South Africa's increasing control of transportation, communication and trade since SADCC's formation. The view was expressed that even in the post-apartheid period, SADCC member states would expect South Africa's central position in regional political economy to continue to be modified.

Now, Namibia has become SADCC's tenth member. Because Namibia was South Africa's last buffer, this signals the eventual end of the apartheid regime. This represents the conjuncture of my research. But does this correlate with the successive conjunctures delineated in the ongoing political economy of the region? There is always some tension between the social scientist's conception of periodicity and ongoing politico-economic processes in the research setting.

In the post-transformation period, it will not be business as usual for international donor agencies. They will be called upon to contribute to the regional development process, refusal of which will be viewed as being counter-transformational. Since these agencies have begun to work with SADCC, there is the possibility of a smooth transition under SADCC's auspices. I expect SADCC to assume an even more prominent role in the post-transformation period.

The book consists of three parts, with a total of nine chapters. Part I begins with Chapter 2, which considers South Africa and southern Africa, outlining the political economy of industrial South Africa with an emphasis on the emergence of secondary industry, and particularly the textile industry. This is a critical conjuncture for gender differentiation in the South African labour force and has significant implications for the southern African periphery.

Part II, which covers Chapters 3 to 6, focuses on Swaziland. Chapter 3 provides an analysis of the Swaziland political economy *vis-à-vis* its pattern of incorporation into the regional political economy, the development of its resource base and the relationship between capital and labour in the industrialisation process. Chapter 4 examines the political economy of agricultural production in Swaziland with a consideration of the development of forward linkages into manufacturing. Chapter 5 focuses on textile employers and managers in factories and cottage industries, concentrating on the regional and global parameters of decision-making, the nature of the labour process in cottage industries and factories, and the mobilisation of female labour. Chapter 6 analyses the results of a survey conducted among female textile workers in cottage industries and factories nationwide to determine their general characteristics. The characteristics of the female labour force and their status in the reserve army of labour will be considered.

Part III, consisting of Chapters 7 to 9, provides comparisons to the Swazi case. Chapter 7 provides a comparative perspective on Lesotho, like Swaziland a former British Protectorate, to illuminate aspects of the Swazi case from an interperipheral perspective. Chapter 8 broadens the comparative framework to examine SADCC's role in providing a regional alternative to the subimperial nature of their relationship with South Africa. SADCC's role in textile industrialisation is considered as well as its possible role in mediating the relationship between development and industrialisation and the impact of structural adjustment programmes (SAPs).

Chapter 9 concludes the book by discussing the significance of textile industrialisation as manifested in cottage industries and factories in Swaziland, and its implications for women and development in Swaziland as well as in the southern African periphery. If indeed a successful transformation of the regional economy is to occur, there must be a levelling of the hierarchy of cores and peripheries through a mechanism that is rearticulative of these economic entities and redistributive of resources among them.

Part I
South and Southern Africa

2 Secondary Industrialisation in South Africa

Swaziland's industrialisation process cannot be analysed without establishing the South African semi-periphery as a context in relation to which Swaziland derives its peripheral status as well as the pace and quality of its industrialisation. After establishing the mechanisms directing South African secondary industrialisation in this chapter, I will consider the Swaziland political economy in Chapter 3. However, the relationship between core and periphery will be explored with regard to the BLS countries' relationship with South Africa via the Southern African Customs Union (SACU).

In the black African context, Swazi women are somewhat unusual in having been exposed to the industrialisation process within the country over a period of several decades. However, they share with other African women an agarian social formation with a strong emphasis on the extended family. In the domestic sphere, women perform many productive and reproductive activities. A combination of factors including head and hut taxes and extreme land expropriation led to male migration. Land expropriation has only occurred in areas of sub-Saharan African with large European settler populations. Another aspect of Swaziland's uniqueness is the intricate tie between its industrialisation and that of South Africa and Europe. One could say that industrialisation in southern Africa represents a series of permutations from the core to the semi-periphery to the periphery.

With increasing attention paid to gender, there seems to be more research done on core industrialisation than on semi-peripheral and peripheral areas. Further, more comparative research needs to be done in the core, between core and periphery, core and semi-periphery and so on. In examining contemporary gender roles in South Africa, it is evident that there has been considerable divergence between the pattern of industrialisation there and that of Europe. Some major features of European industrialisation are that it began in the late eighteenth century, and was ushered in by cottage industries that developed into factories in which the female labour component was

17

predominant. Male-dominated iron- and coal-mining production –
although having been in the background for a few centuries – began
to predominate in the mid-nineteenth century due to technological
advances in procurement and processing and the demand for the
building of railways and providing fuel, respectively. It was at the
point when European industrialisation had shifted to mechanised
mining production that South African mining industrialisation began. In fact, mining ushered in industrialisation in South Africa.

In comparing the European and South African industrial contexts,
J. Tilly and J. Scott's *Women, Work and Family*, which focuses on
England and France, provides a model for socio-historical shifts in the
gender division of labour in Europe from the eighteenth century to the
twentieth.[1] They delineate three such shifts: the family economy
spanning 1700 to 1800; the family wage economy from 1800 to 1900;
and the family consumer economy from 1900 to the present.

The organisation of the *family economy* is characterised by high
fertility and high mortality in marriage; late marriage or celibacy by
some; parental control of resources; and small-scale household organisation of production. The men engaged primarily in agricultural
production but organised their labour so that they could also be
weavers in the cottage industry centred on the household in a labour
process solely involving yarn production. Women and children
participated in earlier stages of the process by carding, combing and
spinning yarn delivered by putting-out merchants from major textile
centres. To keep a weaver working steadily, eight to ten spinners (and
carders) had to be processing within the household.[2] Young adult
women either worked in their own household or that of another family
if there was no work at home.

In early nineteenth century France, textile production became more
centralised by being moved into factories. This modified relations of
production in that males assumed more mechanised jobs and females
relatively unmechanised ones.[3] Spinning, which had traditionally been
a female-designated task, now became a male-designated task. Textile
factory production required that both women and men migrate to
centres where factories were set up. These social conditions led to the
emergence of the *family wage economy*. In this context, it was
important to produce children not for their labour within the household but for the wages they could earn. Nevertheless, fertility and
mortality remained high.

In the family wage economy, married women's work was character-
istically 'episodic and irregular' depending on whether or not the

family needed a supplemental income. When children matured to the point where they could go out to work, a child's labour would be substituted for that of the mother. The wives of miners had fewer job opportunities in mining areas. However, children were often employed there and, in some cases, young adult women. Both categories did both surface and underground work. Since husbands and children worked different shifts under filthy conditions, the married woman served as the co-ordinator of her family's activities as she budgeted family wages, prepared food and washed dirty clothing.

Mining required fixed points of production. Migration was probably motivated by a certain degree of proletarianisation in the sending area. The miner faced no restrictions in moving to a mining area with his nuclear family. However, the miner's wife would have had severely limited employment opportunities during the period of family wage economy.

Interestingly, in the European context, there was a dichotomy between mining areas and textile centres. Unlike mining, textile production was more flexible. However, the development of centres for fibre distribution and marketing actually preceded and fostered cottage industrialisation. When factories emerged, they were developed in those centres and later set up shop in more centrally-located peripheral areas.

In late-nineteenth-century Europe, there was considerable technological change that led to the growth of heavy industry and a higher scale of industrial organisation. The adult male was now the principal labour source. However, an increasing number of clerical jobs were becoming available to women. Wages increased significantly and working-class families now had a living wage. In this period, the textile industry remained a low-wage industry. As European women began abandoning the industry for clerical jobs, foreign-born women began to replace them. Furthermore, with more centralised national governments, health care improved. Couples began practising birth control and the infant and adult male mortality rate decreased. Children were more valued and better educated. Mothers would sometimes go out to work to support their child(ren)'s education or to pay for annual holidays. Tilly and Scott viewed this as representing the *family consumer economy*.

As A. Stadler describes the South African political economy, a very coercive labour system emerged with the advent of diamond and gold mining in the 1870s and 1880s that had pre-industrial precursors.[4] In more recent times, about a century later in fact, South Africa has experienced economic decline due to the high price of oil which has not been offset by substantial increases in the gold price. As a consequence, during this period, labour struggles among black workers have intensified.

Having compared South African industrialisation to European industrialisation more generally, the sections below will consider major conjunctures in the South African political economy. These sections will consider the development of mining and the South African industrial revolution in the period 1866–1901; the formation of the Union of South Africa and the emergence of secondary industry from 1902–18; the changing labour force in secondary industrialisation in the period 1919–47; the National Party's emergence and the institutionalisation of apartheid from 1948–76; the aftermath of the Soweto riots from 1977–86; and, finally, challenges to apartheid by the international community from 1987 to the present.

2.1 MINING AND THE INDUSTRIAL REVOLUTION IN SOUTH AFRICA 1866–1901

In the South African context, diamond mining in Kimberley was initiated in 1866 by teams of diggers, both black and white, hired by prospectors before it became a deep-level mining operation.[5] The conversion to deep-level mining signalled the monopolisation of capital in diamond production. Also, the compound system was introduced in which miners were confined so that they could not smuggle diamonds.

It was the discovery of gold on the Witwatersrand in 1886 that decisively shifted industrial South Africa's core to Johannesburg, where it has remained until the present time. Because South African gold is of low grade and diffusely deposited, deep-level mining was introduced early. It was investors in the diamond mining industry who had the capital to invest in the gold mining industry. However, core countries set a relatively low international price for gold, and in order to work within the limited cost structure of the industry, mining magnates kept labour costs very low. That necessitated the recruitment of black labour from throughout the region.

Labour migrants were housed under the compound system. Only a small percentage were allowed to bring their wives to the mines. For the rest, their wives and children remained in peripheral areas to reproduce the family through agricultural production. Although migrants were paid only for their own reproduction, they had to send remittances to their families because agricultural production dropped to the sub-subsistence level in peripheral areas by the 1920s and 1930s. The separation of the male worker from his family was not a feature of European mining industrialisation.

Textile production in South Africa did not begin until the turn of the century. The form of textile production that emerged was the clothing industry, in which patterns and materials were distributed to subcontractors and outworkers for cutting and assembly. This industry's emergence strongly mirrors Britain's 'second industrial revolution' in that the tailoring trade had been the precursor of fully-fledged factory production.[6] Clothing production to some extent mirrored cottage industry production because cut cloth was put-out for assembly in individual households.

Although some form of cottage industry production was introduced into the reserves in the 1930s, fibre-based cottage industries have emerged in semi-industrial form in the post-Second World War period in peripheral areas of southern Africa. However, unlike the case of the European Industrial Revolution, they seem to be isolated forms that will not portend further industrialisation. Thus, we have a situation in which the articulation of the two sectors was reversed, with mining production occurring before textile production and textile factories preceding cottage industries.

At the time that diamond and gold discoveries were made, most black 'tribal societies' were intact and engaging in subsistence agricultural production. Families of the different ethnic groups were patriarchal, living in homesteads or larger village units. The gender division of labour was such that men engaged in the heavier agricultural work such as tree-felling and ploughing and women in the lighter work such as weeding and harvesting. Children were socialised to assist their parents in performing gender-designated tasks.[7]

2.2 THE FORMATION OF THE UNION AND THE EMERGENCE OF SECONDARY INDUSTRY 1902–18

Stadler characterises the period from 1902–18 as one in which the South African state became more centralised in uniting the republics and the British colonies with the implication that pre-capitalist political structures were undermined.[8] It is also one in which the

1913 Land Act was enacted to restrict land ownership, in conjunction
with the introduction of hut and head taxes, to precipitate male
migration to the gold mines. Similar policies were implemented in
the British protectorates. In segmenting the South African labour
force, small industrialists opened factories in all provinces to employ
local labour.

Although secondary industrialisation began at the turn of the
century just before Union, the four provinces of South Africa had
developed and maintained regional political economies (see Figure
2.1). The Witwatersrand's political economy is based on mining
production with a diversified manufacturing sector. The Western
Cape's economy is based on clothing and other light manufacturing;
the Eastern Cape's on the automotive industry, mohair and wool
production, textile and clothing production and footwear; and Natal's
on sugar processing, textiles and footwear.

M. Nicol points out that capitalism was unevenly developed within
southern Africa as well as in the global context. The first capitalist
penetration into the region was represented by mercantile capital.
Cape Town, being South Africa's oldest city as well as the military,
administrative and commercial centre, has to a large extent continued
to maintain its structural position in the South African economy until
the present time. The mineral and metal exploration and exploitation
was taking place hundreds of miles away.[9] The actual transformation
of the South African economy took place on the Witwatersrand, where
the gold mining industry is based.

Regarding cores and peripheries within South Africa, there have
been substantial shifts in the South African political economy. Cape
Town was the core of the southern African political economy until the
emergence of Johannesburg as a gold mining centre in the late 1880s.
However, Cape Town was for the most part to remain the core of
textile industrialisation until the 1960s, when the Industrial Decentralisation Policy was introduced.

For more detailed consideration of secondary industrialisation,
B. Freund suggests that one should not view South Africa's economy
as having been well-integrated by the time secondary industrialisation
began.[10] From a regional perspective, he argues that there were
sectoral differences in each centre as well as differences in industrial
speciality, sources of labour recruitment, wages and cost structure.

In the Cape, British mercantile capital, commercial and mining
interests were at loggerheads with manufacturing interests over tariff
protection for incipient factories.[11] The mercantile class was heavily

23

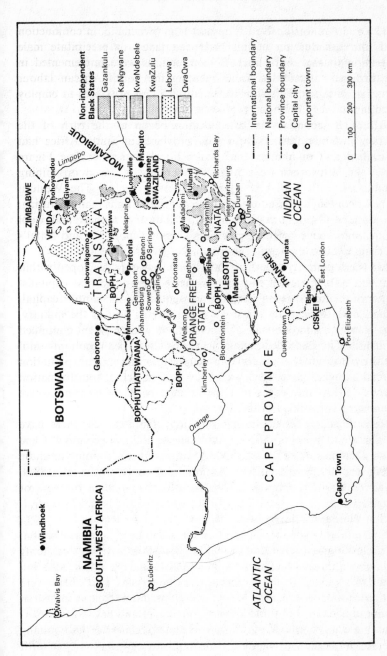

Figure 2.1 Map of Southern Africa

involved in importing British consumer goods into South Africa and did not relish clothing manufacturers engaging in import substitution. Mining magnates, A. B. Bozzolli speculates, might have been opposed to protection because in some instances they owned manufacturing firms in Britain.[12] This was exacerbated by class distinctions between members of the British mercantile class and the manufacturing class as reflected in imperial ties and social club memberships in South Africa.[13] White farmers who would have been natural allies for manufacturers on the issue of protectionism were too far removed from the latter both physically and ideologically to form a united front.[14]

A Commission of Enquiry on protectionism had been conducted in the Cape in 1883 and in Natal in 1905.[15] Just after Union in 1912, the Louis Botha government appointed a Commission of Enquiry to look into the issue nationwide.[16] However, to the dismay of manufacturers, there was a minority report that was adamantly opposed to protectionism, while the majority only half-heartedly supported it.

Nicol suggests that in response to opposition the Cape manufacturers had formed an association in 1904 to be followed by the formation of a nationwide body under the leadership of W. J. Laite in 1917.[17] The Cape Federation of Labour Unions had been formed in 1913 by Bob Stuart.[18] It collaborated very closely with the manufacturers' association to keep wages low and to quell resulting labour unrest.[19] Thus the wages of Cape garment workers remained lower than those of workers in the Transvaal.[20]

Bozzoli's dates for the formation of manufacturers' associations are earlier than those of Nicol. She suggests that the South African Manufacturers' Association (SAMA) in the Cape was founded in the 1890s and the South African National Union Industries Protection League in 1907.[21] Also, in 1907, the official journal of SAMA was founded.

The clothing industry was the last to go into factories. The first clothing factory was established in Cape Town in 1907. The first strike in a clothing factory occurred in 1917. Nevertheless, tailoring, which was under threat of extinction, managed to survive the transition.[22] Thus relations of production were transformed as factory industrialisation became entrenched. Manufacturers were aware that one of the major implications of protectionism was the formation of a large white working class composed of immigrants and proletarianised settlers that could pose labour problems.[23] However, on a note of optimism, they considered labour a potential ally for protectionism and an enlarged consumer market.[24]

In general, the clothing industry was very competitive at the turn of the century because of the low level of technology. The sewing machine had come into widespread use.[25] It was easy for manufacturers to get started in the industry. Furthermore, there was a pronounced division of labour in which different workers within the hierarchy were allocated different duties. These factors posed a number of problems for worker unionisation.

Cape Town clothing industries exhibited the following four types:

1. The retail bespoke tailor who fitted garments for individual customers who might employ assistants, or subcontract work to a middleman or directly to homeworkers;
2. The wholesale bespoke factory that used factory methods to produce garments for individuals, such as uniforms, more cheaply;
3. The wholesale ready-made factory that engaged in mass production of garments from patterns of standard sizes, to be sold to retailers or wholesale merchants; starting with the cheapest clothes and gradually improving quality; and
4. The cut, make and trim factories that cut and assembled cloth and patterns supplied by a retailer, wholesaler or ready-made factory with the production price being decided upon in advance.[26]

All four used the same technology and labour process and were seasonal, with a highly-differentiated division of labour and intense competition.[27] The size of the industry varied widely; however, workers could float from one part of the industry to another.

It was the seasonality of the industry that contributed to the existence of outworkers and small subcontractors, who often worked at home.[28] Even those in workshops often took extra work home.[29] Because of conditions in workers' homes sometimes being insanitary, however, they were viewed as posing a health problem in the spread of smallpox.[30] Slack periods would be signified by their lack of work. In regular factories, there would be slowdowns in slack periods and speed-ups in periods of high demand.

In tailoring, there was a hierarchy of workers who completed different aspects of the labour process. Although the tailor knew each stage of the labour process, most of his workers did not. Whereas women comprised the bulk of unskilled workers, men performed the skilled tasks in the factory and in tailoring.[31] Malays were heavily concentrated in tailoring.[32] Coloured women were predominantly factory workers.[33]

The Southern African Customs Union (SACU) has been at the interface between South Africa and the BLS countries and has been the key vehicle in shaping the political economies of Botswana, Lesotho and Swaziland. The original agreement was negotiated between South Africa and Britain at the time of the formation of the Union in 1910. At the time, the BLS countries were British protectorates designated for eventual incorporation into South Africa as stipulated in the South Africa Act. The rationale for the original agreement was reflective of this future possibility. Furthermore, there was an emphasis on protectionism of South African manufactured and agricultural products.

There had been a few customs union agreements that pre-dated the 1910 agreement, involving various combinations of the Boer republics, the British colonies and protectorates. These agreements allowed each territory to receive the revenue from its imports. At the time of the 1910 agreement it was assumed that the British protectorates would have stable revenues.[34]

As one can see from the perspective of the British protectorates, there were advantages and disadvantages to the SACU. The primary advantage was that they did not have to pay the cost of administration and they could export duty-free to South Africa.[35] The major disadvantage of SACU's inception was their inability to increase revenues derived from the customs pool.

With the full-scale emergence of secondary industrialisation, protective legislation was passed to ensure the sector's successful development. Restrictions were made on exports from the British protectorates to avoid their competition with South African goods. This affected mining and agriculture. However, Swaziland exported tin ore and raw gold; Bechuanaland (Botswana), gold; Basutoland (Lesotho), wool and mohair and the agricultural crops wheat, maize and sorghum exclusively to South Africa.

Clearly, this period was one in which the groundwork for secondary industrialisation was being laid. The segmentation of the labour force by race, gender and class was beginning to take shape around emerging industries. Furthermore, protectionism was being given expression through manufacturers and farmers in the form of legislation and by the Union government in the formulation of SACU. It is during the next period that secondary industrialisation became fully entrenched.

2.3 SECONDARY INDUSTRIALISATION AND A CHANGING LABOUR FORCE 1919–47

It was the Pact government elected in 1924 that passed legislation which would have a profound impact on the development of secondary industrialisation. The government was also responding to the 'poor white' problem created by Afrikaner proletarianisation in rural areas, and subsequent urban migration. State corporatism was emphasised with the nationalisation of several industries to provide employment for the Afrikaner proletariat. The Pact government also formulated a protectionist policy for industry and orientated the development of infrastructure to stimulate manufacturing.[36]

This period also experienced some rather contradictory tendencies. Despite the emergence of manufacturing, there was a concentration of power in the gold mining industry by 1932.[37] Furthermore, despite the 'poor white' problem, the emergence of the Afrikaner bourgeoisie had begun.

Blacks suffered an additional blow to their access to land for farming. The 1936 Land and Trust Act was passed, eliminating black squatting on European-owned farms. Black proletarianisation was having an impact on the gold mining industry in that the rejection rate of potential miners was increasing significantly due to their ill-health and malnutrition.[38] Mozambican labour was often substituted.

For Afrikaner women, their migration often preceded that of males. Due to partible inheritance, sons, in preference to daughters, often received parcels of land to farm. In addition, the destruction of their farms during the Boer War, soil exhaustion, frequent drought and rapid population increase contributed to land shortage among Afrikaners. As less and less land became available, young women began to migrate into urban centres in the 1920s. They were often followed by their brothers and sometimes by their fathers. These young women would send remittances from their meagre earnings to their families on the farm. Afrikaner women were the first to be employed in the textile industry on the Rand at very low wages.[39]

The Pact Government, when elected, implemented a 'civilised labour' policy in which white workers would be given preference in secondary industry. Job reservation was also practised in the mining industry. A battery of legislation was passed to give poor whites the opportunity to be upwardly mobile. Although coloured workers were to receive some dispensation under the 'civilised labour' policy, there was a substantial wage differential between them and their white counterparts.[40]

Some labour legislation was passed before the Pact Government came to power. The Regulation of Wages Act had been passed in 1918. The Factories Act, enacted in the same year, required that clothing manufacturers keep a register of their outworkers, and label goods to indicate that they had not been factory-produced.[41] In 1922, the Apprenticeship Act was passed. The Industrial Conciliation Act was passed in 1924, with the intent to establish an alliance between employers and registered white trade unions – a form of white corporatism – which stipulated the settlement of wages and conditions between manufacturers and workers.[42]

The first order of business of the Pact Government was to pass the Wage Act. Under this act, a Wage Board was set up to make wage determinations for industries in designated areas. Employers were legally bound to conform to these determinations. African workers were excluded from the Industrial Conciliation Act, whereas coloureds were included. Union membership was to conform to certain strict bureaucratic requirements.[43]

The Wage Board sought to improve working conditions in the clothing industry by prohibiting outwork, piece wages, long hours and dirty workrooms.[44] The position of the journeyman or the master tailor was that of an intermediary figure. He subcontracted for merchants and manufacturers and distributed patterns and fabric to outworkers.[45] In the Cape, the journeyman's status remained ambiguous, while in Johannesburg he was a member of the employer's association.[46] Factory industrialisation and labour legislation threatened the existence of the tailoring class. Clearly, the Wage Board was imposing uniformity in the clothing industry. The role of trade unions was to insure that workers got maximum protection under existing legislation for which manufacturers served as a deterrent.

The Wage Board also sought to regulate apprenticeships and paid annual leave, public holidays and sick leave.[47] In fact, Nicol argues that the Wage Act actually mobilised utilisation of the much neglected Industrial Conciliation Act.[48]

The Western Cape and the Witwatersrand were the two main centres for clothing manufacturing. At the end of the First World War, the former employed twice as many workers as the latter. New factories were built during the war to manufacture military uniforms when the British export trade was cut off. However, the 1920s provided a climate on the Witwatersrand that was more conducive to the expansion of the clothing industry.[49] It was then that the Witwatersrand surpassed the Cape in the number of clothing workers employed. By the Second World War, there was a total of 17 000 workers employed in the clothing industry – 8000 in the Transvaal, 6000 in Cape Town and 3000 in the Eastern Cape and Natal.

The mines, requiring a high degree of capital concentration, were a major factor in setting the tone for industrialisation on the Witwatersrand.[50] There, the mining industry generated the development of engineering and related industries. The Rand can be characterised as a high-cost regional economy. Yet, although housing costs were high, there was a vast range of wages. There was a greater need for skilled labour, with white immigrants being a major source of labour recruitment. White miners gradually began to move their families to the Rand.[51] In 1897, twelve per cent of white miners had their families living with them and, in 1912, forty-two per cent.

The fact that white wages were higher in the Witwatersrand than in the coastal areas heightened regionalism and precipitated efforts to unionise garment workers in Cape Town. In analysing class struggle in Cape Town, Nicol argues that the battery of labour legislation passed to regulate secondary industrialisation was more orientated towards industrial conditions prevailing on the Rand.[52]

The Transvaal-based Garment Workers Union (GWU) made two unsuccessful attempts to organise their Cape counterparts in 1930–1 and 1934–8.[53] At first, the GWU attempted to form a parallel union to the Cape Federation of Labour Unions (CFLU), which was considered a 'boss's' union. However, the GWU miscalculated on a strike during the Depression and left victimised workers in the lurch. On its second attempt, the GWU eventually abandoned its strategy of forming a new union instead attempting to oust the leadership of the CLFU. Here again, it was unsuccessful.

In the inter-war years, the clothing industry in the Cape employed a high percentage of young girls who still lived with their parents.[54] There was an equal number of juveniles and adult women in 1926.[55] They also invoked long periods of apprenticeship despite the fragmentation of the labour process.[56] There was some wage discrepancy between coloured and white workers in the Cape although the degree varied.[57] It was not as explicitly racial as was the case in the Transvaal. Skilled workers of both races worked together as well as unskilled workers in the clothing, food and drink sectors.[58]

Nicol observes that there was an increase in the number of women workers during the First World War, particularly black women.[59] On the eve of the Second World War, black women still outnumbered white women slightly. However, during the period, white women outnumbered black women at a ratio of 6:1 in industry throughout the country. In general, there was a rapid increase in white women workers in South African industries after 1925.

Having discussed aspects of the Cape Town clothing industry, the Witwatersrand clothing industry will be considered. In addition to discussing the organising efforts of the GWU in Cape Town, the conditions to which it was responding in the Witwatersrand will be examined. Compared to Cape Town, the Rand had a stronger emphasis on factory production, thereby playing down the role of the tailor. Moreover, factory owners employed a high percentage of Afrikaner migrant women and some 'African' men during this period.

When the GWU was formed in the early 1920s by a Latvian Jewish tailor called Solly Sachs,[60] Afrikaner women represented the nucleus of the organisation. Sachs, a Communist who had faith in the white working class, opted for separate, racially-based unions.[61] The GWU campaigned for legislation that affected the welfare of women such as maternity benefits and the construction of day-care centres.[62] Unions were the principal vehicle for social welfare protection because churches and other organisations were of no assistance.[63]

In a survey of female clothing workers on the Witwatersrand conducted in the late 1920s, H. P. Pollak attempts to discern the family obligations of single white females. She observes that women employed in the food and beverage and clothing industries were predominantly from rural areas.[64] In her sample, sixty-seven per cent of women were single and living with their parents, twenty per cent single and living with other relatives or friends and one per cent living alone. Five per cent of the sample were married and living with their husbands, and seven per cent widowed, separated or divorced. E. Brink indicates that very few women in the clothing industry were married to miners, the most highly-paid industrial workers.[65]

Single women living with their families often engaged in collective social welfare if another family member was ill and/or unemployed. This suggests that they were participating in the family wage economy.[66] The Industrial Legislation Commission recommended that women be paid wages that were two-thirds of those of their male counterparts. However, Pollak's study revealed that women were actually earning only fifty to sixty per cent of male earnings.[67] She recommended that these women be paid a family wage adequate to care for other family members who did not have access to subsistence because of 'the death of the chief breadwinner, unemployment, sickness, desertion, low wages and large families'.[68]

Afrikaner women began to be hired after white men had gone to fight in the First World War. However, instead of being ousted from the clothing industry at the end of the war, they remained because of the increasing productivity of the industry.[69] There were more white women on the Rand than women of any other racial group.[70] Half the women employed in manufacturing worked in the clothing industry. Between 1919/20 and 1922/23, there was extensive mechanisation of the clothing industry, with accompanying deskilling.[71]

Brink elaborates on the factors contributing to the emergence of the family wage economy among Afrikaner migrants. The city held an attraction because of employment opportunities and schools and other social services, which were perceived as vehicles for upward mobility.[72] However, men's wage-earning capacity decreased in urban areas while women's increased.[73] Daughters were more immediately employable than sons, who often wanted to follow specialised trades: to become furniture-makers, mechanics, plasterers, barbers, printers and tailors, which required apprenticeships.[74]

Under the terms of the Industrial Conciliation Act, black women were employees because they did not carry passes, while black men were not. Nevertheless, employers refused to distinguish between them.[75] Moreover, the Factories Act stipulated spatial segregation on the factory floor, thereby inhibiting friendships and informal networks across racial lines.[76]

Secondary industry employed African male labour from a different labour pool than did the mines. Those employed were primarily township dwellers from the Transvaal and Natal.[77] African men later joined Afrikaner women in the clothing industry in the early 1930s, to be followed by small numbers of coloured women in the mid-1930s. However, as late as 1947, African women comprised only eight per cent of the clothing workers in the Transvaal.[78] They had migrated from rural areas within South Africa as well as the British protectorates, including Swaziland.

African women who followed men into the urban centres in the 1930s engaged in beer-brewing and taking in laundry to supplement the family income.[79] However, by the 1940s, black women had become heavily involved in domestic service. In fact, they outnumbered black factory workers. Wages were initially good but later began to deteriorate when compared to industrial wages. The more stabilised white family probably precipitated the shift of black female employment from taking in laundry to domestic service.[80]

The 'civilised labour' policy had an adverse effect on black labour during the Depression, which began in South Africa in 1931. However, by the beginning of the Second World War, there was no longer a pronounced 'poor white' problem.[81] In 1945–46, due to increasing foreign investment, more than half of the industrial labour force was black.[82] Many blacks occupied jobs previously reserved for whites.[83] An ideological gap emerged between blacks and whites in the GWU as racial segregation increased in the clothing industry and in South African society as a whole.[84]

White men, who laid out and cut patterns, were the most highly-paid. White women were semi-skilled operatives who were trained on the job and lowly paid. African men were cutters, pressers and cleaners at wages slightly lower than white women.[85] Black women and men did similar kinds of work, whereas white women performed more strictly defined jobs.[86]

Natal is another area in which the textile industry emerged with a greater emphasis on cotton- and wool-spinning for the manufacture of blankets, rugs, shawls and 'kaffir' sheeting.[87] The finished products were sold to indigenous markets, unlike those in Cape Town and on the Rand.[88] The marketing area extended along the east coast from Transkei to Maputo, encompassing Transkei, Zululand and rural and urban areas of Natal.[89]

The Johannesburg-based Textile Workers' Industrial Union (TWIU), founded in 1932, was the major textile union organising workers in Durban. The TWIU conducted a number of memorable strikes in the 1930s.[90] However, as was the case with the GWU in Cape Town, the textile bosses in Natal distrusted the Rand unions.[91] The TWIU in Durban was heavily composed of Indian workers.[92]

Philip Frame, founder of a major textile conglomerate Frame, made his initial investments in African Textile Manufacturers in 1927 and Consolidated Textile Mills in 1932.[93] The first spinning mill was built by Frame in Pinetown. The investment parastatal, the Industrial Development Corporation (IDC), assisted in the development of plants in border areas to perform the following functions – felt making, wool washing, woollen weaving, knitting and rope-making and matting. In the early 1950s, Durban had only thirteen textile factories. However, by 1970, it had sixty factories and 24 508 workers as a beneficiary of the Industrial Decentralisation Policy.[94]

The composition of the textile labour force in Natal has changed significantly over time. Coloured and Indian men were employed at the industry's inception as well as African men and boys in its heavy section. In the 1930s, white women became a significant presence, although their numbers decreased in the 1940s. In the late 1940s, coloured and Indian women entered the industry, in addition to African men. It was not until the end of the 1950s that African women began to predominate. By the late 1970s, they made up seventy per cent of the labour force.[95] The peak of white worker employment due to the 'civilised labour' policy was in 1933–34 when they comprised forty-seven per cent of the textile labour force.[96]

Before concluding this period, the status of SACU will be considered *vis-à-vis* other developments in the South African political economy. In 1925, the Pact government decided to levy customs tariffs against certain classes of imports. Its aim was to protect and promote secondary industry in South Africa, with the intention that secondary industry surpass gold in export earnings.[97] The British protectorates became members of its currency exchange control unit.[98]

The legislation restricted certain imports from the protectorates, and protected agricultural produce within the country. In the 1910s and 1920s, cattle had been exported by Bechuanaland (Botswana) and Swaziland respectively.[99] Later, to restrict exports of cattle from the protectorates, the South African government imposed a minimum weight requirement that discriminated against the smaller cattle from those territories.[100]

In the 1930s, the South African government introduced controls on agricultural marketing to protect the agricultural produce of white farmers.[101] Examples of some of the producer- and government-controlled marketing boards introduced are the Dairy Industry Control, the Maize Control and the Meat Industry Control boards.[102] The marketing board was a vehicle used by the Hertzog government to pressure Britain into ceding the protectorates to South Africa.[103] S. J. Ettinger views these marketing restrictions as an indication that South Africa was willing to hurt the protectorates economically.[104]

The protectorates were purchasing consumer goods from South Africa as secondary industry got under way and consumer goods began to replace indigenously-produced items. The territories had the dual problem of revenue loss due to protective tariffs and of paying higher prices for consumer goods.[105] In 1925, a twenty-five per cent tariff was placed on cotton blankets and similar cotton cloths that made them prohibitively expensive to inhabitants of the British protectorates. Also, the sale of boots and shoes provided a situation in which the protectorates were subsidising South Africa's industrial protection policy.[106] P. M. Landell-Mills estimates that the South African industrial protection raised BLS import prices by five to ten per cent.[107]

In a customs union arrangement where there is a vast economic differential among member nations, polarisation will occur whereby industries are attracted to the most developed area(s).[108] The protectorates could expect little South African investment. However, the latter developed consumer markets in those territories. Providing an exception, Swaziland's industrialisation began towards the end of this period. This will be considered in Part II.

The period from 1919–47 can be characterised as one in which secondary industry grew substantially. However, the textile industry as a low-wage industry reserved for the employment of poor whites at the beginning of the period had a black majority by the end of the period. One also sees a consistency in South Africa's domestic racial policies and its foreign policy towards the British protectorates in which protectionism and trade quotas were key strategies. The next period is one in which apartheid reaches its apex.

2.4 THE EMERGENCE OF THE NATIONAL PARTY AND THE INSTITUTIONALISATION OF APARTHEID 1948–76

The most significant event after the Second World War was the election of the National Party. The new government embarked on a policy of fully institutionalising apartheid despite the fact that it was antithetical to metropolitan responses to African nationalism after the Second World War. It enacted a number of laws that prohibited inter-racial marriage and mixed residential areas and schools in rural and urban areas. Furthermore, strict influx control regulations were enforced to curb migration into urban areas.[109] The reserves became the foci of peasant revolt, particularly the Transkei in the 1950s.[110] Undaunted by peasant revolts, the Nationalist Government continued to phase-out labour tenancy in the mid-1960s.[111] By the 1970s, white farms were dependent on migrant labour. Manufacturing surpassed mining as the leading sector after the Second World War and provided the highest wages until the early 1970s.[112] Working-class advances were made in the early 1970s that had a spill-over effect on the black community as the mid-1970s approached. Furthermore, Johannesburg experienced some economic decline in the 1960s and 1970s because the most important new industries were being started in 'border areas' of bantustans, or homelands.[113] Moreover, the Energy Crisis in core nations precipitated recessionary trends that Stadler views as having given further impetus to black discontent.[114]

Freund attributes the fear of black predominance in the industrial labour force to the election of the National Party in 1948.[115] In the late 1940s, major industries began deskilling to avoid dependency on black labour.[116] Focusing on labour policy during the 1950s, D. Posel identifies two orientations operating to determine 'native policy'. One was the purist approach followed by Afrikaner workers, intellectuals and professionals, and the other, the practical approach followed by Afrikaner farmers, industrialists and traders. Influx control of black migration into urban areas had to be counterbalanced by the class interests of rural farmers and urban industrialists.[117] Both approaches were represented in the views of successive heads of the Department of Native Affairs including Hendrick Verwoerd.[118]

Textile industrialisation developed rapidly in the 1950s. By 1955, half the textile industries in existence had been initiated in the previous five years.[119] The Eastern Cape, however, had the largest industries. By the 1950s, those white women who remained in the textile industry were employed as supervisors.[120] The 1973 Durban strikes involved a large contingent of textile workers.[121]

The textile industry had a different labour process and experienced more technological innovation than did the clothing industry. Despite the technological lag between South Africa and highly-industrialised countries, considerable mechanisation was occurring. This resulted in deskilling and fragmentation of the labour process.[122] Mechanical looms were introduced as labour-saving devices. Because of the minuscule size of textile exports, the industry was vulnerable to recessionary trends.[123]

In the 1960s, women from the British protectorates were prohibited from entering South Africa to work. Like their female counterparts in the bantustans, they too had suffered from the decline in subsistence agricultural production to varying degrees. In most peripheral areas, there was no employment for women. Some entered South Africa illegally to act as traders and beer brewers on the Rand. Those who were not so daring performed similar tasks in their home areas in addition to making clothes, selling old clothes and engaging in traditional handicrafts.

The Tomlinson Report, published in the mid-1950s, represented an effort by the government to curb urban migration by developing the bantustans. On the one hand, the report resurrects traditional culture, identifies factors contributing to acculturation and assesses the socio-economic and political status of bantustan inhabitants while, on the other, considering strategies for economic development in mining, manufacturing and agriculture.

Observing that there were no African-owned mines in the bantustans, the Tomlinson Report considered options for exploitation of minerals located in those areas. However, there were twenty-four African-owned small-scale manufacturing industries. Furthermore, there were two million peasants or small farmers.[124] In the case of the latter, the Tomlinson Report suggested sugar cane and natural fibre production, and forestry.[125]

In relation to fibre production, South Africa ranked second to Australia in the production of merino wool and third to the United States and Turkey in the production of mohair during the 1960s.[126] Cotton production had begun on a large scale after 1948. The Industrial Development Corporation invested in one of the largest spinning, weaving and finishing cotton mills in South Africa.[127] Some synthetic fibre production had also been developed by British Nylon Spinners.[128]

The Tomlinson Report went further, to strongly recommend that clothing and textile industries be established in the bantustans. Areas of production suggested to be emphasised were as follows:

1. Men's clothing, including tailoring shops and smaller production units for shirts, trousers, coats and overalls;
2. Women's clothing, with dressmakers; and
3. Knitted clothing, including the production of socks, stockings and knitted outer garments.[129]

The Tomlinson Commission preferred that these industries be labour-intensive. Furthermore, it was recommended that the Factories Act be modified to include the bantustans and to allow women to work after 6 p.m.[130]

The Commission expressed some reluctance about encouraging the establishment of spinning mills in the bantustans because of the former's instability and competitive nature.[131] It is clear from the above that the Commission viewed these industries as an incentive for such activities as tailoring and dressmaking as well as large-scale, import-substitution industries. Another dimension to this is that government planners wanted to foster the production of cash crops and the development of industries similar to those in contiguous areas of South Africa.[132] Despite low wages, blacks were viewed as a potentially sizeable consumer market.

The Tomlinson Report encouraged private investment in the bantu-stans[133] and, at the time, suggested the possibility of funding from the International Bank for Reconstruction and Development (IBRD) or the World Bank.[134] Growth points were to be established in which there was considerable infrastructural development of hydro-electric power, roads and a transportation network. Moreover, to encourage local entrepreneurship, credit facilities and vocational training were to be provided.[135] Areas to be considered were Charlestown Location, Standerton, Ladysmith, the Transkei, and Vryburg in the Cape.

Foreign labour was also considered a problem. In 1951, according to the Tomlinson Report, there were about 215 000 foreign Africans in secondary and tertiary industry, 210 000 in agriculture and 225 000 in mining.[136] In 1952, the Native Laws Amendment Act was passed greatly curtailing the entry of foreign Africans into South Africa. In the British protectorates, they effectively prevented female migration to South Africa for employment. This was a significant step towards indigenising the black labour force.

Within the South African political economy, there were three categories of workers:

1. Urbanised workers;
2. Recent migrants intending to settle in town permanently; and,
3. Temporary or oscillating migrants.[137]

The British, as owners of more capital-intensive industries, preferred urbanised workers,[138] and the Afrikaners, migrant workers.[139] Furthermore, there was a dichotomy in preference between skilled and unskilled employment. For skilled employment, urbanised workers were preferred. For unskilled employment, a preference was expressed for migrants because they were less 'cheeky'.[140]

In relation to the reserve army of male labour, urbanised workers and migrant workers represent the floating labour reserve; and recent migrants, the latent labour reserve. Those who are unemployed in urban townships and those unemployed and prevented from leaving the bantustan because of influx control regulations would be members of the stagnant labour reserve.

The female reserve army of labour includes urbanised workers in manufacturing or service industries as members of the floating labour reserve, migrant farmworkers from the bantustans as members of the latent labour reserve, and isolated and impoverished bantustan dwellers and urban squatter settlement dwellers as members of the stagnant labour reserve.

In the clothing industry in the Transvaal, the deskilling of the labour process began almost simultaneously with black women's entry into the industry in the 1940s.[141] Many of the women were former domestic servants who found industrial employment more attractive because of higher wages.[142] Before deskilling began, women were all paid the same, and many learned all aspects of the operation.[143] With deskilling, the labour process gradually became more and more fragmented so that new workers did not know how to sew a complete garment. More fragmentation of the labour process occurred during the 1950s after the rise of the Nationalist Party to incorporate black women at lower wages. By 1951–52, half of all black women and over a quarter of white women in secondary industry were employed in the clothing industry.[144]

I. Berger views the structure of the GWU as reflective of a highly stratified South African society. She contrasts garment unions with craft unions which utilise different strategies for protecting themselves according to speciality. In the clothing industry, it was incumbent upon unions to protect their members from labour substitution and undercutting, either by organising multiracially or by artificially limiting the competition of subordinate workers.[145] This also has regional dimensions.

Because of the segmentation of the labour force by race and gender, as white women were abandoning low-wage textile employment for clerical jobs, the latter were beginning to participate in the family consumer economy and the former were entering into the family wage economy.

By the 1950s, Afrikaner women were moving out of textile employment into clerical, sales and service work. Coloured women became the predominant group, in textiles in particular and the manufacturing sector in general. African women did not enter the industry in substantial numbers until the 1950s. In 1953, all Africans were excluded from joining unions.[146]

South Africa's Industrial Decentralisation Policy, formulated in the late 1960s, was the cornerstone for deindustrialisation of urban areas, particularly the Witwatersrand. The idea, introduced in the 1930s, was initiated in the late 1950s to encourage investment in 'growth points' in border areas near the bantustans. However, the formal policy was introduced as a part of the Physical Planning Act of 1967.[147] Areas affected included the Witwatersrand, Port Elizabeth–Uitenhage, Bloemfontein and Cape Town. A year later, companies were allowed to move into the bantustans.

The former British protectorates (BLS countries) have experienced subtle changes in the dynamics of their relationships with the South African political economy. Lesotho, still a major supplier of labour to the South African gold mining industry, is the most dependent on South Africa. Botswana, with a wealth of mineral deposits, is the least dependent. However, the South African conglomerate Anglo American is exploiting its minerals in joint partnership with the Botswana government. Swaziland, intermediate between the two in terms of its dependency, has a plantation and mining economic base initiated during the colonial period. Swaziland and Botswana send far fewer male migrants to the gold mines. In the former, the number of miners recruited has been stable for many years whereas, in the latter, a programme has been set up to absorb miners into Botswana's domestic economy.

Women in these countries have been prohibited from entering South Africa for employment since 1963. With the independence of the BLS countries, more educated black women have gained access to clerical and service jobs within those countries. However, uneducated women have had to seek domestic employment or work on agricultural plantations or development projects. With the imposition of economic sanctions against South Africa, South African-based manufacturing industries have found it more attractive to invest in BLS economies than to remain in the country's urban areas or its bantustans. Although the incentives are not as attractive as those of the bantustans, there are other advantages. Investors are guaranteed a cheap female labour force, a stable political climate and access to international markets.

As the British protectorates were being granted independence in the second half of the 1960s, post-independence governments began to take stock of the negative implications of SACU for the future economic development of the BLS countries. Each country sent trained economists to renegotiate the agreement in 1969. However, just prior to negotiations, a new sales tax was introduced in South Africa which increased corporate tax and lowered rates of personal taxes for those in higher-income brackets.[148] This raised the price of South African exports to the BLS countries, thereby placing certain commodities out of the reach of the poorer people in those countries. While raising the price of South African imports, they lowered personal income tax for those at lower socio-economic levels. During negotiations, it was agreed that revenue from sales tax be placed in the common revenue pool for access by all parties.[149]

As the time for renegotiation of the SACU agreement approached, all three countries had the political will to withdraw from the customs union.[150] Botswana requested a study to determine the administrative costs necessary should it decide to withdraw. The results of the study indicated that Botswana would have an annual recurrent budget of approximately R150 000. The Botswana government would have to impose slightly higher tariffs. However, it would have a major advantage in purchasing competitively-priced goods on international markets.[151]

One way in which the BLS countries could have been disadvantaged by a withdrawal was if South Africa had decided to bar them from participating in that country's agricultural marketing schemes, to which they contribute small quantities of commodities including wool, mohair, maize and sugar.[152] However, South Africa tempered its harshness in order to project a more accommodating image to the international community.

The renegotiated agreement was more satisfactory to the BLS countries than the original agreement had been. It made provision for an eight-year infant industry protection, duty-free imports for United Nations agencies, non-discrimination in transport charges, and a more equitable marketing arrangement.[153] Most importantly, the BLS countries each received a higher percentage of revenue from the customs pool as compensation for their disadvantaged position with regard to their highly-industrialised neighbour. The Customs Union Commission was set up to represent all four parties and to meet regularly to discuss issues of common concern.[154] Nevertheless, this was not of the same magnitude as the European Community for supranational planning, despite attempts to consider potentially integrative projects.[155]

Infant industry protection allowed for some industrial development in the BLS countries. However, such industries could not survive too far beyond the eight-year period if the companies' average costs were not below those of their South African counterparts.[156] In addition, the BLS countries were entitled to charge an extra tariff against South African goods if they so chose.[157] Because the customs union could now extend protection to BLS industries, it functioned in much the same way as the Board of Industry and Trade whose function was to consider requests for protection by domestic industries.[158] Import restrictions could be imposed by any member country 'for economic, social, cultural or other reasons'.[159] However, the type of industry provided for in the 1969 renegotiation was primarily for export-processing rather than import-substitution.[160] Furthermore, designated bantustans and 'border areas' were given preferential treatment in the transport of consumer goods to urban markets at lower prices.[161]

The geopolitics of the region shifted a few times during the existence of the SACU. The independence of the BLS countries in the second half of 1960s was an isolated phenomenon for that period. The decolonisation process emanating from the North had come to a grinding halt when Ian Smith made the Unilateral Declaration of Independence in Southern Rhodesia (Zimbabwe). All three BLS countries shared a border with the minority-ruled Republic of South Africa. In addition, Botswana shared a border with Southern Rhodesia and South West Africa (Namibia); Swaziland with Portuguese-dominated Mozambique; and Lesotho, in its unique position, was totally surrounded by South Africa. This made the BLS countries very dependent on South African infrastructure.

In the area of infrastructural development, South Africa expressed its designs on the BLS countries. In 1919, Prime Minister Louis Botha considered building a railroad through Swaziland as soon as it was incorporated into the Union.[162] In the post-independence period, when Botswana planned to construct a road to Nata in the North for a ferry link to Zambia, South Africa intervened without success.[163]

South Africa has managed to monopolise water resources in the region by building hydroelectric facilities on major rivers that flow into the BLS countries. They have nineteen dams on the Limpopo and Molopo rivers between South Africa and Botswana and five dams on Komati and other rivers flowing through Swaziland.[164] South African farmers can meet their irrigation needs at the expense of their BLS counterparts. The source of the Orange River lies in the mountains of Lesotho. Originally, considering developing the Oxbow project, the South African government decided against this and built a dam on the South African side of the border because it did not want to be dependent on Lesotho.[165]

In relation to the development of import-substitution industries, South Africa made several attempts to thwart the efforts of the BLS countries to introduce industries of that type. Unsuccessful attempts were made to stop the development of a maize mill in Lesotho and a

fertiliser factory in Swaziland.[166] Swaziland successfully surged ahead
with its plans to start Swaziland Chemical Industries. Lesotho
eventually started its own maize mill. However, there were restrictions
on exports to South Africa. Import-substitution industries had to be
viable in the individual BLS markets in order to survive.

The South African banking system was controlled by two British
banks – Barclays and Standard – whose headquarters for the whole of
southern Africa were in Johannesburg. These banks are the major
banks in the BLS countries as well. Not only did the four customs
union members share the same banking system but they also shared
the same currency. During periods of political instability as in the early
1960s, the South African government made efforts to control capital
outflows internationally but only in narrowly-defined cases in relation
to the BLS countries. At the time of the 1969 renegotiation, all three
countries circulated the South African rand. Ettinger argues that the
circulation of the rand in these countries had the effect of giving South
Africa an interest-free loan.[167] Furthermore, in his view, it impeded
national consciousness and inhibited data-gathering on international
transactions since there is no currency exchange within the Rand
Monetary Area.

Ettinger considers the pattern of South African investment into the
BLS countries to be concentrated in the mining and agricultural
sectors.[168] Anglo American Corporation has investments in mining
industries in all three countries. It has investments in a copper-nickel
mine in Botswana, a coal mine in Swaziland, and, in the 1970s, had
investments in a diamond mine in Lesotho. In agriculture, the South
African conglomerate has investments in Swaziland's timber industry.

Viewing blacks as permanent members of the South African labour
force, the government devised ways of rationalising their segmentation
so as not to be overwhelmed by the black majority. Stricter influx
control regulations gave more definition to the bantustans. Deskilling
in manufacturing and mining led to less dependency on black labour in
urban areas.

For the BLS countries, only contracted male labour was allowed to
work in South Africa. Females formed a separate reserve in those
countries while their black South African counterparts languished in
the bantustans. The renegotiation of the SACU agreement gave the
BLS countries only slightly more space in which to strategise their
development, with South Africa maintaining their dependency. The
next period is a more transitional period in the South African political
economy.

2.5 THE AFTERMATH OF THE SOWETO RIOTS 1977–86

The Soweto riots had a profound effect on the South African political economy. The South African Government was to spend the next decade improving its security apparatus in an effort to try to control the discontented black majority.[169] Then Prime Minister P. W. Botha initiated reforms from above to reach some middle ground against the backdrop of an African National Congress (ANC) guerrilla build-up.[170] He sought more political rights for urban blacks and stricter influx control to segment the urban labour reserve more fully from their bantustan counterparts.[171] However, in the 1983 constitutional changes that provided for a tricameral Parliament, 'Africans' were excluded from political representation. Also the constitution redefined the office of president and concentrated more power in that office.[172] For working-class whites, this conjuncture has signalled the curbing of their upward mobility.[173]

In the 1980s, with coloured women having occupied positions vacated by Afrikaner women, there is evidence that they are now being absorbed into clerical, sales and service work. Black females, being relative latecomers to the industry, entered the lowest rungs of employment at the time that it was mechanising and deskilling. In 1982, black female industrial employment was estimated at 12.8 per cent, with the bulk of the work being in textiles and food processing.

Until recently, domestic service was still the predominant sector. Its decline is documented as follows:

1946 – 93.1%
1960 – 85.9%
1970 – 71.4%
1980 – 33.0%

In addition, 18.68 per cent of African women work in the agricultural sector.[174] However, many of these women are domestics on white-owned farms. Only forty-three per cent of black South African women live outside the bantustans.

As a direct result of the South African Industrial Decentralisation Policy implemented in the mid-1960s, textile and other manufacturing industries were granted incentives to relocate from the Johannesburg area to other areas of South Africa preferably on the borders of the bantustans. Under those circumstances, textile industrialists employed a highly segmented labour force that included Indian males, black males and females, and migrants and non-migrants. There is a significant pay and benefit differential between management and workers, representing the dichotomy between blacks and whites as well as between males and females.

In various instances, black women in the bantustans, single and married, have had to migrate to industrial growth points leaving children behind with mothers and mothers-in-law. This has been documented in the Transkei.[175] These women are paid even lower wages than women in the industrial centres of South Africa because of the fragmentation of the labour process, the deskilling of jobs and the surplus of female labour in the bantustans.

Neither men nor women have reacted passively to exploitation by the mining and manufacturing industries. Based on the recommendations of the Wiehahn Commission in the late 1970s, blacks were permitted to form trade unions. One of the most powerful unions is the National Union of Mineworkers. Also, a variety of textile unions have been formed in which women are active. The Congress of South African Trade Unions is an umbrella organisation that is pro-ANC.

In 1982, a revised plan for the Industrial Decentralisation Policy was made whereby the functional regions were carved out that cross-cut bantustan borders to more adequately address their development needs. Included was a package for longer-term capital assistance, the payment of short-term incentives in cash and the establishment of the Development Bank of Southern Africa.[176] Simultaneously, indirect disincentives remained in force in urban areas. Although P. Wellings and A. Black foresee an acceleration of industrial decentralisation, they do not view the process as fostering economic development in the homelands.[177] Growth points outside the reserves would include East London, Ladysmith, Pietermaritzburg and Atlantis. Those in the reserves include Dimbaza in Ciskei, Isithebe in KwaZulu, Butterworth in Transkei and Babelegi in Bophuthatswana.[178]

In the manufacturing sector, the clothing and textile industry experienced considerable contraction between 1968 and 1978 which Wellings and Black attribute to the passage of the act.[179] Textile jobs are the cheapest to establish.[180] In addition to the job loss suffered as a result of industrial decentralisation, there was additional job loss due to increasing capital intensity. Since no urban area in Natal was slated for industrial decentralisation that province became a recipient of a heavy concentration of manufacturing industries.[181]

Nevertheless, according to Wellings and Black, industrialists were not keen on the Industrial Decentralisation Policy.[182] They suggest that industrialists would have preferred 'deconcentration' to decentralisation. Of course, a cheap and plentiful labour supply was a major motivation for industrial decentralisation.[183]

Wellings and Black further argue that decentralisation was not profitable and they attribute the policy's failure to this.[184] Moreover, South Africa's manufacturing sector had not been competitive on international markets or in capital goods production for regional markets even during the 1960s boom. Also, South African goods had become vulnerable to foreign competition in the home market.[185]

The advantage that the homelands offered investors was that black workers, although less skilled, had no protective legislation.[186] Thus working hours were longer and wages were half of those in urban areas. Furthermore, because women have been more confined to the homelands due to limited access to employment in urban centres, they were perceived as a more reliable labour supply. Men, after receiving training at the employer's expense, could use it as a stepping stone to urban labour markets.[187]

Foreign investment was encouraged in the homelands. Fifty-two per cent of jobs generated were due to Taiwanese investment.[188] Furthermore, the latter's investments in the Transkei and the Ciskei accounted for half of all clothing exports.[189]

The impact of a 'decentralising' industry on a homeland area has a number of dimensions. Blacks are generally excluded from professional or managerial positions. However, it is difficult to attract white managerial staff from the urban areas.[190] Furthermore, whites often feel uncomfortable living in predominantly black areas. Another dimension is the dichotomy between capital-intensive and labour-intensive jobs.[191] The former tend to remain in urban areas and in originally-established growth points; the latter, in the homelands proper.[192] As a final dimension, there is very little vertical or horizontal integration among industries in areas of relocation.[193]

T. Bell postulates a different interpretation of the forces portending industrial decentralisation. He views the process as being spontaneous responses to the market during the 1960s and 1970s in which there was a gradual relocation from core areas in South Africa to semi-peripheral areas and, finally, to peripheral areas.[194] The Witwatersrand was still considered the core.

Placing these phenomena in global perspective, there was a shift in textile production from Western Europe and North America to Japan and the less developed countries (LDCs) between 1960 and 1968. Bell does concede that the Physical Planning Act was the first precipitating factor, in the 1960s.[195] Manufacturing industries had undergone approximately thirty years of primary industrialisation before relocating.[196] The first step in migration was to the Cape in the mid-1960s and second to the South African periphery in the early 1970s. Bell makes a distinction between Durban–Pinetown in its close proximity to Kwa-Zulu as a semi-periphery, and Cape Town, where the nearest homeland is six hundred miles away, as having intermediate status between core and semi-periphery.

Bell suggests that the period in which decentralisation began was one characterised by global recession. South Africa's manufacturing industry was undergoing decline at the time.[197] Economic growth in the manufacturing sector was lower than in the LDCs making its manufacturing behaviour intermediate between the LDCs and developed market economies in general. Furthermore, influx control into urban areas did not undergo any significant changes during the period.[198] His view is that competition from exports precipitated the relocation of clothing and textile industries.[199] Thus, Bell's argument for intensified international competition as a primary factor in precipitating industrial decentralisation is reinforced. He observes that there was negative import-substitution in textile processing functions such as wool scouring, cotton ginning and the dyeing of wool, cotton and cloth, while other sectors experienced some import-substitution.[200]

There has been a third step in industrial relocation in which manufacturing industries began moving to international peripheries instead of confining their movements to the South African homelands. This involves the relocation of industries to the BLS countries. Although economic sanctions against South Africa have been a contributing factor to the continuation of this process, one has to examine how the political economies of South Africa and the BLS countries interrelate.

In the early 1980s, South Africa began to develop trade ties with Newly Industrialising Countries (NICs) in Asia including Taiwan.[201] The latter is a major textile producer that has been suffering from diplomatic isolation since the People's Republic of China gained international recognition in the mid-1970s. Newly industrialising Taiwanese firms began investing in the homelands taking advantage of incentives provided for industrial decentralisation and the encouragement of homeland leaders. Most of their industries produce textiles, clothing and footwear.[202]

The major impetus for the relocation of Taiwanese textile industries is the export restrictions they face under the Multi-Fibre Arrangement (MFA).[203] In many of their South African operations, they would limit the production process to finishing and labelling to qualify goods as being of South African manufacture. Prior to 1985, the United States had been a major market for Taiwanese-produced South African textiles. However, in that year, just prior to the enactment of sanctions legislation, the United States tightened its MFA restrictions. In response to these restrictions, they have targeted new markets in Canada, Europe and South Africa. In the case of the latter, they are competing with domestically-produced textiles.

The decentralisation incentives offered by the South African government are as follows:

- subsidies of up to seventy per cent of interest on the cost of land and building;
- up to five hundred thousand rand for relocation expenses;
- up to a sixty per cent rebate on transport expenses;
- price preference of up to ten per cent from government tenders; and
- the payment of wages of up to R110 for each worker per month for seven years.[204]

These incentives would be attractive to any foreign investor.

Taiwanese industries in the homelands have sometimes set up bogus operations to defraud the South African government.[205] Furthermore, in the homelands, Taiwanese firms are operating in an atmosphere of rampant corruption. Relocating from Taiwan where trade unions are illegal, Taiwanese industrialists are intolerant of them in the homelands. These industries import materials, equipment and spare parts thereby establishing neither forward nor backward linkages. J. Pickles and J. Woods argue that Taiwanese investments in the homelands assist in keeping apartheid entrenched.[206]

2.6 WHITHER THE TRANSFORMATION TO A POST-APARTHEID STATE 1987–PRESENT

South Africa has entered a new phase in its regulation of the African masses. It had responded in bellicose fashion to the SouthWest African People's Organisation and Cuban troops in Angola and to domestic challenges to its hegemony in a variety of forms. The imposition of sanctions against South Africa by a number of countries and international bodies in 1986 resulted in the unprecedented flow of South African-based manufacturing industries into the non-South African periphery. These industries are tapping into the female reserve army of labour defined by its inability to participate in the South African labour market, while men from these areas still migrate to gold mines in large numbers.

Student-led rebellion broke out in 1976 and 1980 in Soweto and other townships in South Africa, initially focusing on the issue of unequal education for non-white racial groups, but later broadened to encompass other manifestations of inequality in South African society. Urban resistance was to re-emerge with a vengeance in 1984, not abating until 1987. Under the State of Emergency, which had been renewed in 1989 but has since been partially lifted, civil liberties had been greatly circumscribed and press curbs strictly enforced.

A number of events in southern Africa earlier in 1989 anticipated the changes that were to sweep Eastern Europe later that year. In the case of Namibian independence, the Soviets and the Cubans negotiated with the United States and South Africa to find a peaceful solution. Because South Africa had tied the removal of its troops from Namibia to the removal of Cuban troops from Angola, both countries were given a timetable for gradual withdrawal of troops. South Africa was able to negotiate the removal of the ANC's military presence from Angola. Furthermore, the FRELIMO government in Mozambique decided in its annual party congress to allow free enterprise in certain sectors of the economy. Thus, the South African government has engaged in a combination of destabilisation and economic co-optation, throughout the region utilising the South African Police, the army and/or proxy guerrilla groups in conjunction with the structural adjustment programmes of the IMF and World Bank.

After the conclusion of UN-sponsored negotiations for Namibian independence, it was suggested that the Soviet Union had discouraged the ANC from continuing armed struggle against the apartheid regime.[207] However, an opposing view was presented in Sechaba, the official organ of the ANC.[208] In any event, the stage was being set for a negotiated settlement in South Africa. Soviet President Mikhail Gorbachev's implementation of *glasnost* and *perestroika* has seemingly brought the Cold War to an end. Now, it is theoretically possible that the West will be able to purchase several strategic metals and minerals from the Soviet Union which were previously available only in South Africa. South Africa not only perceived itself as the only source of strategic minerals and metals but also the bulwark against Communism in southern Africa. I would suggest that South Africa's changed status is one factor that has brought it to the negotiating table. Other factors, of course, are civil unrest, guerrilla warfare, economic recession and international economic sanctions.

Nelson Mandela's release from prison in early 1990 has precipitated a new phase in the transformation process – one considered impossible until the time of its actual occurrence. Mandela has been released to negotiate a new social order in South Africa with the De Klerk government. There have been great expectations of his ability to unify blacks and negotiate with whites, expectations that in some instances are too high. Gatsha Buthelezi has organised members of Inkatha into violent conflict against ANC supporters in an effort to become directly involved in the negotiations. Furthermore, allegations abound of police assistance to Inkatha. The police, to a large extent, tend to oppose De Klerk's efforts to negotiate with the ANC. What has probably strengthened the ANC's hand most is the Pan-Africanist Congress's decision to enter into negotiations with them. The Congress of South African Trade Unions (COSATU) has been very supportive of the ANC's initiatives. The question remains as to the extent to which the South African political economy can be transformed to benefit the masses.

Despite Eastern European moves toward *laissez-faire* capitalism, Mandela's views shortly after his release were more reflective of the goals outlined in the Freedom Charter. He called for the nationalisation of the mines, banks and monopoly industries. This has generated considerable resistance in the South African business community. However, since the call for nationalisation, the South African government has reversed a decision to privatise the major parastatals. In the meantime, the ANC is reviewing its stance on nationalisation.

The ANC would like sanctions to remain intact until its demands are met satisfactorily by the South African government. The demands that have been met are the unbanning of liberation organisations, the lifting of the State of Emergency in all provinces except Natal, the repeal of petty apartheid laws, the release of a large number of political prisoners; and the readmittance of many ANC exiles into the country. In 1991, the 1913 and 1936 Land Acts were repealed, followed by the Population Registration and Group Areas Acts. The ANC would like to have the State of Emergency totally lifted, the release of all political prisoners and amnesty for all ANC exiles. In the negotiation process, the De Klerk government has proposed to have an all-white referendum for a new constitution before having it considered by blacks, whereas the ANC would like a constituent assembly elected to frame a new constitution. In 1990, the EC announced that it would partially lift its sanctions against South Africa to allow new investment, and in 1991 the Bush administration lifted US sanctions despite the fact that all political prisoners have not been released.

South Africa has a sizeable foreign debt. In 1989, the government owed US$11–13bn to foreign banks.[209] Consumers are plagued by high inflation, as manifested in increasing prices of basic commodities and utilities. The price of gold, South Africa's major foreign exchange earner, hovers below $400. This amount is considered the dividing line between economic recovery and continued recession. Now the rand is only worth about 36 cents to an American dollar. Bankruptcies among white South Africans have abated somewhat but still remain relatively high.

Also, there is some division in ANC ranks over whether to engage in a negotiated settlement with the apartheid regime or to continue guerrilla war strategies. It remains unclear at present exactly how the situation will be resolved.

2.7 CONCLUSION

In the period after Union, some regionalistic tendencies were retained in the provincial political economies of South Africa. Furthermore, the racial composition of each province and the proletarianisation of its reserves were different. The early putting-out systems for clothing come closest to the European cottage-industry model. It is questionable whether workers, living in an urban area, were members of a family economy, however. Nevertheless, it is clear that factory industrialisation led to the formation of a family wage economy. Unions were important vehicles for social welfare benefits for women, whose meagre wages could barely cover their own obligations, much less those of other family members. Those white and coloured women – and some 'African' women – who have entered clerical employment may be participating in the family consumer economy.

African women are the most marginalised group in South Africa. They are latecomers to the industrial labour force and are paid some of the lowest wages. Furthermore, these women from different areas of southern Africa began to face restrictions on their entry into South Africa's industrial areas while those from the protectorates were prohibited from entering the country altogether. Because blacks have been so marginally working class, they usually participate in the family wage economy. The family consumer economy is a middle-class phenomenon out of their reach.

During the period of secondary industrialisation in South Africa, there has been increasing segmentation and stratification of the labour force by gender, race and class. The family, as the most basic social unit, is being adversely affected by these processes as individual members face differential participation in the labour force.

SACU provides a mechanism by which South Africa can control the development of the BLS countries for its utilisation of the latter as consumer markets and sources of cheap labour. Furthermore, as an extension of its domestic efforts to control its black labour force, South Africa is also placing similar controls on BLS countries. Moreover, SACU functions as a conduit through which manufacturing industries can relocate in BLS countries. That is reflective of SACU's sub-imperialist nature.

Part II
Swaziland

3 Industrialisation in Swaziland

Chapter 2 focused on the political economy of textile industrialisation in South Africa, to provide a context in which to analyse the emergence and development of Swaziland's peripheral political economy. However, just as South Africa exhibited a different pattern of industrialisation from European countries, Swaziland has experienced a modified version of the South African process. Mining and plantation agriculture began in the former at the turn of the century. Manufacturing has been introduced in two spurts, with agricultural processing beginning in the late 1940s and textile industrialisation in the 1980s. While men figured prominently in early industrialisation, women became involved later.

Peripheries emerge as cores are developed and the latter then begin their incorporation of the former. South Africa, as an emerging semi-periphery in the second half of the nineteenth century, received selective stimuli from Europe until European settlers began to plan an integrated political economy. Swaziland, as a peripheral country, received its earliest stimuli from South Africa and later experienced direct core development from Britain. Although its economy is small-scale by comparison, in the pre- and post-colonial periods, attempts have been made to integrate the Swazi political economy.

Since Swaziland's textile industrialisation has begun so recently, this chapter will provide a context for the contemporary Swaziland political economy. Its political economy can be delineated in somewhat different periods from South Africa's. The period 1881–1909 marks the reign of Mbandzeni and the awarding of overlapping concessions to Boers and Britons; 1910–45 was characterised by mine labour recruitment, land alienation and the development of the plantation economy; 1946–77, by local industrialisation in mining and manufacturing; and 1978–present, periodic economic recession due to incorporation into the global economy, labour surplus and mine labour recruitment restrictions.

3.1 THE AGE OF CONCESSIONS 1881-1909

The BLS countries were equivalent to reserve areas in South Africa until they came under the protection of Britain and subsequently gained political independence. This tied them more closely to British and British South African mining and manufacturing interests and Afrikaner farming interests. However, the incorporation of reserve areas was shaped in part by the political economy of the region in which it was located. In the BLS case, each protectorate experienced incorporation at a different period of time and under different circumstances and developed a different political economy. Furthermore, they became independent within a two-year period, with Swaziland the last to be granted independence.

Until 1881, which coincides with the full ascendency of the Swazi king, Mbandzeni, the Swazi state had remained more-or-less intact.[1] The Swazis had been able to fend off successfully the Boers, the Portuguese and the Zulus. What land concessions Mbandzeni's predecessor Mswati had made, the Boers had been unable to maintain. The latter were faced with the problem of having to repulse indigenous ethnic groups as well as the British in an attempt to establish their hegemony in the Transvaal. As a consequence, they had neither the manpower nor the resources to legislate Swazi boundaries.

In the meantime, with the discovery of diamonds and gold in the Transvaal, the British had designs not only on the Rand but on Bechuanaland and Matabeleland as well. Concessionaires, who were scourging the whole of southern Africa found Mbandzeni amenable to providing concessions to suit a variety of needs – grazier concessions for Boer sheep-herders, mining concessions to Britons and a flirtation with a railway concession for the South African Republic.

P. Bonner characterises the end of this brief period as 'a rapid descent into anarchy'.[2] After the signing of the London Convention in 1884, neither Boer nor Briton could further their designs on Swaziland without the consent of the other. Under the leadership of Cecil Rhodes, those concessionaires who wanted to seek concessions elsewhere chose Bechuanaland and Matabeleland against the wishes of the Boers. Thinking those areas were better endowed with mineral resources, the British were willing to grant the Boers rights to Swaziland as compensation. Bonner has argued that throughout much early Swazi history, the Swazis feared conquest by the Zulus.

Furthermore, they had difficulty with the Bapedi and the Portuguese. Therefore the Swazis and the Boers formed an alliance for mutual protection.[3]

The period of concessions coincides with the rule of Mbandzeni, whom Bonner considers a weak king, chosen by the queen mother in order to maintain her position.[4] He was very favourably disposed towards Europeans and put his mark on more than four hundred concessions for grazing, and agricultural and mineral rights. However, over fifty per cent were for agricultural rights.[5] Often, these concessions overlapped. Bonner suggests that Mbandzeni did this deliberately to avoid further land alienation.[6] Youe, however, argues that the concessions issue presented an even greater morass, in which concessions were not only of different types on the same piece of land but also often overlapped spatially.[7] Concessionaires with conflicting claims formed ties with different members of the royal family. J. Crush observes that factionalism in the royal family over concessions resulted in a series of political killings.[8]

This period was a transitional one in Swazi history. Unlike Basutoland, which functioned as a granary at the inception of South African industrialisation, Swaziland was characterised as a stockyard.[9] In the 1890s, Swazis sold cattle to both white and black buyers. Furthermore, it was during this period that the plough was introduced. With regard to female labour, Crush suggests that the plough's impact was manifested in the utilisation of women's labour over 'an expanding cultivated area'.[10]

Swaziland's economic prosperity was shortlived, however, due to a series of ecological calamities that started in 1894. During a four-year period, rainfall was below normal. Those crops that survived the drought were decimated by locusts; in 1896, the entire harvest was destroyed by locusts.[11] Moreover, rinderpest and East Coast fever decimated the cattle population during this period.[12] For a brief period in the late 1880s and early 1890s, Swaziland produced grain for the Transvaal.[13] However, since this period, it has been a perpetual importer of grain.[14]

In the 1880s, the only significant employers within Swaziland had been the local mines and the larger trading concerns.[15] The calamities of the 1890s gave impetus to labour migration to South African gold mines and farms. In order to fend off hunger, homesteads sent their sons out to work.[16] Conditions in surrounding South African mines were far from ideal. There was considerable corruption in recruiting by labour touts and white mine employers. Working and compound conditions were conducive to high mortality rates. However, most recruits were willing to take the risk. The Transvaal Republic had designs on Swaziland, viewing it as a potential route to the port of Lourenço Marques. Paul Kruger tried to destroy the Swazi monarchy by prosecuting King Bunu for murder.[17] This scheme was unsuccessful. Later, J. C. Krogh's attempted takeover of Swaziland resulted in the imposition of hut and road taxes to force men to migrate.[18]

The monarchy was not opposed to migration in principle but was concerned about how to control it. However, it did not want migration to undermine its position.[19] Because of various problems associated with recruitment, the Rand Native Labour Association sought to gain a monopoly on mine labour recruiting at the turn of the century. The newly-formed Witwatersrand Native Labour Association made a similar effort in 1906.[20] Regent Gwamile wanted all Swazis employed at one mine in order to preserve traditional attitudes.[21] York mine employed a substantial number of Swazi miners.

Nevertheless, L. Callinicos has argued that miners often maintained their same socio-economic position.[22] However, many Swazis worked in the mines only once.[23] Men from homesteads near the Swazi border would slip into the Transvaal and Natal for brief periods to avoid taxation and arrest by the police. Zulu policemen were hired from Natal to patrol migrants resulted in heightened ethnic antagonism. The principal destinations of migrants were the gold mining industry on the Rand and the coal mines and sugar plantations of northern Natal.[24] Other small-scale options throughout the region included domestic service, washing, transport riding (hired transport of livestock and other consumable goods), and extensive public works programmes on roads, docks and railway systems.[25] However, it was only at the end of this period – around 1910 – that mine labour recruiters began to achieve continued success in recruiting Swazi labour.[26]

In 1902, when the British defeated the Transvaal in the Boer War, they became the colonial rulers of Swaziland. Although the British got most of the blame for land alienation in Swaziland, C. P. Youe considers that they attempted to rationalise the problem of overlapping concessions.[27] The Swazi monarchy wanted to reclaim all the land, arguing that temporary contracts were signed by concessionaires. However, the British – resisting the counter-assertions of a Swazi deputation to London – decided to recognise the land claims of the settlers. However, I am inclined to think that British policy was not so innocuous, because it anticipated a similar policy that was imposed on indigenous people in South Africa. The major pieces of legislation there were the 1913 Land Act and the 1936 Land and Trust Act. These acts severely restricted land ownership to about thirteen per cent of the total land area of the country. Crush views the Swazi reserves as having been established to serve South African mining interests.[28]

Another vantage point from which to look at the land partition is that of the settlers themselves. Alister Miller, an early settler and founder of *The Times of Swaziland* and after whom Mbabane's main street is named, espoused the view that the Swazis should have no reserves and suggested instead that a few farms be set aside for members of the royal family and senior chiefs.[29] The land partition was viewed as providing labour for the plantations in Swaziland as well as the mines in South Africa. F. De Vletter suggests that Swaziland's inequality of land distribution precipitated rural migration on a scale similar to that of Lesotho although Swaziland did not supply labour to the South African gold mines on the same scale.[30]

Many settlers during the period shared similar sentiments on land partition. They wanted chiefs to be divested of power over land allocation and labour, as well as the abolition of customs and the dismantling of the political power of the Dlamini aristocracy.[31] However, the settlers eventually agreed to a hierarchical land partition from which chiefs and members of the Swazi monarchy could benefit. Nevertheless, legislation was passed prohibiting the ownership of private property and individual land tenure in the reserves. Furthermore, cattle posts, royal graves and chiefs' homes were to be least disturbed by the partition.[32]

In 1908, British special commissioner George Grey designated thirty-two Native Areas throughout Swaziland.[33] These areas, later termed Swazi Nation Land (SNL), were controlled by chiefs for communal tenure. To be precise about the allocation of land, 56.5 per cent became Private European Land; 39.8 per cent Swazi Nation Land; and 3.7 per cent Crown Land.[34]

A. R. Booth observes that seventy-nine per cent of SNL was composed of poor-to-untillable soil and only fifteen per cent had soils and slopes suitable for crop production.[35] This latter percentage is similar to that of Lesotho. In contrast to the unsuitability of Swazi Nation Land, fifty per cent of settler-designated land was ideal for crops. Furthermore, all known mineral deposits were located in the latter areas. Crush suggests that at the time of partition some determination was made as to the percentage of land the Swazis needed with a view that any surplus population could work in the labour centres.[36]

Because of the method by which land was partitioned, some Swazi homesteads were located on European-owned farms. They were given five years to vacate these farms. However, there were conflicting demands made by chiefs and landowners.[37] The former wanted squatters to perform tribute labour simultaneously with their labour obligations on European-owned farms. Furthermore, there was often not enough land available for the resettlement of squatters on Swazi Nation Land.[38]

The homestead, the basic Swazi residential unit, is composed of members of the extended family living on Swazi Nation Land. This is a settlement pattern followed by all Nguni groups including the Zulus and Xhosas, which provides a contrast to the large, more heterogeneous villages of the Sothos. Status in the homestead is determined by age, sex, seniority and marital status.[39] Homesteads are organised on a patriarchal basis, with the senior male being the homestead head. In that role, he performs the duties of land allocation, care and use of livestock and is the major decision-maker and intermediary between the homestead and the chief and the ancestors.[40]

Each house in a homestead consists of a wife and children whether, monogamous or polygynous, and is entitled to its own fields and livestock.[41] H. Ngubane describes the role of women as follows:

> Women had, and largely still have, prime responsibility for the internal domestic affairs of the family group, including not only the rearing of children, care of the sick, provision of meals and of drink, and cultivation of the fields, but also the maintenance of good relations within the group and between members and their kinfolk elsewhere.[42]

Since land is allocated by the homestead head to his sons on marriage, Ngubane suggests that women, in essence, own the land.[43]

Labour migration, particularly male migration and land shortage, have contributed to the contraction of the homestead since the land partition. Ngubane suggests less mobility for females who might stay at the homestead to assist their mothers.[44] However, after male migration, women began to work as casual farm labourers, and in the 1970s and 1980s, large numbers of young, single women migrated to Swazi towns to seek wage employment.[45]

For expropriated land, K. Matthews delineates four types of white farmer – settler-estate producers; ranch owners; trek farmers; and absentee farmers.[46] Crush indicates that different types of labour tenancy arrangements were made according to the type of farm.[47] Absentee farmers left squatters to their own devices. In the case of the remaining categories, they might employ any one of three options: they might confine squatters to one area of the farm and/or limit their stock; charge squatters an annual rental fee if they refused to work; or pay current farm wage rates.

In an effort to reclaim their land, Queen Regent Gwamile sought the aid of miners to repurchase the land by taxing them £5 sterling per year – the equivalent of three months' wages.[48] This represented the beginning of the monarch's extraction of surplus from the Swazi Nation. The fund was also used to finance deputations to England and for the education of the king. At the time, Swaziland was the most heavily-taxed territory in southern Africa.[49] In 1914, the Native Recruiting Corporation (NRC) granted the queen regent a £5000 sterling loan to repurchase a 6000-acre farm in the lowveld.[50]

3.2 MINE LABOUR RECRUITMENT 1910–45

The Native Recruiting Corporation had begun operations in Swaziland in 1913. At the time, mine labour recruiting entered into a new phase, with recruiting methods that proved to be highly successful.[51] Between 1907 and 1909, 2819 Swazi men were recruited to the gold mines. However, between 1910 and 1912, that figure had increased by more than three and a half times, to 10 339.[52] In non-recruited mine labour, Swazi men represented a quarter of all new hires by 1920.[53] Crush suggests that Swazis had distinct preferences for certain mines.[54] During the period 1912–13, twenty-four per cent of the workforce was Swazi.

Traders became the principal mine recruiters offering as incentives maize, cash and cattle advances. They would send black runners throughout the countryside to advertise and recruit labourers.[55] The standard contract length was six months for underground work and three months for surface work. The latter was preferred by men from the central districts of the country. However, by late 1917, there was a flood of mine deserters back into Swaziland. In one very notable case, fifty mine deserters were arrested in Hlatikulu district, tried and acquitted due to poor mining conditions on the Rand.[56]

Crush observes that labour mobilisation and labour control were problems that dominated the period between 1900 and 1920.[57] The challenges of recruiting and retention were not the only problems. Other dimensions include competition between the gold and coal mining industries as well as between Swazi mines and farms and their South African counterparts.

In so far as colonial authorities were concerned, Swazi mines were secondary to South African mines *vis-à-vis* labour recruitment.[58] One potential source of labour for plantations was the squatters whose homesteads were annexed as Title Deed Land during the land partition. However, squatters would move from plantation to plantation in Swaziland and in neighbouring areas of the eastern Transvaal. Some white settlers owned farms on both sides of the Swazi border with the Transvaal.[59] However, as mentioned above, there were some landowners who left their tenants to their own devices especially if they owned land for speculative purposes.[60]

With the growing success of mine labour recruiters, there was little readily available labour in Swaziland. However, there was an increase in farm wages between 1909 and 1914.[61] Swaziland's wages were higher than those paid to eastern Transvaal farmworkers. However, wages on the local mines and those on the Rand were higher than farm wages on either side of the border. Nevertheless, Rand mine wages remained higher than Swazi mine wages.

Crush indicates that the Swaziland Corporation had a shortage of male labour.[62] The Henderson Company solved its problem by employing women and children. Both categories were considered for their labour potential in the cotton industry just after the turn of the century. They formed the domestic reserve army of labour.

By 1914, the monarchy had recovered 68 000 acres of land from settlers. However, in 1915, the colonial government placed restrictions on Swazi land purchases.[63] Nevertheless, in 1940, the government gave King Sobhuza £190 000 sterling to purchase land in acknowledgement of a growing land shortage in the protectorate. Four years later, he established the Lifa Fund, for which a levy was placed on cattle and cash for more repurchases.[64] In observing that white settlers worried about a Bambatha-type rebellion, Youe suggests that until British colonial rule, the Swazis themselves were too fearful that such a rebellion would precipitate an invasion and incorporation into the Transvaal Republic.[65] Conversely, Crush argues that the Bambatha Rebellion softened the attitude of white settlers towards pushing too hard on the land issue.[66]

It was during this period that settler agricultural production got underway. The colonial government sought to attract British yeoman farmers to the eastern Transvaal and to Swaziland as a part of their anglicisation policy.[67] However, among the settler population, there were both English and Boers. In the early days of plantation agriculture, both groups grew maize, but in the 1910s and 1920s, plantation owners began to diversify their crops to include tobacco, citrus fruits and cotton.[68]

Mining operations were continuing in Swaziland during this period. However, by the 1920s, gold and tin mining were becoming uneconomic. Later, Havelock mine, an asbestos mine, was established near Piggs Peak in the highveld.

In addition to the tax levied by the monarchy, a 'native tax' was levied to fund the infrastructural development of roads and communications systems and irrigation schemes, and provision of agricultural loans.[69] Increased taxes and substantial increases of the human and livestock populations on a limited land base forced men to pursue migrant labour in greater numbers. In 1920, Booth estimates that between twenty-five per cent and forty per cent of Swazi men were working in the Transvaal at any given time.[70]

During King Sobhuza's reign, great emphasis was placed on traditionalism. Liqoqo, a rather informal advisory body to the King, composed of senior princes, chiefs and commoners, became more formalised.[71] New traditions such as Libandla, which met annually for a week in July, were introduced after Sobhuza's installation. To justify his emphasis on Swazi traditionalism, Sobhuza enlisted the aid of a number of prominent anthropologists including Brian Marwick, Winifred Hoernle, Isaac Schapera, Bronislaw Malinowski and Hilda Kuper.[72] The anthropological alliance also precipitated a royalist bias in Swazi anthropology and historiography.

In 1929, Benjamin Nxumalo, Queen Regent Gwamile's brother, founded the Swaziland Progressive Association (SPA).[73] Sobhuza was involved for a while before surmising that it would be a threat to the Swazi National Council (SNC) and withdawing his support. This was at a time when Swaziland was being prepared for Indirect Rule.[74] Upon withdrawing his support, Sobhuza suggested that all complaints to the colonial administration be processed through the SNC. Some members of Sobhuza's age regiment became prominent supporters as members of the conservative elite. They included Prince Mokhosini Dlamini, Mfundza Sukati and J. S. M. Matsebula.[75]

H. Macmillan dates the emergence of the Swazi ideology of traditionalism to the 1920s and 1930s.[76] He defines traditionalism as 'the putting of new content and meaning into old forms and institutions'.[77] Swaziland and Zanzibar are considered to be the only countries in Africa to become independent under a traditional ruler who then became a post-colonial head of state. Macmillan considers the ideology of traditionalism to have triumphed over competing ideologies of African nationalism.[78] The ideology of traditionalism has been particularly oppressive to Swazi women.

I question Macmillan's view that Swaziland and Zanzibar are unique in their traditionalist orientations that influenced the post-colonial political economy. Lesotho and Botswana were ushered into independence by parties formed by members of the chiefly elite. Particularly in the case of Lesotho, Leabua Jonathan was a descendent of Moshoeshoe I, although in an inferior house to King Moshoeshoe II.[79] He proved to be most malleable to the apartheid government in South Africa and to the Roman Catholic Church as independence approached. The ruling party was the Basutoland National Party. The competing parties represented the King (Marematlou Freedom Party) and the Protestant masses (Basutoland Congress Party). This will be discussed in more detail in Chapter 7.

In Botswana, Sir Seretse Khama, son of a powerful Bamangwato chief, became the party leader of the Botswana Democratic Party and the first Prime Minister of Botswana. I find I. Winter's question, 'How do we explain the accession to power of the Swazi rulers?'[80] uninformed about the BLS comparisons. I will take up Macmillan's point about the triumph of traditionalism over competing ideologies in the next section.

The general argument of Crush's book, *The Struggle for Swazi Labour 1890–1920*, is that the period under discussion was a transitional one in which the Swazi Nation lost its economic self-sufficiency and became incorporated into the regional political economy.[81] As compared to Lesotho and parts of the Transkei and Ciskei, Swaziland's incorporation occurred rather late. However, the incorporation process was characterised by intense land and labour struggles. In comparison to other peripheral areas of southern Africa, the Swazi case is unique in that both market production and migration were largely absent.[82]

The early 1930s was not a period of economic prosperity in Swaziland.[83] However, the Great Depression doesn't seem to have been as devastating to Swaziland as it was to Lesotho. During the period, schools and health services were largely in the hands of missions.

3.3 LOCAL INDUSTRIALISATION IN MINING AND MANUFACTURING 1946–77

Booth identifies as major factors precipitating social change and class differentiation the expropriation of Swazi land and the influx of capital after the Second World War. These factors initiated the socio-economic transformation of the homestead. Migrants began to invest in their children's education because of the strong value placed on it.[84]

Booth observes that a number of infrastructural developments occurred during the 1950s, resulting in 60 000 acres of trees being planted and 750 miles of road constructed.[85] He suggests that these infrastructural improvements opened the way for capitalist development in Swaziland. During this period, Swaziland's economy was dominated by British capital in mining, settler farming and irrigated sugar plantations through funding from the Commonwealth Development Corporation and Lonrho.[86]

After the Second World War, the British colonial administration began to acknowledge the vast discrepancy between production on Title Deed Land and Swazi Nation Land. In an effort to alleviate this problem, it set aside two areas – one near Herefords in the northern highveld and the other near Hlatikulu in the southern highveld.[87] However, the project proved unsuccessful. In 1964–65, the first eight Rural Development Areas (RDAs) were demarcated: Nkwene, Maduleni, Sipocoseni, Mpolonjeni, Mahlangatsha, Bulandzeni, Bhekinkosi and Sitataweni. Major objectives included the improvement of infrastructure such as dams, roads and fences as well as the development of village centres and domestic water supplies.

With increasing industrialisation in Swaziland, labour began to respond to its working conditions. The first strike occurred in 1962 at Usutu Pulp Company, when workers demanded a minimum wage. This led to the formation of Swaziland's first trade union, the Pulp and Timber Workers Union.[88] In 1963, striking sugar workers demanded higher wages at Ubombo Ranches in Big Bend, which resulted in a commission of enquiry to identify the factors contributing to the strike.[89] In the same year, sawmill workers at Peak Timbers also went on strike for higher wages. However, according to M. Fransman, the most significant strike was at Havelock Asbestos Mine in which workers not only sought higher wages but also the dismissal of certain management personnel.[90] The colonial government, with the King's acquiescence, retaliated with repression, by arresting union organisers. In the meantime, a second sugar strike began.[91]

The Havelock strike proved most difficult to control. The government declared a State of Emergency and requested a detachment of Gordon Highlanders stationed in Kenya to put down the strike. They interrogated strikers, resulting in most returning to work, and arrested the resisters. After completing this process at Havelock, they repeated it at Big Bend with equal success. Fransman suggests that these strikes polarised the Swazi bourgeoisie, with some supporting the working class and others the monarchy.

At the time of the strikes, there were persistent labour shortages. Booth, focusing more on the sugar strike, attributes it to the suppression of trade union formation by the imposition of an induna-controlled system in which overseers acted as representatives of workers' grievances to management.[92] The colonial government relied heavily on Shangaan labour from Mozambique on plantations.[93] In 1963, women from the British protectorates were prohibited from entering South Africa to seek employment. This forced proletarianised Swazi women to seek low-wage work within their country.

Railway workers went on strike in 1975, and sugar mill workers at Big Bend in 1978.[94] The most violent strike was precipitated by the 3000-member Teachers' Association in 1977 for higher, more stable wages. In their discontentment with government handling of teachers' grievances, over 3000 students rioted in the towns of Mbabane and Manzini.[95] Booth considers worker resistence to be indicative of mass frustration over the move away from democratisation.

Between the 1930s and the mid-1970s, the flow of mine labour from Swaziland was relatively constant at a level between 7000 and 8000 workers per annum.[96] However, mining employment was unrestricted through the period. Most went to the mines when there were agricultural shortfalls. Although Swazis achieved a reputation as good drillers on the mines, they had the shortest, most intermittent contracts because of their participation in the agricultural cycle back home.[97]

Throughout the period that Swaziland had protectorate status, South Africa had designs on its incorporation, in most instances, along with Basutoland and Bechuanaland. While settlers were opposed to Swaziland's incorporation into South Africa, they did not want independence under black majority rule.[98]

As Britain began grooming Swaziland for independence, King Sobhuza hoped to have a constitution that protected the power of the monarchy. When he saw that Britain planned to introduce a more parliamentary form of government, he formed his own political party, the Imbokodvo National Movement (INM). The outgoing colonial administrator, Brian Marwick, was dismayed by Sobhuza's founding his own party to participate in the democratic process.[99] However, the South African government was pleased with the move.

A liberal, pro-capitalist party that sought to neutralise the powers of traditional rulers, the Swaziland Democratic Party (SDP) was founded by Dr Allen Nxumalo and Sishayi Nxumalo, cousins of Sobhuza. The SDP received some support from segments of the settler population and some white South African liberals. The party's founders eventually joined the INM and were appointed to high positions in the Swazi government.

The most radical parties were the Swaziland Progressive Party (SPP) and the Ngwane National Liberatory Party (NNLP). The former was founded by J. J. Nquku and the latter by Dr Ambrose Zwane and Prince Dumisa Dlamini, a nephew of the King. Members of these two parties, who had socialist and Pan-Africanist orientations, eventually merged into the latter party. The NNLP sought to organise the Swazi working class. One of its high-ranking members had had strong ties to the ANC and the South African Communist Party (SACP).[100] However, unlike in Lesotho, a Communist party was never formed in Swaziland.

Swazi independence was delayed until 1968, two years after Lesotho and Botswana became independent.[101] The INM won a resounding victory in which it filled every seat in parliament. R. H. Davies, D. O'Meara and S. Dlamini espouse the view that two separate administrative systems have developed since independence in which the King presides over the Swazi Nation and the Swaziland government.[102] It has been emphasised that the monarchy and the senior chiefs exercise considerable authority because they control the allocation of Swazi Nation Land.[103] According to Winter, the INM was supported by eighty-five per cent of peasants on Swazi Nation Land.[104] The NNLP received some support from the emerging Swazi working class but did not receive enough votes in any constituency to actually win a parliamentary seat.

The post-independence government's priorities included the repurchase of land and the localisation of the bureaucracy and lower-level management in the private sector.[105] The King established separate monitoring committees for the public and private sectors. Macmillan sums up the situation by saying that traditionalists viewed the presence of foreigners in jobs as a threat to national unity.[106] Not only were the latter competing with Swazis for jobs but also for Swazi women and Swazi Nation Land. By 1979, localisation was achieved for eighty-five per cent of the bureaucracy. Many Zulu-speaking South African teachers lost their jobs and had to leave the country. Localisation still remains a burning issue.

In the educational system, SiSwati was introduced into the curriculum in the 1960s to replace Zulu.[107] Furthermore, secondary education was placed under state control to maintain traditionalism.[108]

The Rural Development Areas Programme (RDAP) continued after independence. Its major objectives were to improve the quality of life and the economic prospects in rural areas through long-term development schemes.[109] The RDAP was fully launched in 1970.[110] This time, maximum- and minimum-input areas were delineated. Maximum-input areas were designated on the basis of the people's interest in development, the ecological homogeneity of the area and its population density. The areas designated were Northern, Southern, Mahlangatsha and Central, potentially affecting 33 600 people and 4000 homesteads.

Minimum-input packages included the centralisation of a variety of services. Of major concern were the improvement of extension services, the construction of offices, stores and staff housing as well as input sheds and dip tanks and the purchase of tractors for hire pools. Furthermore, much emphasis was placed on land use planning for purposes of rationalising production on arable and grazing land.

In 1977, the Rural Development Areas Programme expanded from the four original areas to include fourteen additional areas thereby constituting fifty per cent of Swazi Nation Land. Assistance for various geographical and technical areas was forthcoming through the United Kingdom, the World Bank, the United States Agency for International Development, the African Development Bank and the European Development Fund. The expected outcome was the creation of commercial smallholders to produce maize, cotton and other cash crops.[111]

For the Swazi bourgeoisie, most found freehold land prohibitively expensive due to settlers purchasing land for speculative purposes.[112] In 1972, the Land Speculation Control Act was passed to keep sales from being made to non-Swazis for speculation which furthered the interests of the Swazi bourgeoisie.[113] A control board was appointed to approve land sales. There was considerable South African investor opposition to the bill.[114] The white Minister of Finance, Leo Lovell, was forced out of his position for not supporting it.

The Swazi Constitution was suspended in 1973 because the Ngwane National Liberatory Party won three seats in parliament. Since its founding, the NNLP has been developing a substantial following among Swaziland's small but growing working class. According to Booth, the King's decision centred on the government's lack of success in deporting one of the successful candidates to South Africa where he was allegedly born.[115] In the mid-1970s, ritual murder rates began to increase among wage-earners and school-leavers, which Booth correlates with the suspension of the Constitution.[116]

After suspending the Constitution, Sobhuza sought an alliance with the white settler segment. He was also able to consolidate a secure relationship with monopoly capital through Tibiyo Taka Ngwane, originally a royal trust for Swazi mineral concessions and royalties. Because of Swaziland's strategic location, he sought cordial economic ties with South Africa, on the one hand, while turning a blind eye to ANC insurgency into South Africa via Swaziland, on the other. The formulation of a localisation policy was viewed as a means of cultivating the Swazi *petit bourgeoisie.*

In 1978, the King unveiled a new constitution as a basis for elections. At the village level, villagers would select from a list of candidates those who were to choose members of parliament for Libandla as well as members of the Tinkundla or community councils. Voting was to be conducted publicly. The voters would elect eighty out of 160 nominees to the electoral college who would in turn elect forty Members of Parliament and ten Senators 'from its own ranks'. Political parties and public meetings were banned. Parliament's principal role was to debate public proposals and advise the King.

3.4 PERIODIC RECESSION, LABOUR SURPLUS AND REDUCED MINE RECRUITMENT 1977–PRESENT

In 1977, the South African Chamber of Mines imposed a quota on Swazi labour outflow to the gold mines.[117] Previously, the mines absorbed Swaziland's labour surplus. South Africa was responding to global recessionary trends when Swaziland's political economy was also experiencing such trends. Furthermore, the South African government attempted to wage reprisals against supplier nations by lowering their quota. The major labour-supplier nations later organised the Southern African Labour Commission (SALC) to negotiate employment quotas.[118] By negotiating for mine labour stabilisation, they hoped to make it easier for member countries to do economic planning.[119]

The decrease in opportunities for mining employment precipitated male migration to urban areas where unemployment was already high.[120] However, Swaziland could not absorb all its labour – maybe less than half of it.[121] For those who did find employment, they made more frequent visits to their homesteads and sent higher remittances than those working in the South African mines.

Working conditions in Swaziland were often no better than the worst working conditions in South Africa. Plantation workers often lived in single-sex hostels. However, in urban employment, workers' families could accompany them into town if it was economically feasible. De Vletter found that workers in the latter circumstances were more stable in their work.[122]

In the early 1980s, only six per cent of homesteads were supporting themselves from crop production alone. Supplementary activities include handicrafts, beer-brewing and traditional medicine.[123] Traditional healing continues to be popular, mainly due to the feeling of helplessness and inadequacy among the populace, although it has been officially outlawed.[124]

King Sobhuza had a number of European advisers, among them Nathan Kirsh, a Swaziland-born South African industrialist with investments in both countries.[125] Although holding the bulk of his investments in South Africa, through Swaki, Kirsh owns a maize-milling company, a Datsun and Mercedes dealership, Metro and Swaziland Wholesale and the two largest shopping centres in the country.[126] He is viewed as being most active in the manufacturing and commercial sectors of the Swazi economy.[127] In the aftermath of economic sanctions against South Africa, the Kirsh Group has acted as a conduit for South African manufacturing investment into Swaziland.

In the early 1980s, the manufacturing, hotel and restaurant sectors became the fastest-growing in Swaziland's economy.[128] In 1981, manufacturing was the third largest employer of wage labour in the public and private sectors.[129] Twenty-five per cent of wage labour in manufacturing is female.[130] Women and children are preferred as casual labourers in agriculture.[131] The breakdown for major sectors of employment are manufacturing 17 per cent; agriculture 33.5 per cent; and social services 19.5 per cent.

The British investment prevalent during the previous period is being replaced by South African investment. In addition to Kirsh Group investments, the Anglo American Corporation is heavily invested in mining and forestry in Swaziland. These investments include Swaziland Collieries, Peak Timbers and Usutu Pulp Company now owned by SAPPI, an Anglo American subsidary. Thus, Anglo American controls about ninety per cent of Swaziland's forests.[132]

Other sources of South African investment are in packaging through Neopack, a subsidiary of Barlow Rand Group, Swazi Breweries, a subsidiary of South African Breweries, OK Bazaars, also owned by South African Breweries and four Sun hotels owned by Sun International, a South African hotel chain.[133] Thus, South African capital now has control of forestry and dominates commerce, mining, manufacturing and tourism. British capital is for the most part confined to the sugar industry.

The sugar industry's position in Swazi political economy cannot be underestimated. Swaziland's dependency on sugar production has increased dramatically since independence.[134] In 1982–83, the sugar industry yielded 400 000 metric tonnes, making it the second-largest producer in Africa.[135] The industry is the country's largest employer, with a labour force of 60 000. It is also the largest single user of land and water due to reliance on irrigated agriculture to grow sugar cane.

Because of the development of forward linkages in the agricultural sector, plantations generally have four categories of workers. These include casual labourers in the fields; factory processors; forepersons in field and factory; and clerical workers in factories. Women and children would comprise the bulk of casual labourers; and men, the factory processors.

All has not been well for South African investment in Swaziland. The textile industry began to demonstrate its volatility in the early 1980s when Swazi Carpets relocated to the Transkei.[136] In early 1983, the Kirsh Group decided to build a textile factory, originally planned for Swaziland, in a border area of the Ciskei.

The National Industrial Development Corporation (NIDC) is the primary promoter of industrial development in Swaziland. It espouses the view that Swaziland provides a good investment climate with a stable labour force, low wages and no trade union activity. New investors are given a five-year tax holiday. NIDC provides loans and factory space, and sometimes engages in joint ventures with foreign investors.

The Swaziland Enterprise Development Corporation (SEDCO) provides loans to small business owners in Swaziland and conducts workshops for job training in its major towns. Its training is primarily for small-scale industry. Winter suggests that this too is an avenue for capital accumulation by the Swazi middle class.[137]

The tourist industry was developed in the post-independence period. The Sun hotel chain has a monopoly on major hotels in the country. Of the four hotels mentioned above, three are in the Ezulwini valley south of Mbabane and one in Nhlangano in the southern middleveld. The Protea chain has built a hotel in Piggs Peak in the highveld. Most of these hotels have casinos.

The Ezulwini valley is a good location for the tourist industry. It is a reforested area that has a number of restaurants with different cuisines nestled in the woods off of the Mbabane-Manzini highway. For tourism, the country as a whole is very attractive, providing three game preserves in different areas of the country, including one in the Ezulwini valley, and varied natural scenery. However, Booth indicates that there has been a decline in tourists' average length of stay since the mid-to-late 1970s.[138] The opening of Sun City and similar hotel/casino complexes in the homelands has attracted more South Africans to those areas.

In terms of import-substitution, the Swazi government executed a major coup when a French firm established Swaziland Chemistries in the late-1970s, a firm that produced fertiliser. South Africa used the provisions of the Southern African Customs Union Agreement in an attempt to sabotage this project: the firm was making a profit in 1982, but it failed in 1984.[139]

P. B. Bischoff argues that foreign, non-South African investment has actually increased Swaziland's dependency on South Africa. Newly-investing companies have to buy materials from South Africa.[140] This is reflective of Swaziland's structural position in the world-system. It is a periphery mediated through the South African semi-periphery with the Western, industrial core. The role of the sister institutions, World Bank and International Monetary Fund (IMF) is more central to the process of perpetuating structural dependency of the periphery on the semi-periphery and core than is private investment, however.[141]

Another factor contributing to the orientation of Swaziland's industrialisation is its membership in the Southern African Customs Union (SACU). In 1980–81, SACU revenues paid for the previous year accounted for fifty-one per cent of total state revenue.[142] J. R. A. Ayee suggests that Swaziland and the other SACU members should renegotiate the agreement with the post-apartheid government in South Africa.[143] When it became apparent that Western industrial nations were seriously considering sanctions against South Africa, a Swazi senior official expressed fear of the implications of Swaziland's continued membership in SACU should sanctions be imposed.[144] He wondered if Swaziland would be required to impose sanctions against South Africa.

When SACU was being considered for renegotiation in 1988, a Swazi economist espoused the view that Swaziland should use withdrawal from SACU as a device for negotiating a more favourable position for itself. M. Matsebula suggested that Swaziland had not fully utilised protections granted in the 1969 renegotiation. He recommended the following strategies to increase its leverage:

1. To hold South Africa to the letter and spirit of SACU;
2. To raise Swaziland's customs capability; and
3. To actively develop trade linkages with other countries in the Preferential Trade Area (PTA).[145]

As mentioned earlier, despite the fact that the Swazi Nation now owns about two-thirds of the land, Swazi peasants do not have access to all the land that falls into this category. Although Booth suggests that seventy per cent of Swaziland's population lives on Swazi Nation Land,[146] Davies, O'Meara, and Dlamini indicate that eighty-seven per cent of SNL is used for the grazing of the national cattle herd.[147] This is an issue of concern in addition to the generally inequitable distribution of land.

Davies, O'Meara and Dlamini espouse the view that the traditional chiefs, who in the colonial period extracted tribute from the peasantry, aligned themselves with the monarchy during the post-independence period to form a *comprador bourgeoisie* to extract surplus from the South African monopolies that have invested in Swaziland's economy.[148] Tibiyo Taka Ngwane has provided the monarchy with a conduit to foreign capital investment. Tibiyo was originally set up as a depository for mineral royalties paid to the King for asbestos, iron ore, coal and other minerals. It was reorganised in 1975. At the time, the King viewed it as an economic bastion of traditionalism, charging the fund to 'preserve co-operation with such progressive local leadership as is essential to the development of the modern state, the customs and traditional institutions of the Swazi people so as to prevent the disillusionment and instability which has followed their rapid breakdown in other parts of the world'.[149] The following represents the percentage of Tibiyo's holdings in different concerns:[150]

Havelock Asbestos Mine	40%
Mhlume Sugar Company	50%
Royal Swaziland Sugar Corporation	32.4%
Simunye Plaza	25%
Swazispa Holdings	33.4%
Ubombo Ranches	40%

Tibiyo owns Royal Swazi National Airlines and provides grants and loans to the University of Swaziland, the Swaziland Defence Force and to various cultural organisations.[151] It also serves as an investor in agri-business, industry and tourism.[152] Tibiyo has a number of agricultural projects in Malkerns for livestock production and farming and was the sponsor of a failed angora goat project in Ngwenya. For its agricultural projects, it has utilised repurchased Swazi Nation Land. Despite the propaganda that Tibiyo is owned by the Swazi Nation, it has no public accountability.

In elucidating class formation in Swaziland, Winter divides the *bourgeoisie* into the foreign, settler and Swazi fractions, each having complementary interests. The foreign *bourgeoisie* holds investments in the major mines and plantations; the settler *bourgeoisie* in farming and small-scale commercial enterprises; and the Swazi *bourgeoisie*, particularly the monarchy, functions as a *rentier* class. However, the Swazi *bourgeoisie* is more fractionated, including traders, restaurateurs, large-scale farmers in private enterprise, and professionals ranging from doctors, lawyers and lecturers to teachers, nurses and civil servants. Furthermore, Winter views SEDCO as providing a basis for Swazi *bourgeois* expansion that complements foreign and settler *bourgeois* niches.[153] I tend to disagree with Winter that the three fractions of the *bourgeoisie* are complementary. There are tensions that emerge due to competition and conflicting class interests. This will be considered in more detail in Chapter 5.

The settler *bourgeoisie* is quite fragmented, with individual settlers having achieved degrees of success in farming or commercial enterprises, management or the civil service. Interestingly, there is also a gender gap within the settler *bourgeoisie*. The wives of settler men have often started their own small-scale enterprises with the surplus from their husband's employment.

Swazi women do not have high political visibility. There is no women's affairs ministry or related agency. However, there is one female minister. Nevertheless, women are making some inroads into middle- and upper-echelon positions in the civil service. There are a few female doctors and lawyers and many teachers and nurses. At the university, which has a female vice-chancellor, women have substantial representation. Working class women will be discussed in Chapter 5.

Trade unionism has become a burning issue in recent years in Swaziland. True, there has been increasing foreign investment in the economy. However, the government's strategy has been to keep wages low so that more jobs can be created.[154] This has produced conditions conducive to trade union militancy. To relieve structural tensions between workers and management over wages and working conditions, Bischoff suggests that a system of works councils was developed as a stop-gap measure.[155] Winter observes that a major limitation of works councils is that they are formed at individual firms rather than throughout an industry or between industries.[156] With the re-emergence of union activity during the period, there was a work stoppage by workers at the Ezulwini hydro-electric project in 1982.[157] With the exception of the teachers' strike, women have not been at the forefront of labour activism.

Observing that the monarchy stresses consensus to maintain unity in the Swazi Nation, Bischoff notes that trade unions are considered a threat to such unity.[158] However, industries and other concerns have had to respond to increased union-organising efforts among workers. If forty per cent of workers are willing to be union members, the management must enter into negotiations with worker leadership to form a union. An official of the International Labour Organisation indicated that that management can drag its feet on negotiations until membership falls to well below forty per cent. This has been a common tactic in Swaziland. Employers who do not follow proper procedures can be fined by the Industrial Court, however.

Throughout Swaziland's history, the monarchy has been concerned with reappropriating land for the Swazi Nation both within and beyond its colonial borders.[159] In 1982, the King died in the midst of controversial land-acquisition negotiations with South Africa for parts of the South African homelands, KaNgwane and KwaZulu. The acquisition of these two areas would have doubled Swaziland's land area and increased its population by at least 385 000 people. Whereas South Africa viewed this as an opportunity to impress the international community with its benevolence and to provide an additional buffer against ANC insurgency, Sobhuza viewed it as an opportunity for Swaziland to reclaim some of its conquered land. Swaziland faced pressures from SADCC and the OAU not to go through with the deal. However, the matter was resolved in a South African Supreme Court decision with Chief Gatsha Buthelezi as plaintiff in which the KwaZulu transfer was prohibited.

The death of Sobhuza led to a number of personal power struggles over succession. The Liqoqo, which had previously been a private advisory council to the King, took centre stage in major decision-making for the country during the interregnum. Davies, O'Meara and Dlamini claim that there was a Tibiyo faction that was dominant in the Liqoqo.[160] After much deliberation, Prince Makhosetive, a fifteen-year-old boy, was chosen to assume the kingship after reaching the age of majority. In the interim, Queen Regent Dzeliwa – who was subsequently removed – and the Liqoqo were to serve as the young king's advisory board in ruling the country. However, Macmillan argues that there is neither a *comprador bourgeoisie* nor a Tibiyo faction in Swazi political economy.[161] When King Mswati III was installed in 1986, he removed some members of Liqoqo because of their previous activities including those who had been South African collaborators.[162]

Even after King Sobhuza's death, the influence of the monarchy did not abate. In 1983, two of the King's sons were cabinet ministers. However, Booth suggests that they did not occupy the most powerful positions because the locus of power revolved around the Minister of Agriculture and Co-operatives, A. K. Hlope.[163]

Throughout the decade of the 1980s, Swaziland's economy has been in a state of recession interspersed with periods of relative prosperity. During the early part of the period, Davies, O'Meara, and Dlamini indicate that 5000 additional school leavers were joining the ranks of the unemployed each year. At the same time, there were a considerable number of lay-offs of those in employment. The IMF conducted a study of Swaziland's employment situation and concluded that state-sector unemployment was high compared to peer nations.[164] Concern was expressed about increasing the quota of miners to the South African gold mines.

In 1984, Cyclone Domoina struck Swaziland, causing severe damage to recently-constructed roads and the rail communications system. The South African Defence Force's Corps of Engineers was involved in the reconstruction of damaged and destroyed infrastructure. More recently, it has been involved in the construction of a military hospital in Lesotho.[165]

To forge a further alliance with South Africa in the political arena, Swaziland permitted that country to establish a trade mission there in the mid-1980s. In exchange, there is Swazi diplomatic representation in

Pretoria. In addition to providing consular services and promoting capital investment, the South African Trade Mission is rumoured to be engaging in intelligence activities. The presence of the African National Congress in Swaziland has been fraught with difficulty. Despite Queen Regent Gwamile's involvement in the founding of the ANC, and King Sobhuza's membership,[166] the Swazi government became uneasy about the ANC's presence in the post-Soweto period and its use of Swaziland as a springboard for guerrilla attacks on South Africa.

The rival Pan-Africanist Congress (PAC) was asked to leave Swaziland in 1978 after allegations that it had established an armed training camp in the country. However, the ANC has never been expelled. Instead, its operations in the country were severely curtailed when a higher-echelon official departed in 1981. This coincided with the period in which the Reagan Administration colluded with the South African Government to vanquish its guerrilla challenge. It was then that South Africa began to execute the foreign policy component of its 'total strategy'. It invaded its neighbours on the pretext of reprisals for ANC attacks launched from these countries. Swaziland secretly signed a non-aggression pact with South Africa in 1982 that was only revealed after Mozambique signed the Nkomati Accord in 1984.

However, when South Africa ceased actual invasions, it continued to send Special Branch agents to carry out missions against the ANC. The recent revelations of a black Special Branch agent sentenced to death indicated that he was involved in a shoot-out with the ANC in Swaziland in the mid-1980s. Furthermore, it was revealed that the South African government was recruiting ANC deserters and sending them to their former stations to do espionage work. Ebrahim Ismail Ebrahim, a high-ranking ANC member was kidnapped from Swaziland in 1986, tried in South Africa in 1988 and found guilty of treason for his alleged guerrilla activities while in Swaziland. His conviction was subsequently overturned. A late 1980s jailbreak from Bhunya resulted in an apparent kidnapping of an ANC member who later returned to Swaziland to spy on ANC members. He was a suspect in one ANC murder.

In recent years, the ANC has engaged in some recruitment of local people into its ranks. In Swaziland, the daughter of the English headmaster of one of its most prestigious schools, was arrested as a member of the all-white Broederstroom cell of the ANC. Her brother testified as to the reasons why she joined the ANC. He said that she had a racially-mixed group of friends and was very upset by South Africa's repeated incursions into Swaziland to harm them. During the period of my research, there were border tensions between Swaziland and South Africa. A number of people were shot by the South African police for allegedly crossing the border illegally. In one instance, a man was shot as he walked to his home near a border fence. Moreover, in ANC-related activities, the Swazi police uncovered caches of arms from different sites within the country. In one instance, they arrested three members of the ANC, including a mother of a young baby. The young woman was kidnapped by a South African Special Branch policeman as she left the courtroom. In a few instances, Swazis have been arrested with ANC members for arms violations.

Where does the Swazi government stand on the issue of South Africa? Bischoff presents a view of Swaziland as a southern African country walking a tightrope between the status quo in apartheid South Africa and the progressive tendencies of the Organisation of African Unity, the Southern African Development Coordination Conference and the Frontline States. However, in leaning more heavily towards the latter, it negates the image of Swaziland being another South Africa homeland.[167] Its position of neutrality is further maintained by receiving military aid from the United States, Britain, Israel, Taiwan and South Korea.[168]

Many of the industries that have moved to Swaziland since the mid-1980s have done so to escape sanctions against South Africa. They have the advantage of access to South African and SADCC markets and, in some instances, Preferential Trade Area (PTA) markets. Booth views Swaziland as the principal sanctions-breaker in southern Africa.[169]

In 1977, Swaziland signed a trade agreement with Mozambique for the exportation of sugar and coal thereby avoiding using South African ports.[170] However, by 1983, the Maputo-Swazi railroad was threatened by guerrilla activity from Renamo. This has included cross-border attacks on Swaziland. In Mozambique, it resulted in 12 000 refugees entering Swaziland in 1987–88. Also, in 1987, several Swazi motorists were ambushed and killed on the road to Maputo.

The Swazi Government has received challenges to its authority from a number of quarters in recent years. There has been considerable criticism of the Tinkundla system as an alternative to parliamentary government. A former Vice-Chancellor of the University of Swaziland, Professor Sam Guma ignited the debate by observing during an address to a meeting of the Swaziland National Association of Teachers (SNAT) that most Swazis did not understand the Tinkundla system. Parliament called for a review of the system, since it had initially been suggested by King Sobhuza as an experiment. Major issues to be considered include efforts to make the public more aware of the workings of the Tinkundla system, more direct parliamentary representation of successful candidates in Tinkundla elections, and strategies to curb abuses of the system.[171]

The Liqoqo period effectively ended with the imprisonment in 1984 at Matsapha Maximum Security Prison of its leader, Prince Mfanasibili, and his accomplices. However, political tensions re-emerged in March 1989, when a plot to enable the escape from prison of Prince Mfanasibili and those loyal to him was uncovered.[172] Six senior prison officials and three junior officials were detained under Swaziland's sixty-day detention law to determine what they knew about the plot. At the same time, top government officials, senior police and members of the royal family received death threats and were under tight security.[173] Another prison guard was held when tools for the prison break were discovered.[174]

Shortly before this took place, Dr Ambrose Zwane, former leader of the Ngwane National Liberatory Party, his son Bheki and, later, his receptionist Elizabeth Dlamini were detained under the sixty-day detention law for being in possession of pamphlets supporting an underground political party called PUDEMO (People's United Democratic Movement),[175] a shadowy movement that is anti-monarchy, pro-union and pro-democracy. Paramilitary police had searched Dr Zwane's house and office. Later in March, Daniel Simelane, a union leader employed at Ubombo Ranches, was detained for possession of PUDEMO literature. All were released at the end of their detention with no charges filed. However, this party – which like all other political parties is banned – is thought to have emerged during the period in which Liqoqo was in power as an opposing force. However, PUDEMO's reactivation almost simultaneously with the discovery of the Mfanasibili plot caused some confusion about who was doing what.

In June 1989, a labour dispute erupted when the Swaziland Union of Financial Institutions indicated that its members wanted a fifteen per cent pay rise. However, a scheduled strike was called off by the general secretary because of an Industrial Court injunction against it.[176] Nevertheless, a week later, David Mcina, the general secretary of the union, was detained under the sixty-day detention law. There was considerable public outcry over the detention. Furthermore, the Swaziland Federation of Trade Unions was dismayed by an undisclosed reply to a query made to Prime Minister Sotsha Dlamini. In the meantime, King Mswati III called the nation to a meeting at the Ludzidzini royal sibaya, or cattle byre. At the meeting, the King announced that Sotsha Dlamini was being replaced by Obed Dlamini as Prime Minister. People sitting in the cattle byre shouted 'Bayethe! Bayethe!'[177] The new acting Prime Minister is a former trade unionist who was employed at Swazican as a training manager at the time of his appointment.

The Union of Swaziland Financial Institutions resumed negotiations with employers and accepted a 13.25 per cent pay rise.[178] Shortly thereafter, a number of trade unions were recognised in the industrial sector and a few disputes settled. Dr Ambrose Zwane paid the Prime Minister a visit to discuss the easing of censorship in Swaziland and presented him with a copy of ANC leader Nelson Mandela's book, *No Easy Walk to Freedom*.

Swaziland's labour activism has not abated in the early 1990s. Fifteen people were arrested in 1990 and charged with sedition. Although three of the accused were acquitted, the remainder were given a continuance for the lesser charge of attending an illegal meeting. Two of the latter were released from detention in 1991 after allegedly having been detained for incitement of protests at the University of Swaziland.

3.5 CONCLUSION

Swaziland's political economy has been shaped by late-nineteenth-century land alienation both from within and from outside the country, the exploitation of its natural and human resources and the emergence of the monarchy as a *comprador* class after its independence. To a certain extent, it is a microcosm of South Africa.

Swaziland's incorporation into the regional political economy did not occur without considerable resistence. British mining prospectors and Afrikaner farmers settled in Swaziland in much the same way that they had settled in the Transvaal. After Mbandzeni's concessions and the colonial land partition, the monarchy sought to buy back land as subsequently did the post-independence government. However, by the 1930s, the level of proletarianisation had reached the point of no return. In the contemporary period, the Swaziland political economy is experiencing increasing sectoral monopolisation by South African capital.

Able-bodied male labour formed reserves to be tapped by the South African gold mining industry as well as the domestic mining and plantation sectors in different areas of the country. *Vis-à-vis* male labour, the core–periphery relationship between South Africa and Swaziland represents gradations of economic exploitation as reflected in the male and female reserve armies of labour.

Able-bodied women have been offered fewer options for employment, having been denied entry into South Africa for employment in the 1960s. They were confined to plantation and agricultural processing employment until the 1970s, when manufacturing industries began relocating to Swaziland. However, as sources of male employment are diminishing, relocating textile industries are tapping into Swaziland's female floating and latent labour reserves. In Swaziland, as elsewhere in the world, this is resulting in the disruption of family structure.

The Swazi political arena has been controlled by the monarchy first through a political party and later through direct monarchical control. The monarchy, by creating pockets in the economy for *bourgeois* investment and mobility and through governmental appointment, has been able to maintain its support. However, the growing working class provides a challenge to monarchical hegemony. The organising of newly-proletarianised women will be a crucial factor in tipping the balance against the monarchy.

4 Agricultural Production in Swaziland

This chapter focuses on the political economy of agricultural production in Swaziland. Industrialisation cannot be viewed in a vacuum in the Swaziland political economy. It has had a great impact on the agricultural sector in a variety of ways. There is a hierarchy of farming units in the Swazi context deriving primarily from the skewed dichotomy between Swazi Nation Land and Title Deed Land and gradations on each side. On one side, Swazi peasants – including large numbers of women – engage in subsistence/cash-crop production, for which the majority produce at the sub-subsistence level. On the other, white settler farms engage almost exclusively in cash-crop production on a scale by which they can maintain a Western standard of living. They rely heavily on wage labour. However, the settler-estates represent the largest, most productive farming units. They are monopoly capitalist enterprises financed partially by international capital in conjunction with some local capital.

Crops range from solely subsistence crops through subsistence/cash crops to solely cash crops. Acknowledging the stratification associated with the dichotomy and its gradations, each side adopts a different strategy to enhance its position. In the case of more successful peasants, development planners are infusing more capital to convert them into small cash crop producers. On the white farms and settler-estates, monopoly investors are seeking to diverisfy cash crops to increase profitability.

Despite its high levels of agricultural productivity, Swaziland is not self-sufficient in subsistence crop production. Papayas and avocados grow wild in the country. However, most of the tomatoes, Swiss chard, potatoes, carrots and other vegetables are grown in South Africa.

Maize is the staple subsistence crop that also functions as a cash crop. Among cash crops, sugar is most prominent. However, two textile fibres – cotton and mohair – cannot be discounted. The former is a plant fibre while the latter is the hair of the angora goat. The production of textile fibres has the potential to fuel textile industrialisation. Each commodity will be considered *vis-à-vis* its characteristics, labour requirements, marketing structure and articulation into the

Swaziland political economy. Furthermore, each commodity's production has linkages to the South African political economy.

Swaziland has four ecozones that run from north to south. The highveld is the westernmost ecozone, which is mountainous and constitutes twenty-nine per cent of the country's total land area. At an altitude of 1300 metres, the climate is characterised as humid and temperate. However, three per cent of the land is good arable land, ten per cent of fair potential and the rest is marginal. As a consequence, there is a greater emphasis on cattle herding, with tobacco being the ecozone's only cash crop.[1] This area also contains the largest man-made forest and related processing industries, and an asbestos mine.

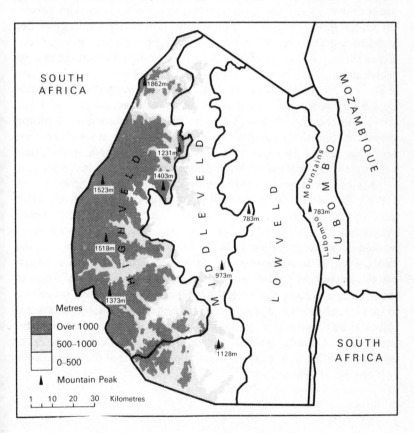

Source: Macmillan School Atlas for Swaziland (1986).

Figure 4.1   Swaziland's Four Ecozones

The middleveld to the east is hilly and subtropical and constitutes twenty-six per cent of the country's land area. Its average altitude is 700 metres and annual rainfall 900 millimetres. About twenty per cent of the upper middleveld has good-to-fair arable soils, as is the case with ten per cent of the lower middleveld. Being the most agriculturally productive ecozone, settler-estates produce citrus fruits and pineapples, and SNL-smallholder farms, cotton, maize, tobacco, groundnuts and bananas.

The lowveld, east of the middleveld and the largest area, covers thirty-seven per cent of the total land area.[2] Its average altitude is 200 metres, with an annual rainfall of 700 millimetres. With rainfall concentrated in the summer months, drought is a constant threat. On settler-estates, sugar-cane, citrus and cotton are produced under irrigated agriculture. SNL smallholders produce dryland cotton. Cattle-herding is also practised. Swaziland's only coal mine in located in the lowveld.

The easternmost area of Swaziland and the fourth ecozone is the Lubombo Plateau which borders Mozambique. It represents only eight per cent of Swaziland's total land area and has a climate and altitude similar to that of the middleveld. The area is quite stony, with only twelve per cent of the region providing good-to-fair arable land.[3] There is a greater emphasis on cattle herding in the Lubombo than on actual crops. However, there is a major cotton project located there.

With the exception of the Lubombo, the ecozones overlap with those in the eastern Transvaal and Natal in South Africa, therefore similar crops are planted in areas of overlap. Maize, as a cash crop, is planted on white-owned farms in the Transvaal highveld, cotton in the middleveld and lowveld areas of the eastern Transvaal and northern Natal, and sugar in the eastern Transvaal and coastal Natal lowveld areas. Since it is more economical for agricultural processing industries to locate near sources of raw materials, most of the maize mills, cotton ginneries and spinning mills are concentrated in these areas. On the South African side of the border, the process of agricultural integration began at the turn of the century. For Swaziland, it did not begin until the late 1950s.

4.1 MAIZE

A Food and Agriculture Organisation (FAO) team viewed maize as being a more popular crop in Rural Development Areas.[4] Because maize is the staple crop of the Swazi diet, there is much government concern that production be increased to accommodate the expanding population. Swaziland's Third National Development Plan, which covered the period from 1978/79 to 1982/83, predicted self-sufficiency in maize production by the end of that period.[5] Currently, maize production is in a state of decline.

However, there have been some successes in maize production at Ntfongeni in Northern Hhohho district.[6] Farmers, under the direction of Taiwanese agricultural specialists produced an average of a thousand bags of maize per household in the 1988–89 season. The project was started in 1983. There are two hundred farmers participating at that site, but there are eight other sites that have not shown as much success. The 1988–89 season is considered to have the highest output of maize on Swazi Nation Land. There were also bumper harvests of potatoes, vegetables and rice.

H. Standing argues that the substitution of maize for the traditional African subsistence crops changed the gender relations of production.[7] Prior to the introduction of maize, the major subsistence crops in West and southern Africa were millet and sorghum. The two crops required the participation of both males and females throughout a somewhat ritualised process of soil preparation, crop cultivation and harvesting.

In Swaziland, sorghum was the staple crop. When it was replaced by maize, women had to engage more intensively in the production process. Men had only one task – the clearing of fields. Once that was done, it was women's work to complete the process. Standing characterises the shift to maize production as being 'individuated, sex specific and secular'; similar to Guyer's West African research. Men perform the ploughing and land-clearance, while women perform the sowing, weeding, harvesting and processing. Women's labour is in demand for sowing and weeding in December and January and for harvesting in April and May. Men work for a much shorter period of time in the agricultural year. This is compatible with their extended periods of labour migrancy.

With the decline in Swazi homestead production throughout this century, it was often the men who would migrate to seek wage employment, leaving the women behind for childbearing, and domestic and agricultural activities.[8] Whereas earlier it might have been possible for men to take leave from work temporarily, as more obligations came to be required at work, they could no longer participate in agricultural production. Thus, women became even more overburdened with agricultural production. Standing suggests that the process of intensification of women's labour as a relatively recent phenomenon may have a longer history than previously believed.[9]

4.2 SUGAR

Whereas maize was a competing cash/subsistence crop to cotton on Swazi Nation Land, sugar-cane was a competing cash crop on Title Deed Land. Sugar-cane production began in the 1950s and covered 23 000 hectares by the early 1980s.[10] Swaziland has been producing sugar up to its quota negotiated according to the International Sugar Agreement.

In analysing Swaziland's industry, it is necessary to view it in historical and regional perspective because that country was a latecomer to sugar production. The sugar plantations which were started at various outposts in tropical areas of the New World after 1650 all depended on slave labour.[11] Natal developed post-slavery plantations using the organisational structure of the slavery model but relying on wage labour. By 1890, sugar was established as the predominant tropical cash crop in Natal at a time when plantation agriculture was breaking down.[12] Maize, wheat, potatoes, grapes and other fruits were also being grown.

The central sugar-mill had been introduced as a new model for sugar production in the 1870s. This represented a differentiation of the major function of growing and milling in the rationalisation of the production process.[13] With this change in structure, the attendant consolidation of land led to the elimination of small outgrower schemes in Natal.[14] Centralisation has also led to the elimination of more peripheral mills.

At the Natal sugar industry's inception, a number of families had sugar plantations, the most prominent being the Huletts.[15] Although having undergone some consolidation in the 1950s and 1960s, it was in the 1970s that national and foreign monopoly capital began buying up the sugar industry. The British sugar firm Tate & Lyle invested in a sugar-mill in Zululand in 1970 only to sell it in 1977 after an investigation by the *Manchester Guardian* newspaper revealed that the company paid poverty wages to its black workers.[16] In the 1970s, two monopoly mining companies, Anglo American and Barlow's, were vying for control of Natal's sugar industry.[17]

Returning to Tate & Lyle's corporate history, it represents the merger of one company that procured raw sugar with a fleet of ships and processed it in Britain, and another that only processed sugar.[18] The merged company had substantial investments in the Caribbean before making its first African acquisitions in Northern and Southern Rhodesia (Zambia and Zimbabwe) when they were members of the Federation.[19] Most procurement was done in Southern Rhodesia and refinement in Northern Rhodesia. The multinational outfit transferred white management staff from South Africa and Mauritius to run these industries. After Zambia's independence in 1964 and the Unilateral Declaration of Independence in Southern Rhodesia the following year, Tate & Lyle formed independent, integrated operations in each country. The Zambian government has bought a majority share in the Tate & Lyle operations there. Tate & Lyle's brief foray into South Africa was mentioned above. Having invested in Swaziland since 1978, the company has an ongoing contract with Simunye Sugar Estate. However, more recently, this multinational company has invested in the National Textile Corporation.

Tate & Lyle began to diversify its operations in the late 1960s and early 1970s due to the wildly vacillating price of sugar, a reduction in domestic consumption, and British membership in the European Common Market. Britain was the only country member that did not derive sugar solely from sugar-beet and was under pressure to abandon cane-sugar. In response to sugar's declining popularity, the sugar multinational established Tate & Lyle Agribusiness to advise and consult with newly-independent governments in Africa.[20] Although originally working on a sugar development project, it diversified into soya beans, rice, vegetables and cotton, and to fishery production. In the late 1960s, the firm was closely associated with the FAO, and in the late 1970s with the World Bank.[21] Tate & Lyle was perceived in Africa as acting in a very self-interested fashion in conducting feasibility studies and negotiating contracts for various projects.

Like Tate & Lyle, Lonrho is a major British multinational with substantial investments in Africa. However, its holdings have always been more diversified.[22] Although Lonrho is not that different from other multinationals in Africa, it is viewed as representing Cecil Rhodes' continental entrepreneurship in embracing Africa from 'Cape to Cairo'. In fact, Lonrho has invested in some ventures that would reduce Africa's dependency on the metropole (the core or the colonial power) such as the oil pipeline from Mozambique to Zambia.

Furthermore, Lonrho attempts to establish good rapport with black leaders in the African countries in which it has investments.[23]

Not only has Lonrho established its own subsidiaries in Africa, it has also taken over other companies while allowing their corporate structures to remain intact.[24] Throughout sub-Saharan Africa, this multinational company owns sugar and coffee plantations, textile mills, motor vehicle assembly plants and agricultural equipment plants. Lonrho has invested heavily in the sugar industry in Africa and has investments in Swaziland's Big Bend Sugar-mill through Lonrho Sugar Corporation Ltd. The company, though incorporated in Swaziland, operates from South Africa. It grows and processes sugar-cane in those two countries as well as Malawi and Mauritius.[25]

The sugar industry cannot be discussed without some consideration of Tibiyo Taka Ngwane's role. R. Levin argues that the duality of structure between Tibiyo and the Rural Development Areas Programme has resulted in the substantial undercutting of the latter.[26] Tibiyo's status as a mineral fee and royalty trust was changed in 1978 to that of a joint investor whose accounts were replenished by dividends from investments.[27] However, it has invested in some industries that have had substantial shortfalls and, as a consequence, has had to receive government subsidies.[28] Levin argues that these subsidies divert funds from projects supported by the Swazi Government.[29]

Tibiyo has invested heavily in the sugar industry. It is a joint investor in the third sugar-mill at Simunye with the Commonwealth Development Corporation on a 50/50 basis.[30] Furthermore, it owns forty per cent of Ubombo Ranches, which supplies Big Bend Sugar Mill. The major shareholder in this case is Lonrho. On a smaller scale, Tibiyo has established two sugar estates, at Sihoya and Sivunga.[31] Furthermore, it controls Vuvulane Irrigated Farms.

All has not been well with Swaziland's sugar industry in the 1980s. In 1982–83, Swaziland produced its quota of 380 000 metric tonnes, of which only 20 000 metric tonnes was consumed locally. Just prior to that time, the European Community (EC) and the United States were the Swazi sugar industry's largest buyers. In the late 1970s, 31.5 per cent of Swaziland's sugar exports went to the EC. However, with Europe's unification, one of its major goals is self-sufficiency in sugar production. Thus, it has preferred to encourage the production of sugar-beet in Europe.

The United States purchased 192 000 short tons of sugar from Swaziland in 1978. However, since 1982, it has been cutting Swazi sugar imports by forty per cent annually. Further exacerbating the problem, US industries are now relying more heavily on isoglucose as a sugar substitute. This has resulted in substantial losses in revenue to the sugar industry.

The dire consequences to the sugar industry projected by Levin in 1986 have not yet come to pass. It was shortly after the publication of his article that economic sanctions were imposed on South Africa. Furthermore, unforeseen circumstances in the global context, in which China could not meet its sugar quota and the United States suffered a severe drought portended a global shortfall in sugar production.[32] Thus, the price of sugar increased. Moreover, with increased foreign investment in the manufacturing sector, local demand for sugar more than doubled. Of course, this has not fully offset losses experienced on the world market. Realising that competition from sugar substitutes and alternatives will continue, the Swaziland sugar industry hopes to expand its local markets and to penetrate SADCC markets. In the case of the former, three manufacturing industries require sugar – Coca Cola, Bromar and Swazican.

In response to declining sugar prices, Simunye Sugar Estate has been planting some alternative crops, including cotton.[33] Ubombo Ranches, which supplies Big Bend, is anticipating cultivating grapefruits on part of its holdings.[34] Vuvulane Irrigated Farms has been cultivating both sugar and cotton since its inception in 1962. The project was originally funded by the Colonial (now Commonwealth) Development Corporation (CDC). In 1986, this project was handed over to Tibiyo. It now consists of 270 smallholder families, most of the households being established twenty years ago, with the original agreement that the farmers should occupy the land for twenty years. However, they have subsequently insisted on staying on the land and being designated as owners of their holdings.

Of the 264 farmers originally settled at Vuvulane, each household received sixteen hectares – eight for sugar and eight for other crops. During the first year, sugar prices were low. The next year, when the price was higher, the ratio was changed to 7:3. The next group of farmers to receive land allocations only received eight hectares each. Farmers are keen to identify uncultivated land that is owned by the project and have in some instances claimed the land for themselves.

For sugar production, Vuvulane has a quota to produce sugar-cane for Mhlume Sugar-mill that takes priority over the production of other crops. When farmers engage in the production of other crops, cultivation charges are deducted from their sugar account. The manager commented that this has often given Vuvulane farmers the mistaken notion that cotton yields higher profits than sugar. Another crop cultivated is maize.

Vuvulane Irrigated Farms owns farm equipment and inputs and provides services at a charge. During the planting season, the estate's tractor operators work overtime to make sure that all the land included in the estate is ploughed. Pesticides are also provided.

Sugar-cane production only requires about three months of labour-intensive cultivation. When the canopy forms over the sugar-cane, it is only necessary to do irrigation work. Thus, farmers can spend the rest of the time cultivating other crops.

Since Vuvulane was handed over to Tibiyo, approximately fifty farmers have not paid regular contributions to the project. It was their understanding that the project had a surplus of E3 million (emalangeni),[35] which they felt should be redistributed to them. The manager argued that the E3 million represented the project's fixed assets at the time of the takeover, adding that the situation had been misrepresented in the newspaper.

Levin suggests that Vuvulane farmers have legitimate complaints about the circumstances surrounding the earlier transfer of the scheme to the Swazi Nation.[36] He argues that it came at a time when there was a decline in world sugar prices. Furthermore, since farmers had to cultivate sugar-cane on seventy per cent of their holdings, they could not make a high profit. Also, although the land was handed over to the Swazi Nation, management remained under the control of the CDC, bringing accusations of colonial lordship.

When management attempted to expel fourteen farmers from Vuvulane in the early 1980s after the scheme's transfer to Tibiyo, King Sobhuza intervened. Subsequently, the High Court ruled against the expulsions. In a more recent incident, management did not attempt to expel those who did not fulfil their financial obligations. As a result, the project has had to receive a subsidy. The manager explained that no attempts were made to expel these farmers because if the land they are cultivating lies fallow, plant diseases could emerge and ravage all the surrounding crops.

In so far as extension services for other crops are concerned, management invites representatives of relevant organisations to come and speak to interested farmers at Vuvulane. Most residents do not have telephones and they live some distance from each other. When farmers are to be advised of a forthcoming meeting, messengers are sent out from the office on bicycles to inform everyone.

Prior to its handover to Tibiyo, Vuvulane Irrigated Farms was one of the few rural areas that fell outside the jurisdiction of the monarchy. In the 1972 elections, the project supported the Ngwane National Liberatory Party, along with sugar workers at Big Bend. One of the criticisms that the FAO team had of the Vuvulane model was that there was a lack of tribal leadership, and as a consequence, farmers involved in the project were not compelled to conform to traditional rules.

4.3 COTTON

Cotton was sporadically cultivated in South Africa after the American Civil War.[37] However, it was not until after 1948 that there was a sustained effort to cultivate the fibre. The cotton industry has grown despite low prices. After a price agreement was reached between growers and manufacturers in 1939, the local textile industry began expanding rapidly.

Swaziland's pattern of cotton production did not completely coincide with South Africa's. In the former, the first recorded cotton harvest was in 1906 and the Empire Cotton Growing Corporation began to produce the crop in 1925.[38] Cotton production reached a peak in the 1930s, but subsequent low prices meant that the crop did not regain its prominence until 1955. Production in 1964–66 represented another peak. A cotton breeder was sent to the Protectorate in 1963.

In Swaziland, cotton has become the major cash crop produced by peasants under dryland conditions and a major foreign exchange earner. The cotton industry emerged during the 1920s but declined in the 1930s due to low prices.[39] Unlike other cash crops such as sugar, pineapples and citrus fruits, which were produced primarily on corporate estates, cotton had been heavily concentrated on white settler farms.[40] Maize was the monocrop produced by peasants on Swazi Nation Land for purposes of subsistence and cash production.

After the Second World War, when cotton prices soared, a new period of prosperity began. In the 1950s, Swazi Nation Land peasants became interested in cotton production. However, it was not until the 1970s that the bulk of cotton production shifted away from white settler farms to SNL homesteads.[41] Successful cotton farming homesteads were also able to produce enough maize for subsistence purposes. The larger irrigated cotton farms were converted to sugarcane production during this period because of high sugar prices.[42]

However, cotton as a crop must not be viewed in isolation but *vis-à-vis* other crops in the context of Swaziland's rural development objectives. Furthermore, some consideration will be given to the development of the cotton industry, its labour demands and its articulation with the manufacturing sector. From a comparative perspective, the dimensions of the industry that interact with South Africa's industry will be considered. With regard to other products, the development of mohair production and the role of maize, citrus fruits and sugar-cane as competing domestic crops are to be considered.

Labour shortages have been a perpetual problem since the inception of Swaziland's plantation economy. However, Kliest suggests that it was the larger homesteads that had more productive members who engaged in cotton cultivation.[43] Thus they had little need for wage labour. In 1980–81, forty per cent of the total hectarage under cotton production was in areas organised in the Rural Development Areas Programme. In RDAs, extension agents promoted maize production. Nevertheless, much cotton expansion among Swazi peasants occurred in areas outside the RDAP where they had little access to extension agents.[44] It is thought that the rising price of cotton was the primary motivating factor. Cotton-farming peasants earn more than five times as much as non-cotton-farming peasants.[45]

Homesteads on which cotton production occurred were usually headed by more mature men between the ages of thirty-five and fifty-five.[46] T. J. Kliest found that there was a negative correlation between deficit maize production and wage employment.[47] Since the majority of labour migrants work in Swaziland's industrial areas, they can make frequent visits home thereby making agricultural and work cycles compatible.[48] Labour peaks for cotton and maize coincide, facilitating the utilisation of homestead labour.[49] More credit has been made available to peasants through banks, co-operatives and ginneries. Thus homestead heads have been able to gain access to high-yielding seeds and tractor rentals to improve cotton production.[50] Moreover, although the ratio between extension agents and peasants is low for assistance in growing any crop, it is higher for cotton-growing peasants.[51]

Since mine labour was restricted in the second half of the 1970s, Kliest, like de Vletter, was optimistic that many of the unemployed could be absorbed into the agricultural sector because of the higher cotton price.[52] However, an earlier study suggested that the unemployed were not producing cotton but simply getting off the land.[53] The Swaziland Cotton Board, an arm of the Ministry of Agriculture and Co-operatives, has argued that a forward-linked industry would provide more stability to the cotton market and inspire more confidence in cotton growers.[54]

With the establishment of the National Textile Corporation, Swaziland has achieved considerable success in vertically integrating its textile industry with cotton production. Bumper cotton production in 1987–88 helped to precipitate Natex's move into Phase II of its spinning factory.[55] Although the mill has access to South African cotton, its expressed preference is to utilise as much Swazi cotton as possible.

Plantation and smallholder production take place with the utilisation of different agricultural techniques. There are more than 11 000 smallholders producing cotton in the country.[56] Plantations or settler-estates tend to use capital-intensive irrigation agriculture, and the smallholders, dryland farming in lowveld areas of the country. Given vast fluctuations in rainfall patterns from year to year, the smallholders tend to produce substantially lower yields. Thirty to forty per cent of cotton production takes place in middleveld and Lubombo areas.[57] Half of the lowveld is drought-stricken for eighty per cent of the time, and the rest for sixty per cent of the time.[58] However, cotton is favoured in areas with low rainfall, and foodcrops are favoured in areas of high rainfall.[59]

Cotton is the most suitable dryland crop because plants have deep roots, enabling them to absorb more moisture and enhancing their drought-resistance.[60] The distribution of rainfall is important, especially during planting and the main flowering period. Excessive rainfall has its problems – early in the planting season, waterlogging and weed infestation; and during ripening, boll rots. Conversely, during drought, the plant simply loses its flowers and does not regain them until it starts raining again. Even though planting often begins in October, the time of harvest can be quite variable depending on localised rainfall patterns. Irrigated cotton requires less water than irrigated sugarcane.[61]

In 1981, a team was sent from the FAO to do an appraisal of Swaziland's cotton industry. Of utmost concern was the establishment of a mechanised weaving industry in Swaziland as well as extension of irrigated agricultural systems to increase productivity.[62] The team estimated that the range of potential cotton-growing was between 36 000 and 60 000 hectares.[63] To expand Swaziland's irrigation capacity, it would be necessary to dam the major rivers flowing through the country from South Africa.[64] Furthermore, the team proposed the establishment of large irrigated cotton estates with a hundred small-holders on each because irrigation is not cost-efficient unless areas it serves have a large hectarage.[65] The FAO team viewed such a project as being likely to attract donor aid.

The FAO team recommended that more smallholders be provided with access to irrigated agriculture.[66] In late 1988, the EC awarded Swaziland a grant of E11 million to develop water facilities in rural areas.[67] The project was to begin immediately and to have a duration of three years. Its objective was to rehabilitate sixteen small and medium-sized dams and then build ten new dams of each size. The project was to target 32 000 people and 35 000 cattle. In late 1989, Swaziland was in the process of negotiating with South Africa for water for Jozini dam near Lavumisa in the south-eastern lowveld.[68]

Intercropping was proposed as a means of maximising soil utilisation, providing subsistence crops and restoring soil fertility. Rape seed was suggested – as well as maize and beans – for the purpose.

The Swaziland Cotton Board, in the Ministry of Agriculture and Co-operatives, oversees cotton production in Swaziland. A small tax is levied against each kilogram of cotton, which is used to support the activities of the Cotton Board. To a certain extent, the board's function is to rationalise Swaziland's cotton production and to supervise research on cotton production in the country's different ecozones. It sets the date by which farmers should have started planting cotton each year. This is done to avoid problems with weeding and the prevalence of pests.

The Swaziland Cotton Board represents the interests of growers, keeps records of membership and the annual cotton yields of small farms and plantations. There is an agricultural experimental station south of Big Bend that caters to the cotton industry. Although the station is understaffed at the moment, the resident entomologist does research on pests that destroy cotton crops. The station is awaiting a staffperson to do research on breeding.

The entomologist at the Big Bend Agricultural Experiment Station indicated that farmers are not really adept at using pesticides. Not knowing how to identify specific pests, they often use broad-spectrum pesticides that not only kill the pests but beneficial insects as well. The experiment station provides extension services to educate farmers in the identification of specific pests for which there are special pesticides.

Swaziland has observer status on the South African Cotton Marketing Board which regulates cotton marketing throughout the region.

Different spinners require different grades of cotton for their operations. The Cotton Marketing Board determines from where and in what quantity spinners can buy ginned cotton based on their specifications. The region served by the South African board is not self-sufficient in cotton production. However, spinners can only import cotton once the regional supply of the required grade is exhausted. More importantly, the Cotton Marketing Board maintains a fund for stabilisation levies on Swazi cotton imported into South Africa.[69]

Cotton farmers have the option of approaching one of two companies operating in Swaziland to get their harvests ginned. J. L. Clark operates several depots in the lowveld but the actual ginning is done at Trans-Natal Cotton Ginnery in Pongola, across the Swazi border in northern Natal. It has a capacity of 10 000 metric tonnes. Cotona, now a Tongaat subsidiary, was set up in Matsapha in 1965 and has a second ginnery in Big Bend. Its capacity is 20 000 metric tonnes. A major concern for Swazi peasants was transportation of their cotton to the ginnery. Their ginnery preference might be determined by which ginnery offered free transportation. In the brief period between 1978 and 1980, the Swaziland Cotton Co-operative Society arranged contract ginning for its members and sold lint cotton to Swazi spinners.[70]

The rationalisation of the labour process in manufacturing is now paralleled by that in agriculture. There is an attempt to create a uniformity of conditions so that there will be a very similar outcome. By planting crops at the same time with the intent of a similar harvest date, processing is facilitated with less expense. Cotona only turns on its engines when cotton-picking begins. However, whereas farming under irrigated conditions would provide a more uniform outcome, the opposite is the case under dryland conditions.

The initiation of the National Textile Corporation in 1986 was a step towards the total integration of the cotton textile industry. Swaziland was thought to be a feasible site for the location of a cotton-spinning mill because it was a moderate cotton producer in the region.

The cotton industry relies on casual labourers who also engage in sugar-cane picking off-season, since both industries are in the lowveld. Most of these labourers are adult females with some children joining in on holidays. Dryland cotton grows from two to three feet tall, within easy reach of children. However, irrigated cotton grows from five to six feet tall and is only within the reach of adults. Cotton yields increase by thirty to forty per cent when irrigation is used.

In 1981, cotton-pickers were paid five Swazi cents per kilogram, which is very low by Swazi standards.[71] In 1989, weeders were paid as little as thirty Swazi cents per row. Cotton pickers are often transported from outside the lowveld. During the 1989 picking season, a truck hauling forty-eight cotton-pickers had an accident, killing eleven people near Siteki.[72] Some convict labour is used for cotton-picking at the Big Bend Agricultural Experiment Station.

The Swaziland government prefers that farm owners hire pickers rather than resort to mechanised picking because that way more people can be employed. In the early 1980s, only the Trans-Natal ginnery was equipped to process mechanically-picked cotton.[73] At the time, Cotona could not add such equipment because there were no provisions for it in the ginnery's plant design.

The year 1987–88 proved to be a record for the Swaziland cotton industry. Farmers produced 26 000 metric tonnes, whereas in the previous season they had produced only 19 000 metric tonnes. The former represents a twenty-six per cent increase.[74] In the 1986–87 season, farmers had produced only 14 991 metric tonnes. Furthermore, there was a substantial change in the distribution of cotton production between the sugar estates and the smallholder farms. In 1986–87, they had produced sixty-two per cent of the total cotton crop. However, due to the low price of cotton for that season, the Swaziland Cotton Board distributed a subsidy to compensate all growers for their losses under the EC's Stabex fund. In 1987–88, they had produced between thirty-five and forty per cent of the total crop. However, the estates – instead of increasing sugar production – had converted to maize production. To give added impetus to cotton farmers to continue cultivation, the price was a little higher than the previous year.

Despite earlier predictions that 1988–89 cotton production would be substantially below the record set in the previous year, early estimates indicated that that crop would actually surpass the previous year's record.[75] The executive officer of the Swaziland Cotton Board attributed the success of the 1988–89 crop to good rainfall in major cotton-producing regions. Earlier predictions were based on an uneven rainfall pattern.

During the 1988–89 season, the South African Cotton Marketing Board conveyed spinners' complaints to Swaziland concerning polypropylene contamination of their lint.[76] Swazi cotton pickers who work as sugar-cane cutters often use polypropylene bags to deposit cut cane. Polypropylene has a textile quality because it is tightly-woven white plastic. When cotton is placed in these bags, it is easy for unravelled polypropylene to interweave with cotton lint. At the spinning mill, it is spun and woven with cotton and can only be detected after dyeing because it does not absorb dye.

The Swaziland Cotton Board recommended that cotton pickers use only solid plastic bags available at local ginneries. The executive director observed that it was not only Swazi pickers who used polypropylene, but South African pickers as well. He added that in periods when there is an oversupply of cotton, spinners are prone to be more discriminating about polypropylene contamination. Nevertheless, the Cotton Board decided to fine farmers E100 if they used the bags.[77]

In the recycling process, cotton seeds procured through ginning are sold to cotton farmers at the end of the season. Cotona can also supply different varieties of seeds available in South Africa. Although experimentation is being conducted to identify the best seed type for cultivation under Swazi conditions, the current favoured seed types are Albacala 72 and 80.[78] Deltapine 90 has recently been introduced from the United States for farmers who use irrigation and/or mechanised picking.

In a joint venture with the National Industrial Development Corporation, the Israeli company Agri Carmel started the Nkalashane Cotton Project in the Lomahasha area in 1984. The project area covers about 20 000 hectares. It operated at a loss in 1985–86 due to drought conditions. In that season, the project produced 994 metric tonnes. In the next season, 1986–87, it increased production by nine per cent, to 1085 metric tonnes. Although the situation had improved even further in 1988–89 due to considerable rain, Agri Carmel still had not recouped its losses.

A staff of forty live on the site and engage in cultivation which, although predominantly dryland, includes a small irrigation component. Agri Carmel employs 1000–1200 pickers for a four-to-five-month period of cotton harvesting. Pickers are paid twelve cents per kilogram, or E5 per day. Seventy per cent of pickers are female. Children work on the project, primarily during school holidays. Pickers combine work at Nkalashane with cotton production on their own smallholdings.

The Swaziland cotton industry shows considerable promise for the development of a fully-integrated textile industry. The greater the level of integration, the more attractive Swaziland will be as a textile centre in the region.

4.4 MOHAIR

To provide a brief history of the mohair industry in southern Africa: the first angora goats were imported into South Africa in 1838.[79] The few surviving animals from the original herd were crossbred with indigenous Boer goats which were highly adapted to the Eastern Cape, where the industry was to become concentrated. South Africa's fledgling industry began to get a boost when British textile manufacturers started to take an interest in mohair. Before the Second World War, South Africa had been the world's largest mohair producer,[80] and it was to reach such prominence again in the 1970s, when it surpassed the United States. It has held that position ever since despite fluctuations in the price of mohair. In the early 1960s, in response to inquiries from Swaziland, the South African mohair industry exported some angora goats to Swaziland.[81]

Angora goats had been introduced into Lesotho during the nineteenth century. Gradually, its herds of goats and sheep grew to make it a major producer of mohair and wool. Although Lesotho's mohair industry will be discussed in greater detail in Chapter 7, some discussion of it is necessary here for comparative purposes. In the late 1960s, Lesotho began to promote mohair hand-processing and hand-weaving in a major women's development project.

As a sister country in southern Africa, Swaziland began to develop angora-goat-herding in the mid-1970s. Tibiyo Trust established an angora farm on a site donated to the government in Swaziland's highveld near Ngwenya, an area topographically similar to lowland areas of Lesotho. Much can be gleaned about the functioning of the project from various consultants' reports submitted between 1981 and 1985.[82] During most of the period, the project had 300–500 goats. The vast majority were angoras, with a few Boer goats being absorbed into the herds. The project encountered a number of problems due to the presence of poisonous plants, the prevalence of certain diseases and unregulated breeding practices.

The flora in the area differed from that of South Africa and Lesotho. There was a lot of *Viburnum lantana* (wayfaring tree) in the area, which is quite poisonous. Angoras also died from prussic acid poisoning (which can result from consumption of frosted sorghum), coccidiosis, heartwater disease and brown stomach worms. Kids did not have as much access to food as did adult goats. Rams were allowed to mate with ewes before mid-May, which resulted in the latter giving birth before the weather was warm. During a couple of seasons, the project lost most of the angora kid population.

The major consultant for the project proposed that herd size be increased and was optimistic that an agricultural extension project could be initiated in which small farmers would begin to acquire herds. This aspect of the project was never to reach fruition, however.

In Lesotho and other areas where communal land tenure prevails, angora goats range freely in mixed herds with sheep throughout the year. Therefore, nutrition and breeding are not controlled and there can be many fatalities from winter cold. Although the Tibiyo project provided somewhat improved conditions, it was not located in the right ecozone.

In general, it is not feasible for Swaziland to develop its own mohair industry. If the country were to become successful in mohair production, Tibiyo would have to develop a more grandiose project that would cater for Swaziland's needs. Lesotho, as a major mohair-producing country, has been unsuccessful in attracting its own scouring plant because of the risk involved for the topmaker – the operator who mechanically scours, cards and combs mohair for industrial spinning. At the inception of Swaziland's angora goat project, planners should have carefully selected a satisfactory micro-environment and made the necessary arrangements to accommodate an expanding herd. Rather than supplying only three per cent of Swaziland's mohair needs, they should have striven to supply a hundred per cent. With mechanical scouring being a remote possibility in Swaziland, they should have attempted to get some of it processed by the South African Mohair Board at a competitive rate until such time that Lesotho could develop its own facilities.

Mohair, as an animal fibre, is processed differently from cotton. Cotton lint is air-blown to remove dirt and other impurities. Animal fibre has a considerable grease content that requires removal with water and detergent scouring. Run-off from scouring plants can pollute the water supply.

In South Africa and the United States, the mohair production process is highly rationalised. It is conducted by private ranchers who have access to up-to-date research on the health, nutrition and breeding of angora goats. Angora goats are sheared twice a year and breed in the early winter so that they kid in the spring. Sheds are provided for the goats during the winter months. Mohair is sold at international auctions at Port Elizabeth and at San Angelo, Texas.

By the late 1970s, a number of cottage industries had come into existence. Droxford Farm supplied about three per cent of the mohair consumed by these industries. The remainder was being ordered from Lesotho and South Africa. The various industries that emerged engaged in weaving tapestries, curtains and cushions. When the Droxford Farm failed in the mid-1980s, some of the cottage industry owners and other interested parties bought up the herds for their own use. One of the goat buyers only uses mohair from her own goats as a supplement to mohair she orders from Lesotho and South Africa, for example, if an order is late or she needs more yarn in a particular colour.

4.5 THE RELATIONSHIP BETWEEN SUGAR AND COTTON PRODUCTION

Clearly, the sugar industry is very prominent in the south-eastern part of southern Africa. Cotton production has for the most part been secondary. To some extent, they are co-commodities. In South Africa, as a response to unstable sugar and cotton textile prices, the textile conglomerate Tongaat, which owns Swaziland's two cotton ginneries, has made investments in Hulett's as well as other types of industries. The Tongaat–Hulett group is very viable as the result of diversification, which included the following assessments in 1987–88:

- the sugar industry was doing well because of the increasing sugar price;
- building materials improved;
- food remained stable;
- textiles were difficult but expected to improve; and
- starch and sweeteners declined.[83]

The Swazi sugar industry, despite its linkages to the South African industry through multinationals, has a slightly different character. Given Swaziland's peripheral status, efforts have had to be made to mollify the Swazi peasantry by providing them with opportunities to grow sugar-cane under contract to Mhlume. Whereas each sugar-mill varies according to its multinational ties and arrangements with growers, the South African sugar industry is so highly monopolised that small growers are excluded from access to the sugar-mills. This is reinforced by apartheid policy and, until recently, the land acts that essentially proletarianised the black peasantry.

4.6 CONCLUSION

The CDC was responsible for initial investment to establish sugar-mills at Big Bend and Simunye during the late 1950s. Subsequently, it was to develop partnerships with multinationals and with Tibiyo, the royal family's national trust. Thus the trend in the Swazi sugar industry has been somewhat unusual. One can speculate that the CDC was interested in developing an integrated sugar industry in a British protectorate for the home market. Tate & Lyle and Lonrho became joint investors who also had investments in South Africa. For both core corporations, the pattern of investment is one in which they invested in the South African semi-periphery, which served as a conduit to investment in the southern African periphery.

Tibiyo is fostering the interests of the monarchy in its efforts to shape and control the Swaziland political economy. This represents a strategy by which the monarchy can tap into monopoly capital to further entrench itself. The trust actually mirrors the multinationals in its investment activities within Swaziland. Its diversified investments include sugar-mills, Ubombo Ranches, Vuvulane Irrigated Farms and, formerly, the Droxford Farm mohair project.

With the decline in international demand for sugar and a relatively low sugar price, the textile industry becomes an important area for alternative investment. Hence, cotton production is bolstered and a cotton-spinning mill is developed. Whereas Lonrho is a diversified multinational, Tate & Lyle embarked on diversification more recently, as demonstrated in the Swazi context with its investment ties with the National Textile Corporation. The contraction of the sugar industry would precipitate sectoral shifts by male and female workers.

Due to the pattern of regional and multinational investment, the South African and Swazi textile and sugar industries are interlinked collectively and individually across international boundaries. Although South Africa's sugar and textiles industries were launched at the turn of the century, Swaziland's sugar industry was not launched until the late 1950s and the textile industry until the 1980s. In the Swaziland political economy, Tibiyo will increasingly diversify its investments as sugar demand decreases and the price continues to drop. Furthermore, South African textile industrialists would favour the expansion of Swaziland's textile industry, while the sugar industry would be concerned about its own contraction.

5 Textile Management

5.1 INTRODUCTION

In examining the industrialisation process in Swaziland, it is necessary to consider the industrialists and the politico-economic context in which they operate. This involves some cognisance of the machinations of the global textile industry. In this chapter, the priorities of managers and owners will be considered as well as the role of women, aspects of the labour process, marketing strategies and intra-industry competition for cottage industries and factories.

Cottage industries and factories have complex historico-economic interrelationships. Cottage industries in European societies were precursors to the textile factories that arrived in the late eighteenth century. The clothing industry emerged in the second half of the nineteenth century. In the South African context, the clothing industry preceded cottage industries, which are now operating simultaneously. In the southern African periphery, due to late industrialisation, the reverse has occurred. Nevertheless, what unites these two industries is the parallelism of the labour process which in one case is unmechanised and the other mechanised, and the employment of women. In the case of cottage industries, substitutions can be made in aspects of the labour process to increase production and/or to reduce production costs. Cottage industries in Swaziland have undergone some historical modification in which the putting-out component is not as prominent as the small-scale factory component.

In the early 1970s, P. Selwyn conducted research on the constraints on industrialisation for small countries such as Botswana, Lesotho and Swaziland (BLS countries) where most investment was made in the agricultural sector when compared to South Africa, the industrial giant of the region. He saw a strong correlation between urbanisation and industrialisation. With South Africa as the industrial core, Selwyn made a basic distinction between internal peripheries and external peripheries in that the latter can be distanced economically by tariffs, trade restrictions and political/military barriers.[1]

South Africa exhibited industrial polarisation internally because most industries were located in the Witwatersrand area. The Nationalist government's efforts at industrial decentralisation actually under-pinned its policy of separate development. Selwyn suggested that industrial polarisation was still quite pronounced as late as the early 1970s, because industrialists were not relocating since the Witwaters-rand area provided the highest concentration of consumer purchasing power for manufactures and cheap railways for the transportation of raw materials.

In the BLS countries, per capita income is substantially lower than in South Africa. In the case of Swaziland, 8000 white settlers inflated per capita income because they owned most of the freehold land and commanded the highest salaries in industry and farming.[2] Selwyn characterised South African income disparities as *social* (*racial*) *inequality* and the income disparities between members of different countries as *spatial inequality*. Moreover, there is a lack of urbanisa-tion in the three countries and, thereby, a lack of growth points. Instead, all three export labour to South Africa. Lesotho exports the highest number of labour migrants to South Africa's gold mining industry.

In 1970, Swaziland generated employment for about a quarter of the growth in its labour force. There, and throughout the region, whites were concentrated in highly-paid managerial positions. Swaziland had many whites represented in its employment statistics as nationals rather than as expatriates. The country has a larger number of industries of a larger size than either Botswana or Lesotho. At the time of Selwyn's research, race relations in Swaziland seemed more akin to those in South Africa.

In peripheral countries, there was a lower ratio of value-added to gross output, which reflects the fact that the BLS countries carried out fewer stages of production than did South Africa. With the Southern African Customs Union, South African-manufactured goods have duty-free access to BLS markets. Swaziland, despite considerable industrial development, did not have many import-substitution industries.[3]

Interviews were conducted by Selwyn with employers to determine their views on investing in the BLS countries instead of in South Africa or Zimbabwe. A major problem in peripheral areas was the absence of an industrial working class. However, in this case, workers from the periphery have limited access to core markets. Selwyn argued that such contact brought wages in the periphery closer to those in the core. However, he suggested that since women do not have access to mining employment in South Africa or any other form of employment, their wages are less influenced by wage levels there.[4] He considered wage margins in Swaziland to be lower than in Botswana and Lesotho because of Swaziland's more developed cash economy.

Localisation of skilled jobs was an issue in all three countries. In fact, a comparison of wage rates does not fully coincide because there have been some jobs in South Africa reserved for whites but held by blacks at lower wages. Conversely, in the BLS countries, with the localisation of skilled jobs, locals are paid lower salaries to do similar jobs.[5]

When investing in the periphery, Selwyn suggested that investors have to have a greater return on their investment than in the core or, in the case of South Africa, the semi-periphery. Furthermore, the risks – which he perceived as commercial and political – had to be minimal. Investment by white industrialists into peripheral black countries necessarily had racial connotations. He observed that most investors approached the situation from a white supremacist perspective. Because of their racial views, investors were very sensitive to nationalistic motivations. They resisted some policies as being antithetical to their interests. Examples were anti-land speculation and racial discrimination legislation.[6] From the South African business management perspective, the BLS countries were considered to be at low risk politically. Investors did not view nationalisation as a real threat.

Utilities usually cost more in peripheral areas, however. Repairs, parts replacement and other support services might be more difficult to expedite due to transportation and communication problems. Selwyn considered these circumstances to be more conducive to monopoly investment into raw-materials-based industries that had multinational ties.[7] He also suggested that 'footloose' or 'runaway' industries would not be attracted to such areas if there were competing locations in core areas of the region. Clearly, he did not anticipate the capital mobility of the 1980s.

Local officials interviewed indicated that the BLS countries provided certain locational advantages to South African industries because they had access to African markets to which the South Africans would not otherwise have access.[8] However, Selwyn did not view this as beneficial to BLS countries, because other African countries were developing their own import-substitution industries and implementing protective tariffs on imports. Membership of the Southern African Customs Union by the BLS countries compounded the issue of their being inhibited from forming other types of economic ties elsewhere in Africa.

Selwyn considered the BLS countries to be in a relatively weak bargaining position *vis-à-vis* foreign investors.[9] He suggested that this problem was compounded by the fact that those governments hired foreign consultants from outside the region via such means as technical assistance programmes. These consultants had fixed ideas about industrial development that had little relevance to local conditions and governments were often forced to make concessions to industries that were not to their benefit. Swaziland was probably viewed very favourably by investors because of its abundant natural resources.[10] Nevertheless, in all three countries considered, there were no significant forward linkages in raw material processing at the time of Selwyn's study.[11] Thus, they were exporting raw materials to core areas for processing, marketing and possible repurchase.

Selwyn suggested the development of some intermediate industry. In fact, one criticism that he had concerning strategies for industrialisation was that industries had not adopted appropriate technologies to local conditions instead of more capital-intensive ones.[12] He considered another major development deterrent to be the mining industry's interests in maintaining the BLS countries as labour reserves.[13]

Selwyn discussed the possibility of a number of subsystems emerging if the homelands were to become independent. He foresaw the creation of a regional development bank, the promotion of inter-peripheral trade and the development of sporadic economic growth. However, he miscalculated whether the BLS countries and the international community would choose not to recognise the homelands as has been the case. Nevertheless, the suggestion of regional integration anticipates the formation of SADCC, which will be considered in Chapter 8. The advantage to regional integration is that it has the potential to promote even development in relation to core and semi-peripheral agencies and investors.

Selwyn thought that peripheral countries should spend less money to attract foreign industrial development and more to develop a local entrepreneurial class[14] by identifying potentially good credit risks.[15] He further suggested that peripheral nations should have joint financial institutions. Selwyn also discussed the possibility of competition between foreign companies and indigenous artisan-type industries. However, with the exception of SEDCO-supported industries, artisan-type industries were generally owned by European settlers.

Selwyn considered the possibility of attracting investors from non-Western areas such as the Chinese, Indians and Lebanese. He viewed the industries started by non-Western investors as being intermediate between Western-financed industries and artisan-type industries. In the African context, considerable animosity has built up against the intermediate position held by the latter two groups of people in different parts of the continent.

C. M. Rogerson suggests that cottage industries in the southern African periphery were originally missionary-inspired for the production of Western handicrafts. In the 1930s, the South African government also emphasised handicraft production in the reserves to alleviate the decline in peasant production. Again, in the 1970s, when urban surplus labour was being dumped in the homelands, it suggested developing such industries.[16] This production included African and European items.[17] In recent years, aid for such projects has become available through the United Nations and other donor agencies in independent peripheral countries. Rogerson considers this trend to represent the development of small-scale production in rural areas.[18]

To a great extent, Swaziland's textile industry is a nascent one. In practice, although most cottage-industry and factory employers are members of the Federation of Swaziland Employers (FSE), they do not perceive themselves as being part of one cohesive industry. Furthermore, Swaziland is not a country in which there is a textile tradition, unlike parts of North and West Africa and Asia, where both cottage-industry and factory production take place. To some extent, cottage industries can be viewed as indigenous, labour-intensive industries, and factories as foreign-owned, capital-intensive industries. However, most of the cottage industries are settler-owned or managed.

Many of the textile factories in Swaziland could be categorised as 'runaway shops' or 'footloose industries'. Although there is little analysis of runaway shops in southern Africa, there is a sizeable literature from elsewhere in the world. In characterising runaway shops, H. I. Safa argues that such multinational firms are attracted to 'countries where low wages, high unemployment, limited natural resources, low levels of unionisation and politically stable regimes prevail'.[19] The country of destination welcomes such industries with the expectation of improving foreign exchange earnings and employment generation, since these industries are largely labour-intensive. The most labour-intensive industries are in the areas of garment manufacture, textiles, food processing and electronics.[20] There is usually a preference for the employment of single, young, female labour. When men are employed, they are usually paid more.

Safa describes the characteristics of runaway shops *vis-à-vis* American labour history. She argues that there are three stages in the process of labour recruitment in the US:

1. Use of native labour;
2. Use of immigrant labour; and
3. Runaway shops.

She suggests that the destinations of runaway shops include the countries of origin of Third-World immigrant labour: that is, Mexico, the Caribbean, and parts of South-east Asia.[21] In the monopoly capital phase, in which such industries are no longer family-owned, the labour process has been fragmented so that the skilled jobs remain in the US and the deskilled jobs are relocated.[22] The establishment of export-processing zones in the Caribbean has facilitated rapid and inexpensive transportation of raw materials and processed goods.

The runaway shop phenomenon is having an impact on family structure. In Mexico, its impact is viewed as being very disruptive because females find it easier to get employment and males encounter great difficulty. The latter are strongly influenced by patriarchal ideology which requires that they be the breadwinners. What seems to be emerging in Mexican *maquiladoras* (export-processing plants) is three-generational matrifocal families.[23] However, in the Jamaican case, where many families are largely female-headed, patriarchal ideology has little or no impact on family structure. Safa proposes some progressive measures concerning working conditions and collective bargaining. However, she realises that such measures could potentially pit workers and countries against each other in the context of the global assembly line.

J. Nash considers the New International Division of Labour (NIDL) to be an outcome of core–periphery interpenetration.[24] This is reflected in the fragmentation of the labour process and results in risk diversification for industrialists. She observes that in the NIDL, women represent the lowest-paid workers in the lowest-paying countries. One outcome is that inequalities emerge according to gender, race and region, as well as between rural and urban areas.

Capital migration has now surpassed labour migration in impact. In conjunction with actual factory production, entrepreneurs have developed putting-out systems to distribute raw materials for homework. Nash speculates that one long-term impact is that factory industrialisation will lead to the eradication of handicraft and business enterprises already in existence.

A. Robert lists several factors that are conducive to textile relocation from member countries of the European Community (EC), as follows:

1. Essential raw materials, such as cotton and jute, were often locally grown;
2. Mature production processes are often more-or-less standardised and call for little modern knowledge;
3. The necessary level of technology was either traditionally present in those countries (spindles, handlooms) or could easily be obtained (cutting machines, sewing machines and irons);
4. Due to these factors, the capital expenditure needed was very low in relation to other forms of industrialisation;
5. The LDCs' limitless 'reservoir' of cheap labour satisfied the labour-intensive industries' search for comparative advantage;
6. Finally, production abroad was greatly facilitated by technological improvements in transport and communications.[25]

Nevertheless, she dismisses the view that import penetration of Third World countries would have a devastating effect on Western Europe's textile and clothing industry.[26] However, she does observe that the EC lost 243 000 jobs in this sector in the period between 1972 and 1977.[27]

The Newly Industrialising Countries (NICs) have experienced rapid industrialisation as a direct consequence of textile production. Taiwan and Hong Kong have emerged as major textile centres. Other Asian countries emerging are Korea and India and, on a smaller scale, Singapore and Pakistan.[28] Robert contends that it is women's economic weakness and social subordination that make them more vulnerable to patriarchal attitudes in such workplaces.

On the restructuring of the global assembly line, Ward argues that boundaries between the formal, informal and domestic spheres, are becoming increasingly obscure.[29] Some women are performing daily in all three. Women, faced with negotiating employment in any combination of these spheres have had to develop innovative forms of resistance. Women doing homework are considered the most isolated and exploited.

A major constraint on the development of non-core textile industries is the Multi-Fibre Arrangement (MFA). It is an international agreement that functions to protect non-competitive industries in the core against competition from periphery imports.[30] It was originally intended to have the opposite impact, in assisting peripheral industry to develop without competition from core imports. S. Burne and

M. Hardingham see its abolition as essential to improving the status of Third World-produced textiles.[31] Although core runaway shops may be a factor in precipitating periphery industrial migration, quotas set under the MFA have motivated these industries to seek relocation in other peripheral countries that do not reach their export quotas.

To analyse the perspectives of owners and managers in both cottage industries and factories, I conducted a series of interviews with most of my informants during my research in Swaziland. There were a few single interviews conducted towards the end that included managers whose factories were not part of the survey. All the interviews were open-ended and some of the same types of opinion emerged repeatedly. The following sections consider cottage industries and factories separately.

5.2 OWNERS AND MANAGERS IN COTTAGE INDUSTRIES

In the post-independence period in most underdeveloped countries, small-scale development planners have sought to employ women in introduced handicraft industries that process indigenous raw materials for international markets. The handicrafts include traditional garments, tapestries and rugs, and other household items. Because these projects are often based in villages where there is no running water or electric power, appropriate or intermediate technologies are often adopted. Handicraft industries sponsored by small-scale donor agencies often take the form of co-operatives. However, in Swaziland, most of these industries are privately-owned.

The oldest cottage industry in Swaziland was started in 1947. However, the vast majority of such industries existing today were begun during the 1970s. Most of these were started by married European expatriate women. Cottage industries have tended to be located in rural areas of the country and on the premises of the employer. These industries engage in spinning and weaving and use the most appropriate technologies. Cottage industries often provide the only means of employment for rural women.

Cottage-industry owners are usually long-term residents in Swaziland who own Title Deed Land. One woman married a white Swazi national and moved to the country twenty years ago. Another was married to an expatriate who had had an assignment in the country with a donor agency and decided to continue living there. Yet another has lived in the country for nearly half a century after moving from

South Africa with her husband, who was engaged in a major afforestation project. As a final example, a long-term European immigrant to South Africa decided to move to Swaziland to start his own cottage industry. In addition to South Africans, the nationalities represented among cottage-industry owners include Britons, Germans and Americans.

Anthropologists and other social scientists have tended to ignore white minority groups in peripheral contexts. The most notable exception that comes to mind is some research on white South Africans done by members of that group. In Swaziland, although race relations appear cordial, there is little social interaction between the European settler community and Swazis. In fact, they seem to form two distinct solitudes. Swazi female domestic servants to some extent interpenetrate the two solitudes. There are some white Swazis who speak Siswati, however. The coloured and Indian communities are also quite separate. The most common arenas of interracial interaction outside the workplace is in the bars and at discotheques.

Cottage-industry owners exhibit positive racial and gender attitudes and respect for Swazi culture. However, prior to Swaziland's independence, the European settler population was very intransigent in maintaining its political and economic power. H. Kuper suggests that during the initial period of contact Swazis did not classify whites by colour, viewing them instead as a separate species.[32] It was those Swazis who had the greatest exposure to Western institutions who began to see the world through a racial prism. Dichotomies emerged between white and black, landed and landless, and 'civilised' and 'barbarous'.[33] Furthermore, the Swazis began to distinguish ethnicity among whites whether they be Briton, Afrikaner or Jew and the character traits of colonial officials fulfilling specific social roles. Today, the land issue and localisation policy remain some of the most racially-sensitive issues in contemporary Swaziland. In the post-independence period, Swaziland has been viewed as the most politically conservative of the BLS countries.

European settler women, although well-educated, find it difficult to obtain public and private sector employment because of Swaziland's localisation policy. A number of them are married to men who earn a high income, thereby providing capital for investment in their cottage industries. To make a place for themselves in the working world, they seem to expand the domestic context – their home, their land. Most of the cottage industries are located on land that is also cultivated for cash crop production.

Some expatriates think that the Swazi industrialisation process should be along 'appropriate' lines and should be Swazi-owned. An expatriate woman was critical of the course of industrial development in the textile industry. Commenting that all the cotton-processing firms in Matsapha Industrial Estate were South African-owned, she said that she had been on a tour of one of the industries and had seen a few women standing around watching machines. She suggested that what Swaziland needs is small-scale, labour-intensive industries located throughout the country that produce goods for basic consumption.

Cottage-industry owners usually hire a Swazi manager for their enterprise(s) who has proved to be a very reliable employee. Although such a person can serve as an intermediary, owners often have close contact with their long-term employees because they work alongside them during the labour process. Moreover, when finishing is done, the owner is always there to see that the merchandise is suitable for shipping or display.

Textile owners, because of their close relationship with their staff, seem more attuned to personal illness and family problems that arise with the latter. They also seem more sympathetic in instances in which staff need to leave early or be absent from work. They simply let them know how the time can be made up. A number of cottage-industry owners indicated that they offer flexitime because so many of their employees are involved in childrearing and other domestic activities. Also, shops and government offices close at the end of the working day leaving no time for employees to conduct their business after work.

The cottage industries that typify Swaziland and the rest of southern Africa are clearly adapted to the conditions of the rural political economy. Although workshops are set up on the owners' premises, in a number of instances, spinning, crocheting and knitting are put out to women in more remote areas. These are the most tedious aspects of the labour process. Most industries have their own outlet(s) and also market through shops in urban areas.

Surprisingly, few textile-producing co-operatives have been formed in Swaziland. One woman indicated that her business had actually evolved from a co-operative. About twelve years ago, she and members of the Swazi and European communities in her area decided to pool their handicrafts and display them in a building on her property. The items varied in quality, with some lying on the shelves for months. She began selecting the best items for display and eventually started giving high-quality raw materials to members for processing. Also, a partly government-owned cottage industry attempts to foster co-operative formation in conjunction with the chief handicraft officer in the Ministry of Commerce and Industry.

Burne and Hardingham suggest that co-operative ownership benefits more people than does private ownership, with the proviso that co-operatives must be run democratically and not dominated by an elite.[34] But they admit that there are some circumstances to which co-operatives are more suited than others. Cases in which co-operatives are unsuitable would be in countries where there is extreme poverty. Often, villagers could not afford to make the initial investment necessary for membership. Swazi rural women are less marginal.

One informant suggested that I should not confine my research solely to textile production, arguing that the strong grass-weaving tradition exhibits the greatest similarity to textile production. Several grasses have been used to construct household furnishings and utensils such as mats for sitting and sleeping, churns and baskets. Large grass floor mats, table placemats and handbags are most commonly produced for tourist markets.

Mohair, cotton and wool are the most commonly used fibres in cottage industries. Three industries are heavily orientated towards mohair tapestry-weaving. One industry produces washable cotton rugs, another spins cotton yarn and yet another weaves cotton cloth.

Cottage-industry owners do make an attempt to buy natural fibres within the SADCC region whenever possible. In interviews, they play down their buying from South Africa. For example, those who use mohair say they tend to buy from Lesotho Handspun Mohair, which was formerly a CARE-sponsored co-operative. One owner buys Lesotho's mohair clip (a season's crop of mohair) from the South African Mohair Board in Port Elizabeth.

Wool is the main fibre used for the knitting of jerseys, and the yarn is usually purchased from South Africa. However, some jerseys are made from handspun mohair. Cotton has the benefit of being more durable and easily washable, and is just coming into vogue as a speciality fibre.

When the Tibiyo angora goat farm project failed in the mid-1980s, some cottage-industry owners bought the goats. One woman who had purchased fifty goats now has a herd of a hundred. She uses fibre from her herds to supplement mohair she orders from abroad. She indicated that if she were to have a herd large enough to satisfy the needs of her cottage industry, she would require two thousand head of goats. However, this owner observed that angora-herding is particularly labour-intensive because they are not well-adapted to the Swazi climate.

With the introduction of the National Textile Corporation – a cotton-spinning mill to be discussed in the next section of this chapter – cottage industries began to consider the utilisation of cotton fibre since it is grown and processed locally. A donor-sponsored industry was already producing handwoven cotton cloth. A cotton-spinning industry buys direct from the ginnery. However, a cotton-rug industry orders dyed cotton yarn from South Africa because it does not have a reliable water supply for dyeing. Thus, the introduction of the spinning mill has not been disruptive to the labour process.

Globally, natural fibres still have the major share of the fibre market *vis-à-vis* man-made fibres despite predictions to the contrary. This gives female fibre processors – both spinners and weavers – a means of making a livelihood. However, Burne and Hardingham caution against spinners and weavers attempting to cater exclusively to international markets.[35] They argue that reliance on one fibre makes them vulnerable to fluctuations in international fibre markets, to competition between natural and man-made fibres, and to mechanisation in developed countries that replicates Third-World manual techniques.

Looms are not manufactured in Swaziland or in any of the SADCC countries. They are, for the most part, purchased from Europe and New Zealand. Spinning wheels are now manufactured at the Manzini Industrial Training Centre (MITC). However, at the time of my research, this was not widely-known. Furthermore, there had been no recent production at MITC.

In so far as the labour process is concerned, most cottage industries tend to put out the most tedious aspects of the labour process such as spinning, knitting and crocheting. Weaving is performed almost exclusively in the factory context. Most Swazi women learn to knit and crochet in school. With regard to the labour process, since women do not have a weaving tradition, they usually start by spinning and eventually move on to weaving. They are taught by women who have been employed in the cottage industry for a long time. The owner produces patterns, which are attached to the backs of looms to guide weavers. Experienced weavers usually can weave without patterns because they have memorised the designs.

The most diversified cottage industries combine workshop production and the putting-out of raw and unfinished materials as well as the production of non-textile products. Furthermore, they usually have a sizeable and well-located outlet. One of the most diversified industries is a cottage industry based in Malkerns whose sphere of economic activity extends in a twenty-five kilometre radius of the management facility.

The Malkerns site includes a workshop for six seamstresses, a shop, offices and storerooms. Beads and yarn are put out to women who return every Monday to exchange finished goods for more raw materials and to receive their pay. Furthermore, the owner is in partnership with two other women and owns shops at a major hotel near Mbabane and in a shopping mall in the capital.

The informant who suggested the idea of viewing grass-weaving as textile production had formed a working relationship with grass-weavers living on a mountain some distance from her business. Lutindzi grass abounds in the area. My informant was able to reach an agreement with the grass-weavers to produce mats for her shop. She told them the shapes, sizes, colours and quantities she wanted and supplied them with dye. The informant would visit them periodically to buy their mats. As each woman presented her mats, the cottage-industry owner would do a check for quality control and show women what should not be done as well as encourage what should. In one instance, she asked a woman who had done very good mats to stand and explain to the group how she had made them. Rejects would not be purchased. The informant commented that the women under-produce for her shops; she could sell three times what they are currently producing.

The newest, smallest and least-diversified cottage industry has expanded over a period of a several months from three employees to six. At the beginning of my field research, the women were only doing cotton-spinning. By the end, they had diversified into mohair-spinning and were beginning tapestry-weaving. Not displaying items in shops, the owners have relied heavily on foreign mail order sales.

Certainly, raw materials that are put out compete with women's domestic and agricultural activities. P. Teal argues that since most spinners are part-time, integrating their spinning with the domestic and agricultural cycles, it is of low quality, thereby influencing the quality of the finished product. Spinners usually cannot make a living wage in their work. Teal traces a scenario in which the weaver decides to buy yarn from a spinning-mill to avert financial ruin.[36] He benefits, the mill benefits, rural herders benefit – but the spinners are eliminated from the total labour process. To resuscitate spinners, Teal proposes some intermediate technology between manual and mechanised spinning to increase the quality and rate of production of cottage-industry-produced yarn.

As yet, this is not a problem in Swaziland. Teal is analysing a situation in which mill production intervenes in the manual labour process. Furthermore, the spinners he describes seem to be involved in less structured enterprises than those described in Swaziland. One point that is illuminated by the above is that in the Swazi context there is a continuum, of which industrialised and non-industrialised activities form the two poles. Cottage industries engaging almost entirely in factory-like production would be closer to the industrialised pole, while independent producers utilising traditional materials are closer to the opposite pole, and village-level development projects with handicraft components close to the centre.

In spite of the fact that cottage industries are controlled by the expatriate community, there is considerable competition among these industries. New cottage industry owners did not want to display their products widely because of fear that their designs might be copied and sold by those with more capital. One textile producer banned another from her property because the latter was trying to steal trade secrets in her absence. In a few instances, it was strongly hinted that one woman was 'out for herself'. Later, I discovered that woman paid her employees some of the highest wages in the entire textile industry.

There is little vertical integration in these industries. Most raw materials and equipment are procured from outside the country. In one case, the owner of a cotton-spinning cottage industry approached the owner of a cotton-rug-weaving industry about selling her yarn to him. He said that her price was too high for him to sell his finished rugs at a reasonable price. He could buy machine-spun yarn much cheaper. She, in turn, had wanted to pay the cotton-spinners in her employ well.

In terms of diversification, some cottage-industry owners have made more headway. Those industries that have diversified, for example, by doing sewing, beadwork and grass-weaving, can hedge their bets against insolvency by emphasising one area if the other proves unprofitable. There are a number of problems that might emerge – a cut-off in the supply of raw materials; mass resignations by workers; inaccessibility of a putting-out site due to rain-damaged roads, and so on. This gives the cottage-industry owner flexibility in determining the direction of the enterprise.

There was much discussion of the role of design: who should be involved and why they are not. Design work is generally not performed by Swazi women. Since cottage industries are primarily expatriate-run, I am certain there is some sensitivity on the part of owners to charges that this is one way in which their workers are being exploited, by being deprived of skills. Design was invariably linked to creativity. Some managers and owners expressed the view that because art education was not stressed in primary and secondary education in Swaziland, women do not know how to channel their creativity. One woman said that women do not bond well in exchanging ideas and coming up with new designs. A number of cottage-industry owners have indicated that they have attempted to teach design to adults in the industry but their efforts have been thwarted by bureaucracy.

The owners of two cottage industries are actively involved in designing tapestries. One member of a couple is an artist. Unlike Basotho tapestries, which tend to reflect foreign-designed local scenes, Swazi tapestries tend to have a more European flavour, with a preference for abstract designs and pastel colours. One cottage-industry owner won an award from the South African Wool Association for her design work.

In Lesotho, a sister cottage industry to one in Swaziland encouraged its weavers to design their own tapestries by doing *litema*, abstract geometric designs which are engraved on the façades of traditional houses in some areas of Lesotho. The effort was very successful because it was a design the women had seen or actually engraved into their house facades in a different medium.

Small-scale industries must be flexible in design and technique in order to gain entry into and maintain their position in international markets that are fashion-sensitive. Forward linkages must be facilitated by encouraging smallholder fibre cultivation, the formation of small, labour-intensive village production units, and the development of appropriate technologies that will not limit flexibility in production.

Here, the role of the putting-out merchant must be considered. Unlike her pre-industrial counterpart, the contemporary putting-out merchant is an international arbiter of style. Being interlopers between core and periphery, putting-out merchants make modifications in handicrafts in the areas of colour, size, raw material and function, to fit the decor of the Western middle-class living-room or lounge and must therefore be acutely aware of changes in fashion trends.

In their role as employers, putting-out merchants risk some loss of raw materials and equipment when they distribute them. To minimise loss, they weigh all the materials put out as well as the finished products and leftover materials. One woman said that some of the mohair from her cottage industry is regularly stolen for private use.

From the perspective of marketing, there are some speciality shops that sell handicrafts as well as open markets located throughout the country. One speciality shop is owned by an expatriate woman in Mbabane. Her shop has a more artistic orientation, with an emphasis on paintings and sculpture. Gallery shows are held there monthly, with openings for the artists. The owner prefers not to sell tapestries because she does not think they exhibit much creativity. One exception is tapestries produced by a cottage industry in Lesotho.

For these industries to have a variety of African crafts on sale, they must import them via South Africa. In South Africa itself there is a high demand for African art from throughout the continent. In textiles, there is a demand for African prints. Zambian and Tanzanian cloth has entered the markets of neighbouring SADCC countries. One retail outlet owner said that in the pre-sanctions period, she used to travel all over the continent to buy African artefacts and textiles. However, as the rand began to plummet, such travel was no longer feasible. She now imports via Johannesburg. Another retail-outlet owner indicated that she travels to Zululand to buy from producers but would be reluctant to travel elsewhere outside Swaziland unless accompanied by a man.

South Africa is an important regional market for African handicrafts of all kinds. One shop owner said that an outgrowth of the current crisis in South Africa is that there is now a reorientation of perspective in which white South Africans feel more a part of Africa, as opposed to being Europeans who happen to live on the African continent.

A business management programme in Manzini has a handicraft shop in which ninety per cent of the merchandise is manufactured in Swaziland. The manager, a Swazi woman, does not buy directly from producers, although she buys regularly from the local market. She encourages producers to come to her shop, however. The vast majority of customers who patronise the shop are expatriates.

Marketing is extremely important in making handicrafts visible and selling them. Trade fairs are held at national, continental and intercontinental levels for purposes of establishing new handicraft markets. Quality control exercised in primary production is a key determinant to an item's popularity. Recently, middle-class preferences have tended toward plastics and pastel colours. At the local level, some women producers have begun to recycle colourful plastic bags by substituting them for grass weavings.

Cottage industries are generally low-wage industries, with substantial mark-ups occurring once items leave the hands of producers and travel through the marketing apparatus. It is the middleperson and the retailer who receive the greatest remuneration for handicrafts going through conventional channels. There is pressure on putting-out merchants to keep prices low in order to make handicrafts attractive on international markets. Overhead costs include packaging, shipping and customs duties. Cottage industries may be constrained from becoming more forward-linked simply because of the cost factor.

At the local level, tourism provides a means of marketing handicrafts. In the Ezulwini Valley, there are a number of hotels and restaurants along the Manzini–Mbabane road, and many of the hotels have gift shops. Furthermore, market areas for independent producers have been set up alongside the road. At weekends, South African tourists are the major customers at these restaurants, shops and markets. Also, tourists sometimes visit remote cottage industries to observe production and to buy handicrafts.

Teal addresses the problem of rural cottage industries in which there is a fibre-spinning tradition that caters to rural markets. He suggests that the construction of roads to give isolated communities access to the outside world also make their production vulnerable to competition. Since most handicrafts produced by cottage industries are not indigenous to Swaziland, there are no rural markets for them. Beadwork and grasswork, which are traditional Swazi crafts, usually appear in modified form for Western consumer use.

For most of their history, cottage industries were not considered to be full-fledged industries and escaped rigid wage regulation by the government. A committee met in 1990 to schedule wages for the different job types in cottage industries. In addition to being relatively unregulated until recently, cottage industries – because of their intermediate status – have proved difficult to unionise. An official of the Swaziland Manufacturing and Allied Workers' Union (SMAWU), who attempted to unionise workers at one cottage industry, said that it was difficult because they had no real tools to down and no boss present to whom they could communicate their demands. On the day the union called a strike at this cottage industry, the owner was in his house nearby oblivious to any problems at the workshop.

De Vletter observes that Swaziland has some of the most liberal legislation towards labour unions.[37] It provides for an industrial court to adjudicate labour disputes. Unions can be formed if forty per cent of the labour force agrees to membership. Employers, for the most part, have been anti-union and have dragged their feet when they have been approached about trade union formation. At the time of my research, there were no trade unions in cottage industries or textile and clothing factories in Swaziland. However, by 1991, there were more than a hundred cottage-industry workers in SMAWU, while efforts were underway at the National Textile Corporation. The regulation of cottage industries has strengthened the union's hand.

Independent producers were not included in this study. As indicated earlier, they and factory workers occupy opposite poles of an industrial continuum, with cottage-industry workers being intermediate. Furthermore, the 'factory pole' represents the formal sector and the opposite pole, the informal sector. Cottage industries are transitional, both historically and contemporaneously. In a survey of the women's handicraft training programme, Pauline Woodall, who was then director of the National Handicraft Training Centre, speculated that 100 000 women were involved in handicraft production in Swaziland.[38] Women's representation in the informal sector is viewed as being high because it does not conflict with their domestic and agricultural duties at the homestead while providing them with a means of income generation. L. Loughran and J. Argo found that most informal-sector female handicraft producers are older women; younger women shun this sector because they do not consider it to be lucrative.[39] In the literature on the informal sector, the predominant view is that women participate in it because they do not have access to the formal sector due to male bias in employment, education, residence, and so on.[40] Loughran and Argo observed that the Swazi government has not been successful in introducing co-operatives, resulting in rural women preferring to work alone or in loose associations.[41]

There are approximately 200 Zenzele or 'do-it-yourself' associations that are involved in rural development projects throughout the country. Their total membership is about 4000, with membership in individual associations numbering from ten to fifty. They collect dues and have regular meetings in which they co-ordinate their handicraft activities. The Zenzele associations do sisal-weaving, sewing and vegetable gardening.[42]

There are two United Nations (UN) projects with handicraft components that target women and the rural poor. The first is the Women In Development (WID) project founded at Ntfontgeni in the northern highveld. Started in 1975, there are project sites at five other rural locations, all in UN sponsored RDAs. At these project centres, training is offered to women in batik dyeing, tie-dyeing, screenprinting, sewing, machine-knitting, leathercraft and shoe-making, and mohair- and wool-weaving.

Training sessions last four a half months. At the end of training, women can take out loans to buy sewing machines and other equipment. Loughran and Argo found that by 1986 sixty-two post-WID women's handicraft groups had been formed,[43] but most of the clothing manufactured was considered to be of such poor quality that it could not be sold in urban markets in Swaziland. The WID groups also produce school uniforms, as do a number of sewing groups – including St. Theresa's Catholic Mission, the Council of Swaziland Churches, the National Handicraft Training Centre and Manzini Industrial Training Centre. However, they are finding that the market is becoming saturated. An expatriate involved in one of the branch projects was not only concerned about market saturation but also about the indebtedness of the women who had out taken bank loans to buy equipment. Many were so indebted during their first months of work that they could not meet loan payments. Russell, Dlamini and Simelane found that despite the fact that female participants in the project were generally not very poor, twenty-five per cent could not afford to pay for equipment.[44]

The other UN project orientated towards rural development is the People's Participation Project (PPP) sponsored by the Food and Agriculture Organisation. The project attempts to target the poorest of the rural poor, many of whom are women. Cotton-farming is one component of the PPP, as well as the development of cottage industries and handicraft production.[45] In fact, at a number of project sites, the WID project serves as the cottage industry and handicraft component for the umbrella UN project.

Independent producers have a number of options for selling their crafts. They can sell them directly in the market, to retail outlets in Swaziland, or they can travel to the major cities in South Africa and sell them on the street. One cottage-industry project manager, lamenting over the fact that some of her producers had gone to South Africa to sell their wares, commented that in order for producers to make a profit, they must purchase items in South Africa to bring back to sell in Swaziland.

Russell examines the marketing efforts of primary producers who are not members of formal organisations – those most closely akin to traders in west, central and east Africa.[46] Conducting her research at marketing outlets in Swaziland and South Africa – as well as in individual homesteads – she finds that producers are confronted by a hierarchy of relationships based on gender and race in the network of exchange from producer to consumer. She also identifies markets for various handicrafts produced. Handicrafts made from raw materials indigenous to rural Swaziland, such as grass baskets and mats, would be sold to middle-class South African whites; crafts made from purchased materials, such as quilts and knitted and crocheted items, to urban Swazis. Thus, these handicrafts have distinct markets, unlike other handicrafts sold in the country.

Vis-à-vis the gender division of labour, men are the transporters of women to South Africa. Furthermore, it is men who control the curio market in Swaziland. They cater to the South African tourist market and have stalls set up near the major hotels in the Ezulwini Valley. They carve in stone and a rare, protected wood called *kiaat*.

The women who trade in South Africa are the most affluent and receive the highest profits for their wares.[47] They tend to be middle-aged and married to men who have skilled or semi-skilled occupations. To increase their profits, some of these women barter their wares to South African housewives in exchange for second-hand clothes, which they in turn sell in Swaziland.

The major towns in Swaziland have markets where people can buy locally-produced handicrafts, clothing and food. Sellers come from throughout Swaziland and southern Mozambique to the Manzini Market. Swazis and expatriates buy here. The owners of speciality shops often visit the market to select the best items to sell in their shops at a substantial mark-up.

In response to the view that Swazi women are not willing to work as cheaply as Asian women, a Swazi official at a training centre responded that whites have a monopoly on the handicraft industry and will not let blacks be fully involved. She is encouraging Swazi women in her programme to explore creative ideas and to do market research prior to mass production. This is an effort to produce more Swazi small-businesspeople.

The Business Management Extension Programme trains young Swazi men and women in management techniques and provides workshop space for them to launch their businesses. Among the seven industries on the site, two were textile-related. An official of the programme suggested that there is a problem in encouraging Swazi entrepreneurs because the general populace is accustomed to consuming goods produced in South Africa. He also pointed out that even support industries in Matsapha Industrial Estate are not owned by Swazis.

To conclude this section, the artisan-type industries of which Selwyn speaks are owned by expatriates. They provide women in remote areas with employment opportunities that they would not ordinarily have. I would suggest that because of the selective development of Swazi Nation Land in the Rural Development Areas Programme, many rural areas have been neglected. The capitalisation of parts of designated RDAs has peripheralised non-capitalised areas and non-RDA areas. In non-capitalised areas, rural conditions are conducive to the investment of expatriate women in cottage industries. They are tapping into the latent labour reserve. This reserve is constituted by women living in the immediate vicinity of the cottage industry. However, through its putting-out mechanisms, the industry reaches the latent labour reserve that lives within a wide radius of the actual workshop.

In the next section of this chapter, consideration will be given to textile factories.

5.3 MANAGERS OF FACTORIES

In cottage industries, because each industry performs a similar and nearly complete labour process, I have characterised them as a whole. In mills and factories, more specialised functions are being performed. Here, I will consider each industry and its labour process in relation to the development of forward linkages in Swaziland. First, however, some relevant literature will be discussed.

Selwyn surveyed sixteen industries in Botswana, the same number in Lesotho and thirteen in Swaziland in the early 1970s.[48] Of the forty-four industries thus surveyed, a quarter were categorised as textile, wearing apparel, and leather industries. In a more recent analysis of firms investing in Swaziland since September 1985, de Vletter found that, by nationality, six were Taiwanese and an equal number South African, and that approximately half of fifteen new firms manufactured clothing or textile products.[49]

Swaziland's manufacturing industry accounted for nearly a quarter of the gross domestic product (GDP) in 1983.[50] It is the largest private sector employer after agriculture. A quarter of workers in this sector are female. In the first half of the 1980s, Swaziland experienced an economic slowdown in which industrial decline resulted in substantial job losses in the manufacturing sector. Many of the firms that had invested between 1972 and 1983 were considered 'footloose industries' or 'runaway shops'.[51]

In the South African context, there appear to be three types of textile industries engaging in relocation to Swaziland:

1. Successful South African firms located in urban areas that have been able to develop more cost-efficient operations through mechanisation that need outlets to international markets, sometimes pursuing them through SADCC countries;

2. European and American firms with branches in urban areas and in homelands in South Africa that face direct pressures as a result of laws fostering disinvestment in their own countries and who decide to relocate; and

3. Asian- and South African-owned fledgling firms located exclusively in the homelands where they are heavily subsidised, that establish labelling factories in SADCC countries to facilitate their access to international markets.

Clothing and textile factories employ the majority of female factory workers in the country. There are nine such factories in Matsapha Industrial Estate, employing a total of over 3000 women (see Appendix I, Table A1). These factories perform a number of functions. They include a cotton ginnery, a cotton-spinning mill, six clothing factories and a zip factory.

Cotona has two ginneries in Swaziland, one located in Big Bend in the lowveld and the other in Matsapha Industrial Estate. The ginneries are owned by Tongaat, a South African textile firm based near Durban. Cotona started its first ginnery in Swaziland in 1965. However, it does not have a monopoly on cotton-ginning in the country. Some farmers living close to the Natal border take their cotton to the Pongola ginnery. The manager of Cotona speculated that twenty-five to thirty per cent of Swazi cotton was ginned in Pongola.

The ginning process is very capital-intensive in separating cotton lint and seeds. The seeds are piped to an area where they are packaged for resale. The lint is cleaned and compressed into bales. The machinery is run for approximately eight months a year. A hundred and fifty-nine men are employed at Cotona. They are involved exclusively in the production process. Women employed there have clerical jobs.

Swaziland has its own Cotton Board in the Crop Production Division of the Ministry of Agriculture, which oversees cotton production in the country. The manager of the board indicated that there are more than 11 000 small cotton producers registered with the Board, the vast majority of whom do dryland farming. The board levies taxes on each bale of cotton produced to finance its operations.

However, it is the South African Cotton Marketing Board that decides annually on the price of cotton, based on world market prices published in *Cotton Outlook* in Liverpool. They average the November and March prices. The Board allocates cotton to textile manufacturers on the basis of their grade and quantity requirements. Because southern Africa is not self-sufficient in cotton production, after all the regional allocations are made it authorises the importation of more cotton from other countries.

National Textile Corporation (Natex), the cotton-spinning mill, relies on cotton allocations from the SA Cotton Marketing Board. In projecting the image of being a Swazi enterprise, Natex places a lot of emphasis on the fact that it processes Swazi-produced cotton by purchasing cotton from Cotona and Pongola. However, Natex requires a higher grade of cotton than is generally produced in Swaziland and it purchases some Israeli cotton.

Natex was established in Swaziland in 1986 with South African investment by the Kirsh Group and the assistance of British technical experts, having previously been based in South Africa. The managing director has said that the major consideration in investing in Swaziland was the fact that Swaziland was the only one of sixty-one cotton-producing countries worldwide that did not have a cotton-spinning mill. In Swaziland, the Kirsh Group has received funding for its expansion from the National Industrial Development Corporation of Swaziland and the World Bank.

The managing director is British and so are his managerial staff, with the exception of a Tanzanian quality control specialist. There is one expatriate female in management. The clerical staff are coloured. The personnel officer is a Swazi woman. Natex had around 500 employees (about 300 of whom are female) in 1988. It is clear that gender and ethnicity are very important in determining factory hierarchy.

The managing director says there is a very special relationship between women and textile production, giving three reasons:

1. They can perform minutely-detailed handwork;
2. They have the ability to do two things at once; and
3. They can do repetitive work for long periods of time.

He considers women more reliable workers than men, indicating that, in Swaziland, the former often pay their children's school fees. He says he adheres to a policy of equal pay for equal work. This is a view commonly expressed about female textile workers, in which their gender-based socialisation is confused with innate characteristics. As for equal pay for equal work, women are segmented in terms of the jobs they perform.

The managing director, who ran a textile mill in Lancashire twenty years ago, says he has a predominantly female, well-educated labour force. The spinning-mill never shuts down, with three overlapping 12-hour shifts a day. Employees work for four days a week, have every fifth day off and four days off at the end of each 28-day period. In other words, they work a 48-hour week. On my first two visits I found eighty-five per cent of employees to be female, but most of the supervisors were males. When a new person in management was asked about this, he said that technical staff are only in the mill for a quarter of the operating day. Should anything go wrong, the men would be able to repair the equipment. Literacy is also important. In the event that a technical problem cannot be solved, those involved will have to write it down to inform supervisors of the problem on the next shift. There is an emergency generator in the event of a power failure, which is a frequent occurrence during the summer months.

Natex is a highly capital-intensive spinning mill with the latest technology. In separate processes, the baled cotton is sorted and mixed, then it is blown out, carded, reduced in size by the speed frame (roving), taken through a ring frame and wound on to spools. Yarn wound on smaller spools is transferred to larger spools for export.

Ideal conditions for weaving require a high temperature and high humidity. These conditions, and the dustiness of areas of the mill, contribute to the general discomfort and long-term health problems of workers. Electric looms are set up with a number of spools of yarn placed so that the yarn is drawn in through a series of needle eyes to be woven by airloom. Women working at the ring frame indicated that focusing on needle eyes was damaging their eyesight.

It takes one warp beam half an hour to produce cloth. The cloth produced is of a polyester and cotton blend. They may be blending cotton and wool or mohair in the future. In 1988, Natex was phasing in additional aspects of the labour process such as weaving, making up and finishing. Subsequently, it phased in dyeing.

Natex's primary market at present is South Africa. The managing director indicated that he would like to penetrate the European and American markets eventually. As a concession to Swazi traditional fashion, *emahiyas* (traditional toga-like garments) will eventually be manufactured. The managing director observed that if they catered solely to the Swazi market, the mill would be in operation for only four hours a week. In the long term, Natex is planning to open a number of mills, each employing 300-500 workers, throughout the country.

The managing director says that his employees get top salaries in Swaziland. He also discussed a package of benefits and services to which they are entitled. They are provided with health services by five British doctors at the Occupational Health Service. Women workers get free pre- and post-natal care and their infants can receive medical care until they are six weeks old. No one has to walk more than 1.25 kilometres to take a *kombie* (van) to work. Hot meals are available in the cafeteria twenty-four hours a day. Since many of the female employees have not worked previously, Natex offers training in such topics as personal hygiene and family planning.

When asked about the spinning mill's relationship with cottage industries, the managing director replied that his employees were better-educated and that handicraft production is associated with a lack of education. However, he conceded that handicraft producers get a discount on yarn that is spun by Natex.

An appraisal report prepared in 1984 by the Commonwealth Development Corporation is very revealing about the original proposal for Natex (then Swatex). As mentioned in Chapter 3, Nathan Kirsh is a Swazi-born South African industrialist who has considerable investments in Swaziland. The Kirsh Group's subsidiary there is Swaki, a maize-milling company. It was through Swaki – in conjunction with the Swazi government, the World Bank and the Commonwealth Development Corporation – that the cotton-spinning mill was originally proposed, thereby making it a Swazi-owned company. This gave it potential access to marketing under the Preferential Trade Area for Eastern and Southern Africa (PTA).

Although, as Booth suggests, the Kirsh Group was eager to establish a cotton-spinning mill in Swaziland to avoid sanctions,[52] the appraisal report provides a different rationale for making such an investment. It argues that South Africa was experiencing a severe yarn shortage in its textile industry.[53] Some textile conglomerates were doing their own spinning to fulfil their manufacturing quotas. However, for the smaller textile firms, yarn was perpetually in short supply and such firms would have to pay a twenty-five per cent tariff on imported yarn. Before investing in Swaziland, the Kirsh Group started a similar mill in Zimbabwe. Nevertheless, economic sanctions against South Africa would not only prohibit the import of South African goods but also the export of certain goods to South Africa from affected countries. The Comprehensive Anti-Apartheid Act of 1986 stipulates a ban on the importation of South African textiles. In the case of Swaziland, investment and trade with South Africa was facilitated by the Southern African Customs Union despite sanctions.

Ostensibly, Swatex would use cotton produced in Swaziland, thereby making it a pivotal industry in the vertical integration of the textile industry. However, the report observes that the quality of Swaziland's cotton has deteriorated in recent years. Forty-five per cent of cotton production is on plantations and the remainder on smallholdings. They suggested ways of improving production on the latter, such as the appointment of an agronomist/breeder at the Big Bend Agricultural Experiment Station and the introduction of high-quality seed cotton from South Africa. Swatex proposed representation on the Swaziland Cotton Board and that Cotona and Swatex be signatories of the South African Cotton Marketing Agreement to stabilise the price of cotton and to provide an alternative source of supply if there were a poor harvest.

The report made provisions for an expatriate staff and highly-trained workers to be hired because of the capital intensity of the operation. No provisions were made for localisation of expatriate-held positions.

Nathan Kirsh is probably the most influential South African businessman who has had a long history of investing in Swaziland. He is the founding president of the Federation of Swaziland Employers. However, remarks made during a speech at a dinner commemorating the twenty-fifth anniversary of the FSE in 1989 provoked comment from the secretary-general of the Swaziland Federation of Trade Unions. Kirsh's remarks were: 'In many countries where trade unions became vehicles to achieve political power, there have been disasters that destroyed their economies and their prospects for a better future. This could have happened in Swaziland but it did not. [For] this, to some extent at least, the Swaziland Employers Federation can take credit.'[54] The trade union's secretary-general questioned the potentially disastrous effect of trade unions and credited the Swaziland government and the International Labour Organisation's (ILO's) Workers' Education Project with creating an atmosphere in which trade unions could be formed. In the same speech, Kirsh suggested that the Government grant automatic work permits to expatriate wives, whose positions would eventually be localised. The secretary-general felt that such preferential treatment was not justified, observing that it is not extended to Swazi expatriate wives abroad and that there is a high unemployment rate in Swaziland.

At the beginning of August 1989, Kirsh announced plans to invest one billion emalangeni into the textile industry in Swaziland over the following seven to eight years. In addition to Natex, which represents a E125 million investment, a new Spintex factory costing E63 million was to have been constructed by the end of 1990. This factory would also receive funding from the International Finance Corporation of the World Bank, the Dutch development corporation (FMO), and the German development corporation (DEG). The Kirsh Group speculates that thousands of jobs will be created, making Swaziland a major textile-producing country, like Mauritius, which now has a labour shortage.[55] In 1991, these plans had not been fully implemented. However, more phases of production have been introduced at the original Natex site and the workforce has doubled in size.

In relation to forward linkages to the cotton-spinning-mill, YKK is a Japanese-owned subsidiary that was established in Swaziland in 1976. It produces zips, primarily for the South African market. The only local textile industries to which it sells zips are Injobo and two Taiwanese textile firms. The company's plans for expansion into South Africa were obstructed when the Japanese government put a ban on further investment in South Africa in 1986. However, it has selling agents there.

As textile industries relocate from South Africa to surrounding countries, YKK finds that its marketing patterns are changing. The personnel officer indicated that a big factory in Durban, one of YKK's largest buyers, which employs 7–8000 people, was relocating to Botswana.

Using the latest technology, YKK produces nylon, metal and plastic zips as well as buttons, rivets and plastic buckles. Importing polyester from South Africa, it produces 2.5 million zips per month. Most machines are computerised, with employees monitoring their action. Machines weave the polyester into tape, dye the tape the desired colour, and sew on the nylon element or impress on the metal element. YKK produces all its capital goods in Japan, thereby enhancing vertical integration within the industry. The Swaziland factory ranks twentieth among YKK plants.

The company employs 110 people, sixty per cent of whom are female. They work from eight a.m. to five p.m. and only do an extra shift when they have more orders than they can handle. The company adheres to the Japanese management style by providing incentives for workers to remain in its employ for long periods of time. The five members of the senior-level management are Japanese who have been in Swaziland for varying lengths of time. The factory manager has been employed there for eleven years. Twenty to thirty staff members have been employed for ten years or more, and some of these are original employees.

With regard to the business climate in Swaziland, YKK did not make a profit for the first seven or eight years. Although the company experienced a bad year in 1984, it is now highly profitable. The personnel manager thinks that the five-year tax holiday is not long enough for newly-investing companies. One limitation is that YKK does not have access to PTA markets because it is not fifty-one per cent Swazi-owned.

Injobo is a large clothing factory in Matsapha Industrial Estate. Originally, it was a branch of a South African textile firm that relocated in Swaziland for the purpose of relabelling South African garments 'Made in Swaziland', for sale on international markets. It failed in late 1987 and was purchased by Eastbrook, an American firm. The production manager said that the new management had had a difficult time converting the labelling factory into a legitimate business. It had to fire the least productive workers who knew only how to sew labels.

Injobo manufactures flannel shirts, polo shirts and elastic shorts. When skill levels are heightened, it will manufacture fancier shirts. Eighty per cent of manufactures enter the American market. (It is rumoured that their flannel shirts are sold to J. C. Penney.) Fifteen per cent of manufactures are sold on European markets and the remainder in South Africa. They plan to concentrate their marketing in the European Community in the coming years. However, in 1991, Injobo is teetering on the edge of bankruptcy.

The production manager admitted that there was a substantial wage discrepancy between Injobo and an equivalent industry in South Africa. Machinists in South Africa are paid R130–140 per week whereas machinists in Swaziland are paid E47 (R47). He observed that South Africa would be a very expensive textile producer if it were allowed access to international markets.

At the time of my first visit to Injobo in April 1989, the firm had 700 employees. The production manager indicated that the number would increase to 1000 over the ensuing three-month period. By mid-June, the figure had increased to 900. He speculated that the firm could easily exceed a thousand. Recruiting is done by word of mouth in the factory, employees often bringing their relatives and friends. Although most of Injobo's workers live in the Manzini–Matsapha area, a few live in Mbabane. The production manager would like to eliminate the latter because the workers there exhibit a high rate of lateness and absenteeism. He views the public transportation system as being a limitation on further expansion.

Injobo wants workers to have achieved a high educational standard. The production manager said that they must speak English, know some mathematics and have manual dexterity. However, he speculated that because Injobo is more labour-intensive it hires at a lower standard than Natex. The former had recently spent E30–40 000 on training. Three out of four foremen had had previous work experience in South Africa. To my suggestion that the Swaziland government sponsor textile training, the production manager replied that he was opposed to the idea because it would significantly increase the cost of labour.

Ethnicity is an important factor in the composition of the factory hierarchy. Members of fourteen nationalities are on the board of directors of Eastbrook. The chairperson is a Pakistani. At Injobo, the managing director and the production manager are white; the personnel director and the financial officer, Swazi. There are some coloured clerical staff. Most of the foremen are Indians hired from Durban.[56]

Swaziland has higher scheduled wages for textile workers than Lesotho – about sixty rands higher. During 1989, a fourteen per cent rise was agreed by the government. The production manager indicated that there were options for relocation in other countries in the region. He said that if the firm should close suddenly, it would like to leave its workers well-trained and employable. Since many South African textile industries are relocating to the BLS countries, Zimbabwe and Mauritius, there is the assumption that another textile industry would replace Injobo.

In terms of the vertical integration of the Swazi textile industry, Natex is viewed as a welcome addition. Injobo stands to benefit from the cotton-spinning mill's production of cotton/polyester blend cloth, whose manufacture had begun only in 1989. At the time, Injobo was relying heavily on flannel material imported from South Africa.

In relation to competitors, Injobo was experiencing a problem in 1989 with Oriental, a neighbouring company owned by the Taiwanese. The production manager said that Oriental had continued to label goods manufactured in South Africa despite the efforts of the Swazi

Government and the United States Customs Service. He added that he had little confidence in either agency on this matter, even though a US Customs official had visited Injobo.

During the period of my research, there were a number of sweat-shop-like textile factories owned by Taiwanese in Matsapha Industrial Estate. There were communication problems with the Taiwanese management of these factories because managers could not speak English very well. Oriental and Pan-African were sister companies owned by a Taiwanese firm with a branch in the South African homeland of Qwa Qwa. Their original site, near Injobo, could not be expanded so the firm was allocated a second site at another location in the estate. All the cutting for the sister companies was done at Pan-African. The two companies manufacture polyester pyjamas and shirts. At the time of my visit to Oriental, it was having a labour dispute which a representative of the Industrial Court was attempting to mediate. Thus the firms were having difficulties with the Government concerning their labelling operations *and* problems with their workers. By the end of 1989, both Oriental and Pan-African had ceased their Swaziland operations.

Francois Fashions, started in 1987, manufactures knitted jerseys (sweaters) for both sexes. They market primarily in Canada and the United States, although some of their goods are sold locally. The headquarters of the company, which does its own marketing, is in Durban.

The 120 employees work from seven a.m. to five p.m. on weekdays. They use hand-powered knitting machines to knit skeins of a synthetic fibre called koran into jersey components, and to sew the components together. They have a few electric-powered machines and are expecting more to be transferred from Durban from where the koran is also imported. Finishing is done on site for export. This industry comes closer to being a cottage industry because the process is very labour-intensive.

Sanctions are the reason why many textile factories are in Swaziland. The country as a whole, however, did not implement sanctions against South Africa. Although Swaziland is generally perceived as having been a beneficiary of sanctions, its sugar revenues were considered to be lower in part because it had to use South African ports. The presence of runaway shops that were sewing labels on South African-manufactured textiles made Swaziland vulnerable to allegations of sanction-breaking.

5.4 CONCLUSION

Selwyn, in analysing constraints on industrialisation in the BLS
countries, did not anticipate the polarisation of industry within these
countries as they began to more fully urbanise and industrialise. To a
certain extent, industrialisation in the periphery is a microcosm of that
process in sectors of the South African economy.

Cottage industries and factories have separate domains in the Swazi
context – one rural, the other urban. Although both are constrained by
the Multi-Fibre Arrangement, they employ female workers from
different labour pools and manufacture consumer goods for distinctly
different markets. To a large extent, cottage industries represent
privatised efforts at rural development where alternative projects do
not exist. Whereas they are not potential runaway shops, there are
cases in which they have been taken over by larger, more profitable
cottage industries.

The technology is very appropriate in the case of cottage industries.
The labour process is simplified to the point where women can be
trained relatively quickly in the initial stages of production. If they
remain employed long enough, they can learn the entire labour
process. It is possible for them to take their skills elsewhere and to
use them independently. Their manufactures, tapestries and other
household items appeal to the core middle-class speciality market.

In the textile factories, there is an emphasis on capital-intensive
technology to the extent that little labour is employed. In the clothing
factories, labour-intensive technologies are not much different from
those used at the turn of the century, and they require the employment
of large numbers of women. In terms of forward linkages, the textile
factory is ahead of the clothing factory. The former is performing
many of the functions of cottage industries at a very rapid rate, for
sizeable consumer markets.

Managers and owners of cottage industries and factories therefore
face different constraints under which they operate in Swaziland.
Cottage industries are more 'indigenised' with the possibility of
multinational linkages within the region. However, it is highly
unlikely that such an industry would up sticks and move to another
area of the southern African periphery.

However, factories are much more highly capitalised and receive
various incentives from the Swaziland Government. If management
feels that it is not meeting maximum profitability in that location, it
can easily relocate to another urban or semi-urban area to set up shop.

Clearly, the balance of power is in management's favour. Taiwanese textile industries tend to be the most marginal operations and are as a consequence highly mobile.

6 Female Workers in Cottage Industries and Factories

6.1 INTRODUCTION

There is a paucity of literature on women and work in southern Africa. Until the 1970s, the vast majority of social science literature dealt with male labour migrancy to the South African gold mines. At that time, there was a shift of focus on to women in the family context in peripheral areas – local labour reserves within national labour reserves. However, women had participated in semi-industrial employment in some areas of the southern African periphery since the 1960s and even earlier in others. Cottage industries were the major semi-industrial employers for women in Botswana, Lesotho and Swaziland as well as the South African homelands. It was not until the 1980s that South African textile industries began to tap systematically into the female labour reserve. Many problems related to women and work in southern Africa still await in-depth research.

C. Murray focuses on the family as a unit that has been disrupted by the migratory labour system throughout southern Africa.[1] Reviewing some of Isaac Schapera's research in Botswana, he observes that there has been a substantial increase in the percentage of female-headed households since the inception of the migratory labour system. In examining the work of William Watson and Jaap Van Velsen, he argues that the tribal structure – and by implication family structure – has been maintained. In considering the literature on family disruption, Murray also views kinship structures as remaining intact over time, allowing for a number of role substitutions and extensions as well as the reconstitution of traditional roles at a later stage in the developmental cycle of the family. He calls this a dissolution/conservation contradiction.[2]

B. B. Brown, a political scientist conducting research in Botswana, also focuses on the impact of male labour migration on women in the context of the family. She views the women's role as subsidising foreign capital by remaining in the confines of the country and engaging in household production and reproduction.[3]

Brown observes that marriage patterns have changed considerably since the 1920s. During that period, parents selected spouses for their children. Most people got married at the time and marriage conferred considerable status. Childbearing occurred only after engagement.[4] By contrast, in the 1970s, marriage was delayed until a later age primarily due to male outmigration. Migrants, who were in and out of Botswana between shifts, only married at thirty – ten years later than marriages half a century before. Today, most women have borne several children by the time they finally marry. This situation is exacerbated by the fact that men in their thirties tend to ignore female members of their cohort to marry women in their twenties.[5]

Schapera's research in Botswana in the 1920s and 1930s indicated that labour migration began to have an impact on Botswana society in the 1940s. In 1936, only six per cent of the population were labour migrants and in 1943, ten per cent.[6] In attempting to correlate the rate of labour migrancy with the rate of female-headed households, Schapera found that whereas the Batswana (the people of Botswana) did not condone childbearing before marriage during the pre-colonial period, by the time of his initial research there was greater acceptance of the practice.[7] In 1943, twenty-three per cent of unmarried women of child-bearing age had borne children. For Brown, in 1978, the figure was fifty-four per cent. In addition, seven per cent of households were headed by single women and sixteen per cent by widows. Thus nearly a quarter of established households were headed by women.[8]

Surprisingly, Brown found that Batswana women had a number of employment outlets. Five per cent were working illegally in South Africa.[9] In one district, a quarter of able-bodied women worked in South Africa, primarily as domestics. Such illegal migration did not begin until the 1940s because chiefs had previously curtailed women's migration.[10] Of course, women must have experienced more difficulty in entering South Africa after they were barred from labour migration there in 1963.

Female heads of household in Botswana face problems because of unequal distribution of land, livestock and labour as well as sex discrimination in employment. Furthermore, within the domestic context, Brown sees an increased nucleation of the family which militates against utilising an extended family network to perform tasks such as childcare, cattle-herding, and crop cultivation and harvesting. By implication, her view indicates that the nucleation of the family is an irreversible process in response to male labour migration.

Unlike Swazi society, which is homestead based, Sotho societies, including those in Lesotho and Botswana considered above, are village-based. In fact, Botswana villages tend to be larger than Lesotho villages. Furthermore, in both countries, some villages have become major towns, necessitating less migration. Thus villages have more extended kinship networks. In Swaziland, due to land partition, towns were established by white settlers and the colonial administration and were in separate areas from Swazi Nation Land. It has only been in the last decade or so that more Swazi families have moved into towns.

Studies of women and family in Swaziland have focused on the homestead as the traditional locus of production and reproduction.[11] With regard to migration, the homestead has also become the sending community for labour migrants. Furthermore, there has been the tendency to view the homestead as an ideal type from which members are periodically assigned to seek wage labour to sustain the welfare of all its members. However, B. Rosen-Prinz and F. Prinz's findings suggest that younger male members of a homestead, because of rules of primogeniture, often make a personal choice to migrate to improve their economic circumstances.[12] Their earnings are usually not distributed throughout the homestead but are given to their nuclear subunit.[13] Ngubane views it as serving a social welfare function to the migrant in times of unemployment or business failure.[14]

Unlike its sister countries, Lesotho and Botswana, Swaziland began domestic industrialisation in the post-Second World War period and was able to reverse the ratio between South African migration and domestic migration in its favour by the 1960s.[15]

Rosen-Prinz and Prinz's research was a part of an International Labour Organization (ILO) study of male migratory labour in the southern African region. Because of the emphasis of the project, they neglected to examine female migration. In fact, their data reinforces the view that women form a social support group for men at the homestead. They cite 1966 Census data indicating the inequality in sex ratios in rural and urban areas – 70.7 males per 100 females in rural areas and 147.4 per 100 females in urban areas.[16] Rosen-Prinz and Prinz attribute this to the tendency of male domestic migrants to leave their families at the homestead because they cannot afford housing in Swaziland's urban areas.[17] In contemporary Swaziland, sex ratios in urban areas are almost equal.

Rosen-Prinz and Prinz observe the same process of role substitution and extension espoused by Murray. Children have often functioned as substitutes in traditional male tasks such as ploughing and herding. However, as children are increasingly attending school, women have taken over these tasks.[18] Yet, they only partially embrace the dissolution/conservation contradiction in acknowledging that the number of migrants increases in inverse proportion to cash crop production.[19] Obviously, women became overburdened with agricultural production as a result of role extension. Ngubane suggests that the most economically viable homesteads are those formed by monogamous couples with close relations with their children and who work together in the fields.[20]

To reinforce the neglect of female migration, Rosen-Prinz and Prinz emphasise women's dependency on males in Swaziland. They argue that women are dependent on their fathers, brothers, husbands and sons for access to land and credit.[21] What happens when they are denied access to resources because they have no husband? I consider the husband–wife relationship as being primary for adult women's access to resources.

M. Neocosmos delineates four structural types of homestead on the basis of a country-wide study comparing economic characteristics of homesteads on Swazi Nation Land: these are poor, lower-middle, upper-middle and rich homesteads. Poor homesteads produce at sub-subsistence level and have the highest concentration of labour migrants; lower-middle homesteads produce at the sub-subsistence level but compensate for shortfalls with petty-commodity production; upper-middle homesteads produce at the subsistence level; and rich homesteads produce at subsistence level, employ wage labour and utilise more expensive equipment and sometimes irrigation facilities.[22]

Neocosmos considers the vast majority of labour migrants to be male, and rural petty-commodity producers to be female. As examples of petty-commodity production, Neocosmos suggests jersey-knitting, beer-brewing and grass-weaving.[23] Thus it is among lower-middle homesteads in which such production is concentrated. Although one can speculate that female petty commodity producers are prime candidates for labour migration, I think that female migration is more widespread.

P. McFadden views migration as a major feature of colonial and post-colonial incorporation of indigenous economies.[24] She highlights land alienation as the key factor leading to the proletarianisation of the Swazi peasantry. In considering female wage labour, she observes that

women participated in wage labour as far back as the 1920s. Their first
wage labour employment was in agriculture and domestic service.[25]

The focus of McFadden's study is Swaziland's pineapple industry,
which was controlled by Libby's at the time. She documents the
squalid living conditions, high crime rate, low wages and exploitative
working conditions for women who were, for the most part, seasonal
migrants without any other source of income. She also observes the
emergence of what she calls 'working class' marriage in which an
employed woman has a live-in boyfriend who does not work and is
dependent upon her income.[26]

For the most part, these women had migrated permanently from
their homesteads.[27] Half of them were from Shiselweni, and a quarter
each from Hhohho and Manzini.[28] Many had illegitimate children who
would be outcasts in their home areas.[29] McFadden attributes the high
rate of illegitimacy to a breakdown in morality.[30]

There were two categories of workers – field and industrial. Libby's
employed a predominantly female labour force in both. In each
category, there were casual, seasonal and temporary workers.[31] A
small percentage of the labour force was permanent and entitled to
limited fringe benefits but even they were not entitled to paid maternity
leave. They were granted unpaid maternity leave for three months, for
which they were not permitted an extension. Non-permanent workers
suffered loss of seniority when they were rehired by the company.

Seasonal workers remained in the area between the end of the
picking season in November and the start of planting at the beginning
of the year. They engaged in beer-brewing and prostitution to tide
themselves over until their wage was resumed.

At the time of McFadden's research, workers had no vehicle for
improving their lot. Trade unions were banned in Swaziland. Furthermore, the Swaziland government had a small share of stock in the
company and did not want to jeopardise its vested interest by assisting
the workers.[32] What one can conclude from McFadden's study is that
women workers were being exploited by Libby's as an international
concern with government assistance in relation to their wages and
working and living conditions, as well as by skilled workers and their
unemployed boyfriends.

A. Armstrong conducted a country-wide survey of women engaged
in wage employment in Swaziland. Four hundred women were
interviewed at forty establishments including agricultural plantations,
mines, factories, banks, clinics and the civil service. The Swazi
Government is the largest employer of women in the country and

employs thirty-five per cent of wage-earning females compared to twenty-seven per cent of wage-earning males.[33]

Armstrong finds that in the female labour force there is a dichotomy between professional jobs, such as nursing and teaching, and unskilled agricultural employment.[34] Female labour force participation has grown substantially in the last two decades. Most female wage workers are young and occupy newly-created jobs. Older women have not had a high degree of access to the labour force and often generate cash income by engaging in childcare for payment from working parents.[35] Armstrong concludes her study by suggesting areas yet to be explored: for example, the comparability of male and female wages as well as the discrepancy between wage-earning and non-wage-earning females such as handicraft producers.[36] She suggests a profile of the emerging Swazi female wage worker as being 'independent, struggling on her own with her family and childcare responsibilities, burdened physically and financially, but enterprising, hard-working and determined'.[37] As I discuss relevant areas in my own survey, I will refer to comparable data in Armstrong's.

It is clear from the above that the family has been undergoing some degree of nucleation with a tendency towards female-headedness in response to the twin processes of industrialisation and proletarianisation. Usually proletarianisaton in rural areas precipitates labour migration. Males have been migrating to industrial areas since the turn of the century. However, females have faced a number of restrictions to their movement *vis-à-vis* South Africa as well as their own homesteads or villages. Furthermore, due to the current pattern of industrialisation, job creation and wage differentiation, males and females are becoming increasingly at odds with each other in forming marital relationships and raising children.

A survey was conducted among fifty-five textile workers in Swaziland to determine the characteristics of the female labour force in cottage industries and factories. Included in the survey were twenty-two cottage-industry workers and thirty-three factory workers. Before analysing the data, it is necessary to give a description of the cottage-industry and factory contexts. As indicated in the previous chapter, cottage industries are generally family-run businesses located on the premises of the employer. In the Swazi context, they are rarely co-operatively-owned. Cottage industries are relatively unmechanised and workers perform a number of specialised tasks including carding, combing, dyeing, spinning, weaving and finishing. With the exception of newly-employed workers, most know every aspect of the labour process. There appears to be more flexibility in time allocation to perform aspects of the labour process. There is also considerable interaction between employer and employee. The employer knows general background information on most of the workers. Few males are employed in cottage industries.

The factory context is a different type of setting. Management's offices are either in a separate building or a separate section of the factory. Although there is more emphasis on mechanisation in factories, it varies according to the type of factory. Clothing factories are less mechanised than cotton-spinning mills and zip factories. The former simply consist of sewing machines, cutting machines and tables. The latter are more mechanised, consisting of modern technology that serves the same functions as the separate aspects of the labour process in cottage industries. Most of this technology is computerised. Workers are trained to feed, monitor and repair these machines to minimise interruption to the labour process. Whistles signal beginnings and endings of work and breaks.

Factory settings are more hierarchical, with workers actually dealing with intermediaries rather than upper-echelon management. In clothing factories, there is usually a quota on the number of garments to be sewn in an hour. Therefore the pace of work is much more rapid than in cottage industries. In the clothing factory, some men are employed as cutters; in the cotton-spinning mill, they are in supervisory positions and do machine maintenance.

Factories also are preoccupied with security and the prevention of strikes. In Matsapha Industrial Estate where the two types of factory are located, they are surrounded by high walls with a check-in point at each entrance. There are women and men employed as security personnel.

6.2 GENERAL CHARACTERISTICS

Industries were surveyed in Pigg's Peak, Malkerns, Hlatikulu, Ngwenya, Ezulwini and Matsapha. Among the most general characteristics considered are age, educational level and residence. The mean age of women who participated in the survey was 27.7. The youngest woman was 16 and the oldest 47. Women employed in cottage industries were generally older than those employed in factories. The mean age was 32 for the former and 23.3 for the latter. Thus, women employed in cottage industries are on the average about nine years older than women employed in factories. Women in the clothing factory were slightly younger than women employed in the cotton-spinning mill. For women employed in the former, the mean age was 23.4, and the latter 26.6.

The maximum level of education achieved by female textile workers was 12 years, with the mean being 8.5 years. Sixty-nine per cent of respondents had between 8 and 12 years of education. In cottage industries, the maximum was Form 4 (11th grade) and the mean 6.4 years (Standard 6) and, in factories, the maximum was Form 5 (12th grade) and the mean Form 3 (10th grade). In the clothing factory, the maximum was Form 5 (12th grade) and the mean Form 2 (9th grade). In the cotton-spinning mill, the maximum was Form 5 (12th grade) and the mean was Form 4 (11th grade). I would conclude from the above that factories employ younger, better-educated women than cottage industries and that the cotton-spinning mill employs older, better-educated women than does the clothing factory. Some relevant answers to an open-ended question elsewhere in the questionnaire indicate the educational aspirations of some factory workers. They are as follows: 'I would like to attend the university to get a degree. I need a scholarship to get a Bachelor of Arts in Law' and 'I am concerned with furthering my studies so that I can become a nurse.' Clearly, some of these women have considerably higher aspirations.

Because Swaziland is a country in which urbanisation is confined to small towns, it is more difficult to distinguish between rural and urban areas. Mbabane and Manzini are the largest towns in Swaziland, with populations of approximately 40 000 and 45 000 respectively. Other towns are considerably smaller. In this instance, I made the urban/rural distinction on the basis of the availability of consumer goods. Thus most major towns fell into the urban category. Nevertheless, this is still rather arbitrary considering that many small communities are within walking distance of 'urban' areas. Overall, sixty-two per cent of respondents resided in rural areas and thirty-eight per cent in urban areas. In the case of cottage industries, sixty-eight per cent were rural dwellers and thirty-two per cent urban dwellers and, in factories, fifty-two per cent rural dwellers and forty-eight per cent urban dwellers.

6.3 WORK EXPERIENCE

To establish a chronology for women's work, all respondents were asked how long they had been employed outside the home. Percentages were as follows: 10.9 per cent of women had just entered their first job; 16.4 per cent had worked for only one year; 10.9 per cent had worked for two years; 23.6 per cent for three years; 7.3 per cent for four years; 1.8 per cent for five years; 1.8 per cent for six years; 5.5 per cent for eight years; 3.6 per cent each for nine years, ten years and twelve years; and 1.8 per cent each had worked between fourteen and seventeen years, and twenty-two and twenty-four years. The mean period for employment was five years. In cottage industries, four per cent of women were employed in their first job; in factories, fifteen per cent. This illuminates the fact that cottage industries are older than textile and clothing factories.

Although most Swazi women are recent entrants into factory employment, many of those employed have had some previous work experience. Women were asked about their employment prior to entering their current job. Thirteen per cent had previously held a textile-related job; four per cent had had government employment; eleven per cent had been domestics; sixteen per cent had held other service jobs; nine per cent had held other factory jobs; seven per cent had held jobs in agriculture; and two per cent had worked in the hotel industry. For thirty-eight per cent of women textile workers surveyed, their current job is their first job. In Armstrong's study, fifty-four per cent of women surveyed had participated in wage labour before their present job.[38] A breakdown by cottage industry and factory is illustrated in Table 6.1. It appears from this table that the textile industry is the fastest-growing industry for female employment in Swaziland, with more than a third of all workers in textile factories having their first job and having worked at that job for less than a year.

Table 6.1   Previous Employment (percentages)

	Cottage Industry	Factory
Textile employment	4.5	18
Government employment	4.5	0
Domestic employment	18	6
Non-domestic employment	13.6	21
Non-textile service employment	4.5	3
Agricultural employment	22.7	0
Hotel employment	4.5	3
Not applicable – first job	27.7	48

Since Swaziland has begun industrialising more rapidly in recent years, I was interested to determine women's work preferences for working alone or with others. Originally, women were doing handicrafts in the home. The introduction of cottage industries removed women from the home to work collectively with other women in a factory-like setting. However, some cottage-industry jobs do allow women to work alone in the workplace. Only nine per cent of respondents in the survey preferred to work alone; seventy-five per cent preferred to work with others; and sixteen per cent had no preference. Results for cottage industries and factories were similar. In cottage industries, nine per cent preferred to work alone, about seventy-three per cent with others, and eighteen per cent had no preference. In factories, nine per cent preferred to work alone, about seventy-six per cent with others, and fifteen per cent had no preference. Clearly, the vast majority of textile workers are favourably disposed towards working with others.

6.4 INCOME AND OTHER RESOURCES

Female textile workers' monthly income ranged between E24 and E290. The mean is E151. The range for cottage industries was between E30 and E180, with a mean of E103; for factories, a range between E72 and E290 and a mean of E175. The wage scheduled by the Swazi government for trainee spinners and weavers is E24.23 per week or E96.92 per month, and more experienced weavers E35.54 per week or E142.16 per month for work in cottage industries.[39] In factories, a textile preparer should be paid E37.26 per week or E149.04 per month, and a sewing machinist II E39.09 per week or E156.36 per month. Those surveyed are being paid scheduled wages.

When asked if they could support their family on their current income, fourteen per cent said they could and eighty per cent said they could not. Workers were asked what they thought their proper income should be. The proposed income ranged between E100 and E1000 with a mean of E317. Obviously, respondents consider their wages to be too low. A mini-survey was conducted of manufacturing industries in Matsapha Industrial Estate that were not included in the earlier survey. Of the fifteen industries in the mini-survey, six were textile-related industries. The tabulation of survey results appears as Table A2 in Appendix II which lists the number of workers, percentage of females employed and average monthly wages. Clearly, industries with the highest concentration of males are higher-paying than the textile industry as a whole.

In enumerating monthly expenses, clothing expenditure ranged between E5 and E160 per respondent, with a mean of E50; food expenditure ranged between E0 and E220 per respondent with a mean of E40. Seventy-three per cent of respondents paid no rent, but for those who did pay, it ranged between E5 and E80. The mean was E10. Forty-six per cent of respondents paid no utilities. Those who did paid between E10 and E170, with a mean of E22.

I had originally hypothesised that many women textile workers were married to labour migrants employed in South Africa, particularly gold miners. Only fourteen per cent of all respondents had husbands who were migrants. However, they represented seventy-three per cent of all married women in the survey. The mean age of women with migrant husbands was thirty, which is above the mean age of 27.7. Nine per cent of women employed in cottage industries had migrant husbands; twelve per cent in factories. When asked where their husbands worked, only one respondent indicated South Africa. The husbands of the remainder resided in Swaziland. All the men sent remittances to their wives. The maximum remittance was E450 and the mean E35.22. In Armstrong's survey, sixty-three per cent of women received cash remittances.[40]

In terms of job promotion providing women workers with an additional income, most respondents were not optimistic. Only thirty-one per cent of all respondents thought that they would be promoted in the near future. For women in cottage industries, thirty-six per cent responded that they would be promoted; for women in factories, twenty-seven per cent responded affirmatively. In the further breakdown between the spinning mill and the clothing factory, the figures were fifty-six per cent and seventeen per cent respectively.

To supplement their income, forty per cent of all women workers had an additional job. No one engaged in beadwork, a more traditional craft, however. Since there is considerable seasonable employment available, women were asked if they engaged in cotton-picking. No one did.

In cottage industries, forty-one per cent of women had additional jobs and, in factories, thirty-nine per cent. Cottage-industry workers divided their activities among grasswork, a more traditional pursuit, jersey-knitting, in which yarn was probably put out by the cottage industry for which they worked; or other tasks such as beer-brewing, skein-picking and doily-making. At the cotton-spinning factory, sixty-seven per cent had additional jobs and, at the clothing factory, twenty-nine per cent. In the case of the former, the work schedule gives workers larger blocks of time in which to engage in additional employment. However, in the clothing factory, there is a uniform five-day week. Table 6.2 indicates the type of work pursued.

Table 6.2   Additional Jobs (percentages)

Work Type	Cottage Industry	Factory
Glasswork	14	0
Beadwork	0	0
Jersey-knitting	14	0
Cotton-picking	0	0
Other	14	36

Respondents were asked if they cultivated cash- and food crops at their homesteads. Eighty-two per cent cultivated crops. Of the respondents who cultivated crops, maize was the crop most frequently indicated. It is generally cultivated in the middleveld and highveld. Four per cent cultivated sugar cane and two per cent cotton, the only exclusive cash crops represented. Sugar-cane and cotton are generally cultivated in the lowveld, where little industrialisation has occurred.

Ninety per cent of cottage industry workers cultivated crops, while seventy-six per cent of factory workers did. Of crops cultivated by cottage industry workers, ninety per cent cultivated maize and thirty-two per cent other crops, including pumpkins, sorghum, groundnuts and sweet potatoes. None cultivated sugar or cotton. In the factories, seventy-three per cent cultivated maize, six per cent sugar-cane, three per cent cotton and forty-eight per cent other crops, including jugo beans and soybeans, groundnuts, sweet potatoes and cabbages. In the cotton-spinning mill, one hundred per cent planted maize, none cultivated sugar-cane or cotton and eighty-nine per cent cultivated other crops, including beans, groundnuts (peanuts) and sweet potatoes. In the clothing factory, sixty-two per cent planted maize, eight per cent sugar- cane, four per cent cotton and thirty-three per cent other crops. One clothing factory worker, in discussing additional work activities, said: 'I normally participate in overtime work like making balls and skein-picking to earn extra income. I also grow vegetables at home, especially spinach, cabbages, carrots and pepper.'

Fifty-six per cent of respondents had cattle. Twenty-seven per cent had goats, sixty-six per cent chickens, and eleven per cent other livestock such as donkeys, ducks and pigs. None had sheep. In cottage industries, 63.6 per cent of women had cattle, whereas in factories, fifty-two per cent did. Clearly, these wage labourers are not as proletarianised as their counterparts in other areas of southern Africa. Furthermore, there are obviously sustained relationships between town and country in the case of urban workers.

6.5 FRINGE BENEFITS

Fringe benefits provided by the employer are of considerable interest. Only thirty-six per cent of respondents had coverage for medical and dental care; sixty-four per cent received none. In most cases, this would be only medical care. For female cottage industry workers, fourteen per cent had medical and dental care; for factory workers, fifty-two per cent. In response to an open-ended question, one factory worker commented, 'Medical coverage is only provided for minor illnesses at work. Otherwise, we pay for our own medical care'. Thirty-eight per cent of all female workers received paid maternity leave, while sixty-two per cent received leave without remuneration. For cottage industries, it was thirty-two per cent and for factories, forty-eight per cent. Sixty-five per cent of employees received contributions to employee pension funds and twenty-nine per cent did not. For cottage industries, sixty-eight per cent received pension contributions, and factories, seventy per cent.

6.6 EXPENDITURE

According to government statistics, forty-three per cent of Swazi homes had access to tap water.[41] Armstrong's study indicates that seventeen per cent of agricultural workers and thirty-nine per cent of non-agricultural workers had access to electricity.[42] The high percentage of respondents not paying for utilities may be those without electricity and tap water. However, there would be some respondents who would have one utility and not the other. When asked about expenses for water, firewood and paraffin (kerosene), sixty-six per cent of respondents said they paid nothing. For those who paid, the range of payment was E1 to E72. Although some respondents may have supplemented utilities from consumer energy sources, the data indicate that those purchasing water, firewood and paraffin are paying between ten and forty per cent less than those paying for utilities. Table 6.3 indicates the breakdown of average expenditure between cottage industries and factories.

Table 6.3   Average Expenditure (in Emalangeni)

	Cottage Industries	*Factories*
Clothing	25.00	59.30
Food	27.70	49.60
Rent	0	17.06
Utilities	17.50	17.30
Water/firewood/paraffin	1.53	4.33
School fees	9.06	10.10
Transport	10.08	14.75
Other	0	10.60

All cottage-industry workers surveyed indicated that they paid no rent. Just over half of all of factory workers (54 per cent) paid no rent.

Figure 6.1 represents the percentage of expenditure in major categories of all respondents. They could only save 2.5 per cent of their income.

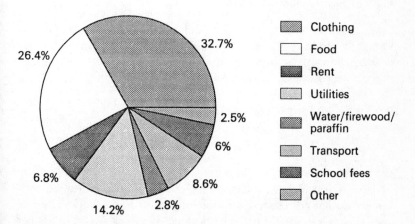

Figure 6.1   Relative Expenditure: Average Expenses (percentages)

6.7 WORKING CONDITIONS

Respondents were asked what were the channels for lodging a grievance in the workplace. During the period of research, no textile industry had a union. Indications are that employers are quite resistant to unions in the textile industry. Forty-two per cent of respondents viewed the personnel officer as the person with whom they could lodge a grievance; eighteen per cent indicated a works council; and nine per cent indicated a variety of other means which included talking to the manager, supervisor or representative of the work group. Cottage industries are quite small so there was no personnel officer to respond to grievances. In factories, however, sixty-seven per cent of respondents designated the personnel officer as the avenue for filing a grievance. (Usually, the personnel officer is black.) Eighty-six per cent of cottage-industry workers relied on the secretary, the representative, the supervisor, the owner or the manager. Only one cottage industry had a works council. Some respondents, in both cottage industries and factories, were uncertain about the process of lodging a grievance.

In another part of the questionnaire, respondents expressed their grievances against their employers. Cottage industry workers made the following comments:

> We get our wages on the tenth. We cannot express our grievances and receive a positive reaction. We want our wages to be increased and to have annual increments.

> Wages are not fixed. They are paid according to output, i.e., the finished product. There is no paid leave or any leave at all. We cannot budget our expenses since the wages are not fixed. Sometimes, we get wages as low as E40.

Factory workers made the following comments:

> There must be paid maternity leave, better working hours and additional pay.

> I have a transport problem – and use public transportation. My wages do not correspond with the long hours that I work. The rate per hour is too small for the work done. We work twelve hours per day, four days per week, twenty days per month.

Only men are promoted here. The government should give women opportunities to develop skills in handicraft-making, dress-making and other occupations where women can be self-employed.

The salary is too low even for a living wage. Women here are grossly underpaid. I was one of the first employees here but have not yet been promoted even though other women have been promoted who came long after me.

These comments reflect some differences in working conditions in cottage industries and factories. Obviously, there is considerable pent-up dissatisfaction.

The Swaziland government does permit the formation of trade unions although it gives them little support. There are a number of unions that come under the umbrella of the Swaziland Federation of Trade Unions. An official of the Swaziland Manufacturing and Allied Workers Union was interviewed to determine whether efforts had been made to unionise textile industries in 1989. He indicated that efforts had been made at both factories surveyed and at one cottage industry. In the case of the former, one factory had gone into liquidation, thereby bringing unionising efforts to a halt. In the case of the other, management vehemently resisted unionising efforts. As mentioned in Chapter 5, the union official suggested that cottage industries are problematic for union organising.

6.8 EMPLOYMENT TRAINING

Employment training is essential to building a skilled and productive labour force. Workers surveyed were asked whether they attended training courses in preparation for their textile jobs. Only fourteen per cent had attended a training course before starting their jobs. Those respondents who had had training were asked where it took place. Eleven per cent named their place of employment; four per cent said Manzini Industrial Training Centre; and, two per cent each named the Council of Swaziland Churches and the National Handcraft Training Centre. One woman did not remember where she had been trained. Ninety-six per cent of respondents indicated that they wanted further training, while the remainder said they did not. Clearly, the majority of female textile workers would like to improve their skills and many employers are neglecting to make such an investment in their labour force. However, sometimes training does take place informally in cottage industries and may not be recognised as such by employees.

The percentage of women in cottage-industry employment receiving training during the period of employment was five per cent and, in factories, twenty-one per cent. Fourteen per cent of women in cottage industries had taken a training course after starting the job, compared to thirty per cent of factory workers. Furthermore, ninety-one per cent of cottage-industry workers and all the factory workers wanted further training. The clothing factory has spent a considerable sum of money to train its workers to sew garments.

6.9 EMPLOYMENT ALTERNATIVES

Having earlier provided a sketch of the types of employment from whence these women came to the textile industry, it is also important to determine what employment alternatives they wish to explore. While eighteen per cent were undecided, sixteen per cent wanted to keep the same job; fourteen per cent wanted another textile job; fourteen per cent wanted to become secretaries; and sixteen per cent wanted government jobs. The remainder of respondents wanted jobs as domestics; as non-domestic service employees; as accountants; and as nurses. It is significant that thirty per cent of respondents would like to continue to work in the textile industry. A few respondents who wanted another textile job mentioned Natex as a possibility. Nevertheless, neither cottage-industry workers nor factory workers explicitly wanted to work in the other type of industry. For the employment alternatives of women in cottage industries and factories, Table 6.4 gives the percentages in each category. Thirty-six per cent of cottage-industry workers wanted to continue working in the textile industry, while only twenty-seven per cent of factory workers did.

Women in Swaziland have been viewed as being less mobile than men in seeking wage employment. When asked whether they would be willing to migrate to enhance employment opportunities, eighty-six per cent of respondents said that they would consider migration, while fourteen per cent would not. Of those who would consider migrating, sixty-two per cent preferred to relocate somewhere in Swaziland and five per cent in the Republic of South Africa. For cottage industries, it was fifty-nine per cent for Swaziland and five per cent for South Africa; and for factories, sixty-one per cent and twelve per cent respectively. Forty-four per cent of women employed in the cotton-

Table 6.4   Employment Alternatives: Cottage Industries and Factories
(percentages)

Employment Alternative	Cottage Industry	Factory
Same job	18	15
Another textile job	18	12
Domestic employment	9	0
Non-domestic service employment	9	6
Secretary	0	24
Accountant	0	9
Nurse	9	6
Wants to leave but undecided	27	6
Government	9	21

spinning mill would consider relocating in Swaziland and fifty-six per cent in South Africa. For the clothing factory, seventy-nine per cent of women would consider moving elsewhere in Swaziland and four per cent to South Africa.

Cottage-industry workers overwhelmingly preferred to migrate within Swaziland where, in most instances, they would be paid higher wages than they were presently getting. Workers at the cotton-spinning factory were the only group of women who expressed a preference for moving to South Africa. They were also the most highly-paid factory workers, who are probably aware that even higher wages are being paid for the same type of work in South Africa.

Clearly, there is a hierarchy of female labour in Swaziland that is reflective of the female reserve army of labour. Female workers view migration not only in terms of geographic mobility but also social mobility. Younger, educated rural women might consider migrating to Swaziland's industrial areas. Women at the top of Swaziland's industrial hierarchy would be more likely to seek employment in South Africa.

6.10   TRANSPORTATION

The distance between home and workplace was of particular importance as it relates to mode of transportation for respondents to and from work. Only 10.9 per cent of respondents live on the premises of their place of employment; 14.5 per cent live one kilometre away; 7.3 per cent live two kilometres away; 3.6 per cent three kilometres; 9.1 per cent each for four and five kilometres; 7.3 per cent live six kilometres away; 3.6 per cent eight kilometres; 1.8 per cent nine kilometres; and 16.4 per cent ten kilometres. The remaining 16.3 per cent live from twelve to twenty-five kilometres away. The mean distance from work is six kilometres, and 54.5 per cent live within five kilometres of their place of employment.

For cottage industries, distances average 4.6 kilometres and, for factories 7.7 kilometres. It is only in the case of cottage industries that workers sometimes live on the premises.

Fifty-six per cent of respondents went to work by bus; twenty-six per cent on foot; six per cent each for private car and company *kombie* (van). The remaining twelve per cent lived on the premises of their employers. Table 6.5 represents the breakdown for cottage industries and factories.

Table 6.5   Mode of Transportation (percentages)

	Cottage Industry	*Factory*
Car	5	6
Bus	50	61
Company *kombie*	0	9
Living on/near premises	31	24
On foot	14	0

This reinforces the view that, on average, workers in cottage industries live closer to their workplace. However, distances are not as great as one might expect. It is the relative isolation of most cottage industries that allows them to tap into an extensive rural labour pool. The bus is the principal mode of transportation for both cottage industries and factories.

When asked if they were satisfied with the public services they received, for example, roads, transportation and schools, seventy-three per cent of respondents said they were. Of women working in cottage industries, eighty-two per cent said they were; of women in factories, sixty-one per cent said they were, and for the clothing factory, fifty-eight per cent. Women in factories probably have greater expectations for infrastructural development.

Roads linking major towns in Swaziland are all tarred. Furthermore, the country has a very good public transportation system linking these major towns. However, in a few remote areas, where cottage industries are located, roads are unpaved and in very poor condition. Buses run infrequently.

6.11 MARRIAGE AND CHILDREARING

Marriage, either by customary or civil law, is not common among women workers in textile-related work. By the time women reach their early twenties, older women put pressure on them to get married. Barring that, they suggest having a child. However, there is the general view that nowadays men are more reluctant to make a marital commitment. They usually prefer that their intended spouse have a child before *lobola*, or bridewealth, is negotiated. Many of the young women working in textile employment are in their twenties, unmarried and have children. They view their employment as the major avenue for providing for their own needs and those of their child(ren).

The ideology of traditionalism is pervasive in every aspect of Swazi life and particularly affects the status of women. Through the legal system, women are given subordinate status to men.[43] Marriage in Swazi society confers certain privileges to women through their husbands. They can have access to land and credit. It was the wish of most Swazi women in the survey to be married or to remarry if they had been married previously.

Western middle-class feminist notions have only been incorporated by middle-class Swazi women, many of whom are single. Working class women are relatively unexposed to feminist ideology but have to live relatively autonomous lives.

In marriage under civil law in Swaziland, men can only take one wife. However, in the case of customary law, a man may marry polygynously. In the context of the survey, a couple who are cohabiting without having made arrangements for customary or civil marriage are not considered to be married. Of all respondents, sixty-six per cent of women were single, twenty per cent married, five per cent separated or divorced, seven per cent living with a boyfriend, and two per cent widowed. Among cottage-industry workers, the breakdown is sixty-eight per cent single, eighteen per cent married, nine per cent separated or divorced, none living with a boyfriend, and five per cent widowed. Among factory workers, sixty-one per cent were single, twenty-four per cent married, none separated, three per cent divorced, nine per cent living with boyfriend, and three per cent widowed. These percentages correlate closely with the results of

Pollak's study discussed in Chapter 1 (see p. 30) except that in the case of the former, single women have more children.

For the cotton-spinning mill, thirty-three per cent of female workers were single, fifty-six per cent married and eleven per cent widowed. There were no women who were either separated or living with a boyfriend. At the clothing factory, seventy-one per cent were single, thirteen per cent married, four per cent separated, eight per cent living with a boyfriend and four per cent widowed. From the above, it appears that one's ability to be married has socioeconomic implications and that different types of textile industries have access to different segments of the female reserve army of labour. This suggests a dichotomy between rural and urban textile workers. Whereas the cottage industry labour force is composed of a majority of homestead dwellers, the factory labour force has a higher proportion of town dwellers.

It is significant that there are more married women working in the cotton-spinning mill. The mill represents the most skilled and highest-paying job for women in the textile industry. Because it has more exclusive hiring practices, it has probably tapped into Swaziland's floating labour reserve, attracting some women from other jobs with a long history of work experience in the towns.

Returning to cottage industries, women in rural areas did not live with boyfriends. Live-in relationships are more prevalent in the towns. Above (see p. 138), McFadden called this type of conjugal relationship 'working class marriage'. I would suggest that women continue to live in their father's homestead if they are unmarried. Furthermore, the ideology of traditionalism is given a purer expression in rural areas and would militate against a woman living with her boyfriend. However, illegitimacy occurs in both urban and rural areas.

Women were asked whether they planned to marry, because one cannot assume that marriage is a universal goal for Swazi women. When unmarried women were asked whether they planned to marry or to remarry if married previously, seventy-one per cent said they did, and four per cent said they did not. Twenty-five per cent of respondents were married survey-wide. For cottage industries, sixty-eight per cent said they wanted to be married, nine per cent did not, and, for twenty-three per cent of cases, the question was not applicable. For factories, seventy-three per cent wanted to be married and twenty-seven per cent were already married.

One question elicited open-ended responses from women about their views on being married or remarrying. Twenty-four per cent viewed it as being 'natural' or normal practice giving the following responses: 'It's natural'; 'It is part of nature to get married'; 'It is part of Swazi custom to get married'. Thirty-six per cent said that they wanted to establish a family: 'I want to settle down and have a family of my own' (she already has five children); 'I need a man in order to raise a family'. Twelve per cent said that they wanted to be in a relationship with one man: 'I want to have children with one man' (she is single with no children). Seven per cent said that they wanted to be married in order to be in a position to co-operate with their husband: 'I want to solve problems jointly with someone'. Seven per cent viewed marriage as primarily an economic arrangement: 'I want to have a good life'. Four per cent of respondents wanted protection: 'I want marriage for its own sake and in order to have a future'. Six per cent were concerned about the legal implications: 'I want to become a lawful wife'. Four per cent did not answer the question. It is surprising that even though such a high cultural value is placed on marriage, so few respondents are married. In analysing recent census data, Table 6.6 has been adapted from the 1986 Census.[44]

Table 6.6   Population by Age, Sex, and Marital Status (percentages)

Age	*10–19*	*20–29*	*30–39*	*40–49*
Female				
Never married, with children	12	52	22	9
Married	1.9	23	26	21
Male				
Never married, with children	2	38	31	16
Married	0.03	11	26	26

Source: Central Statistical Office.

Clearly, from the above figures, more than half of women in their twenties are not married but have children. Armstrong cites a study by Gary Ferraro that concludes that women are getting married in their late twenties, as is the case for men in Botswana.[45] In my more general observations of Swazi society I have found cases in which women were either married or involved in a permanent relationship with a man in which the man refused to support children born of previous relationships.

Swaziland's birth rate is 3.2 per cent per annum, claimed to be the highest in the world.[46] In an evaluation of Swaziland's Family Life

Association, A. Rwomire found that about half of his sample was still single, with the average male age being 28.9 and the average female age 27.2.[47] All the family planning services are concentrated in the Manzini–Mbabane industrial corridor.[48] Not only was the rest of Swaziland underserved, but also members of particular age groups, such as adolescents.[49]

Regardless of marital status, eighty-two per cent of respondents have children. Sixty-eight per cent of single women have children and all the married women in the survey. Women in cottage industries have a maximum of eight children and a mean of 2.6; women in factories, the maximum is five and the mean 2.1. Eighteen per cent of all respondents had no children; eighteen per cent one child; and eighteen per cent two children; twenty-two per cent had three children; sixteen per cent had four children; four per cent had five children; two per cent had six children; and two per cent eight children.

The mean number of children per worker was 2.29. Among married women, the mean was 3.5; and among women who had never married, 1.9. In cottage industries, the mean was four children for married women and two for women who had never married; and for factories, 3.12 and 2.36 for the above categories respectively. In Armstrong's sample, the mean number of children was 2.57.[50] For agricultural workers in her sample, the mean was 2.6 and non-agricultural workers, 2.54. For women who were or had been married, the mean was 3.35 children and, for those never married, 2.13. Comparable statistics in my survey are a little lower than Armstrong's.[51]

In cottage industries eighteen per cent had no children; eighteen per cent had one child; fourteen per cent, two children; eighteen per cent, three children; eighteen per cent, four children; five per cent, five children; five per cent, six children; and four per cent, eight children. In factories, eighteen per cent had no children; eighteen per cent, one child; twenty-one per cent, two children; twenty-four per cent, three children; sixteen per cent, four children; and three per cent, five children. No one had more than five children.

In the clothing factory, twenty-five per cent had no children; twenty-one per cent, one child; twenty-one per cent, two children; thirteen per cent, three children; sixteen per cent, four children; and four per cent, five children. Again, no one had more than five children. At the cotton-spinning mill, no one surveyed did not have children; ten per cent of the women had one child; thirty per cent had two children; fifty per cent had three children; and one per cent had four children. No one had more than four children, however. From the above, one can discern that women employed in cottage industries have higher birth rates than women in factories, and that women employed in the clothing factory had a higher birth rate than women employed in the cotton-spinning mill.

When respondents were asked whether they wanted more children, fifty-three per cent said they did and forty-seven per cent said they did not. In cottage industries, fifty-five per cent indicated that they wanted more children, while forty-five per cent did not. In factories, the percentages were identical. In the cotton-spinning mill, thirty-three per cent of female workers wanted more children while sixty-seven per cent did not. In the clothing factory, sixty-two per cent wanted more children while thirty-eight per cent did not. In Armstrong's survey, half of the women wanted more children.[53]

The women were asked whether they used some form of birth control. Only thirty-three per cent indicated that they used some birth control, while the remaining sixty-seven per cent did not. For cottage industries, eighteen per cent used birth control, and in factories, forty-two per cent did so. In the cotton-spinning mill, seventy-eight per cent of women used some form of birth control, and in the clothing factory, twenty-nine per cent. Women employed in the spinning mill tended to be older than those in the clothing factory. Furthermore, the formers' employer provided workshops on family planning. In Armstrong's survey, twenty-one per cent of agricultural workers used contraceptives and 29.5 per cent of non-agricultural workers. She, like Rwomire, suggests that more family planning information is needed.

When asked about social services not provided by the employer, such as hospitals, clinics and counselling services, seventy-five per cent said that they were satisfied and twenty-five per cent dissatisfied. For cottage industries, seventy-three per cent were satisfied, and in factories, seventy-six per cent. Despite the similar levels of satisfaction with social services, rural areas tend to have no hospitals and fewer clinics and counselling services.

6.12   DOMESTIC DIVISION OF LABOUR

Household production and reproduction are essential to the maintenance of the Swazi labour force. Women working in industrial contexts are often overburdened with domestic activities because they have a smaller kinship network to utilise. Respondents were asked about particular chores they performed and whether they received the assistance of other family members. Ninety-six per cent of female textile workers cooked; ninety-three per cent cleaned; and forty-six per cent engaged in childcare. In relation to agriculture, sixty-nine per cent engaged in crop production and twenty-two per cent in animal husbandry. Sixty-two per cent fetched water and firewood. Eighteen per cent engaged in other domestic activities such as house construction and maintenance, beer-brewing, knitting, dressmaking and yard sweeping. Table 6.7 indicates the breakdown between cottage industries and factories in relation to domestic duties performed; Table 6.8, domestic duties for those employed in cotton-spinning mills and clothing factories; Table 6.9, domestic duties of husbands in cottage industries and factories; and Table 6.10, domestic duties of children in cottage industries and factories.

Table 6.7   Domestic Duties: Cottage Industries and Factories (percentages)

Duty	Cottage Industries	Factories
Cooking	95	97
Cleaning	100	96
Childcare	50	38
Crop production	82	64
Animal husbandry	23	15
Fetching water/firewood	77	48
Other	14	18

Table 6.8   Domestic Duties: Factories (percentages)

Duty	Cotton Mill	Clothing Factory
Cooking	100	96
Cleaning	100	88
Childcare	100	38
Crop production	89	54
Animal husbandry	22	12
Fetching water/firewood	77	48
Other	22	17

Table 6.9   Domestic Duties: Husbands (percentages)

Duty	Cottage Industry	Factory
Class I – cooking, cleaning, childcare	5	18
Class II – crop production, animal husbandry, fetching wood/water, other	9	15

Table 6.10   Domestic Duties: Children (percentages)

Duty	Cottage Industry	Factory
Class I – cooking, cleaning, childcare	45	21
Class II – crop production, animal husbandry, fetching wood/water, other	41	21

When asked if their husbands engaged in cooking and cleaning, only thirteen per cent of respondents said yes. When asked the same question concerning their children, thirty-six per cent said that their children assisted them with cooking and cleaning. Twenty-six per cent of children assisted with animal husbandry. There is a dichotomy between cottage-industry workers and factory workers, in that the children of the former assist them in domestic chores while the husbands of the latter assist them, although to a lesser extent.

Women workers were asked who was the principal decision-maker in their household. Sixteen per cent of women said they were; twenty-two per cent said their husbands were; thirty-two per cent said that their fathers were the principal decision-makers; four per cent identified their fathers-in-law; eighteen per cent said that their mothers made major decisions; four per cent, their mothers-in-law; and four per cent, their grandfathers. In cases in which the female worker is the principal decision-maker, I would speculate that she is a female head of household. If the husband is mentioned as being the principal decision-maker, he has probably established a home apart from his parents' homestead.

If the father-in-law or mother-in-law plays that role, it is likely that the female worker lives at her husband's homestead. If the mother or grandfather is the principal decision-maker, she is probably living in her parents' homestead. Even if women are not actually residing in a homestead, they probably live close enough so that they can visit often. In fifty-four per cent of responses, the woman's father's family plays a major role in decision-making, whereas in only twenty-nine per cent of responses did the husband's family exert such influence. In any event, four-fifths of female textile workers make decisions in consultation with family members or in-laws regardless of where they live. Table 6.11 indicates the percentages for factories and cottage industries.

Table 6.11   Principal Decision-maker (percentages)

Decision-maker	Cottage Industries	Factory
Yourself	18	15
Husband/boyfriend	9.5	27
Father	36	33
Father-in-law	4	4
Mother-in-law	23	15
Grandfather	9.5	0
Not applicable	0	6

In the dichotomy between cottage industries and factories, fathers and mothers-in-law become prominent in decision-making in the case of the former, and fathers and husbands or boyfriends in the case of the latter. The latter are more nucleated and patriarchal.

6.13 CHILDCARE

Childcare is a major concern for women wage labourers. Traditionally, when Swazi women lived among their extended family at the home-stead, childcare could be shared. However, with labour migration, one may not have kin in close proximity. Respondents were asked who takes care of their preschool child(ren) while they are at work. Thirty-three per cent of respondents had either no children or no preschool children. Twenty-two per cent had made arrangements with their mothers; seven per cent with a more distant female relative or in-law; eleven per cent with their mothers-in-law; and only two per cent with their sisters. Twenty-two per cent had a hired babysitter and four per cent used a crèche. Overall, it appears that the maternal relatives share childcare equally with crèches (24 per cent). In cottage industries, thirty-two per cent relied on a mother or sister, nine per cent on a hired babysitter and four per cent on a crèche. In factories, twenty-one per cent relied on a mother or sister, thirty per cent a hired babysitter and three per cent a crèche.

The discrepancies between cottage industries and factories reflect an urban/rural dichotomy. More women working in cottage industries rely on their mothers and sisters because they live closer to their homesteads than do women working in factories at Matsapha Industrial Estate. By the same token, factory women rely more heavily on hired babysitters because they do not have relatives available. Very few women of either group relied on crèches, probably because of their relative unavailability. Table 6.12 gives a breakdown of designated babysitters for both cottage industries and factories.

Table 6.12 Childcare (percentages)

Babysitter	Cottage Industry	Factory
Mother	27	25
Mother-in-law	9	12
Sister	4.5	0
Other female relative/in-law	4.5	3
Hired babysitter	9	2
Crèche	4.5	3
Not applicable	45	25

As mentioned above, those cases that fell into the 'not applicable' category were ones in which respondents either did not have children or had children who were of school age.

6.14 CHILDREN'S EDUCATION

In the context of the questionnaire, upward mobility can be viewed in relation to a woman's success in the workplace. Another perspective, which is related to the above, is the advancement of a worker's offspring. When female textile workers were asked about educational goals for their children, forty-nine per cent wanted them to finish secondary school; forty per cent wanted them to graduate from university; and 5.5 per cent wanted them to undertake a vocational training course. However, most of these women could not afford to assist their children in realising these educational goals. Of those women who had children, only eighteen per cent said that they could afford their children's total education. Table 6.13 indicates the break-down between cottage industries and factories for the educational aspirations of female workers' children.

Table 6.13   Children's Educational Achievement (percentages)

	Cottage Industry	Factory
High school	64	42
Vocational school	9	3
University	23	52
No answer	4	3

Clearly, factory workers have higher aspirations for their children than do cottage industry workers. However, there was no significant discrepancy between the two groups of women in terms of their inability to pay for their child(ren)'s full education. Only eighteen per cent of cottage industry workers and twenty-one per cent of factory workers, could afford to pay, by their own estimation.

To determine whether respondents were perpetuating Swazi tradition in the socialisation of their children, I asked if they were teaching children handicrafts. Fifty-four per cent said no; eighteen per cent taught only girls; four per cent taught children of both sexes. For twenty-four per cent of respondents, the question was not applicable.

6.15   CONCLUSION

Although Murray and Brown provide different interpretations of the relationship between family structure and labour migration in the southern African periphery, the family has undergone a profound transformation since mine labour recruitment began at the turn of the century. In the ensuing period, the periphery has experienced the effects of underdevelopment, which have not left women and children unscathed. Women have found that they too have to migrate to find wage employment to support themselves and their children, often without a husband.

The characteristics of the Swazi female textile labour force can be considered a subset of Armstrong's female industrial labour force. She dichotomises professional and unskilled workers and focuses on the latter. She characterises unskilled workers as young women in newly-created jobs who are usually unmarried and struggling with family and work. Older women are viewed as being less desirable for recent industrialisation and have become the babysitters for younger women.

McFadden addresses the stratification of women within the pineapple industry, in which there is a dichotomy between field and factory workers. Although both categories experienced seasonal employment, field workers were the most exploited. They were totally uprooted from their homes, lived on the premises of the pineapple industry in very squalid conditions and were paid very low wages. These women often resorted to what McFadden called 'working class' marriage in which unemployed men engage in temporary liaisons with them in order to have access to cash.

In my own study of the textile industry, there is a dichotomy between factory and cottage-industry workers. The former tend to be younger, more educated and more recent entrants into the labour force. Most are single with one or two children. They tend to have greater aspirations for themselves and their children. These women, for the most part, are not as proletarianised as women in the pineapple industry because they still have access to crops and livestock. Many of these women hire other women to care for their children. They have varying fringe benefits at work and no union representation.

By contrast, in cottage industries, women are on the average older, have more children and live in their own homesteads. They are not as mobile as factory workers but have higher aspirations for their children. Living in their own homesteads, they have access to child-care and direct access to fields, crops and livestock. They too engage in additional cash-generating activities. In summarising the question-naire, there are lower percentages of women marrying with each succeeding generation and/or marrying at a later age. Some demo-graphers have indicated that this is a regional trend. I attribute the decline to a number of factors:

- the lack of self-sufficiency of the homestead as a productive unit capable of supporting polygynous households;
- the decline in polygynous marriages;
- a high rate of male unemployment in the country;
- male employment concentrated in the industrial areas of Swaziland or South Africa, requiring their absence from the homestead for extended periods of time; and

• young women having to fend for themselves and their children in the areas where they seek employment which, for the most part, do not coincide with those of the men.

It is obvious from the survey results that a high value is placed on marriage. Women who have a number of children express hopes of eventually marrying and having a family. Some of these women will marry, especially those who are recent high school graduates and those who have had a child or children by one man with whom they live or maintain a relationship.

When a woman assesses her future prospects for economic security, marriage figures prominently in the equation. This is particularly the case in the non-Euro-American context, where neither men nor women are paid a family wage. It is even more necessary to have a dual-income family to cater to the needs of children because there is no social welfare system to provide added support to female-headed households.

Tilly and Scott's socio-historical categories for the organisation of work in the family unit do not correlate with Swazi structure nor that of families in other peripheral areas of southern Africa. Parents and children do not participate collectively in handicraft production for sale, as in the *family economy*; most children are too young to work, as in the *family wage economy*; and, most households are headed by females who do not earn a family wage as males do in the *family consumer economy*. Whereas Tilly and Scott's categories are not applicable to Swazi family structure and that of other areas of the southern African periphery, despite some historical similarities, I think it is more applicable to core contexts – and some semi-peripheral contexts, for example, white South Africa.

Part III
Comparisons

7 A Lesotho Comparison: Elusive Industrialisation and Labour Migration

7.1 INTRODUCTION

In Chapters 2 and 3, the semi-periphery–periphery relationship between the political economies of Swaziland and South Africa was established to provide a context for analysing women and textile industrialisation. This chapter is devoted to an analysis of the Lesotho political economy for purposes of interperipheral comparison. In some of the literature on Swaziland, it has been suggested that instead of comparing it to Botswana and Lesotho a more apt comparison is Zimbabwe.[1] Certainly, Swaziland's sizeable European population distinguishes it from Botswana and Lesotho. However, there are historical similarities among these countries.

For sixty-three years, the three protectorates were ruled by the British High Commission and were subject to some of the same colonial policy. Legislation regulating the taxation and migration of men and women was applied to each. All three are considered to be more-or-less ethnically homogeneous. However, they did have different domestic resource bases and were articulated into the South African political economy at slightly different times and under different circumstances.

To varying degrees, each Protectorate has served as a reserve to the South Africa gold mining industry. However, their participation in gold mining has occurred in inverse proportion to the development of their domestic political economies. Thus Swaziland and Botswana did not send as many migrants nor as high a percentage of able-bodied males to South Africa as did Lesotho. Basotho (Lesotho nationals) women are probably the most proletarianised of women in BLS countries.

Lesotho gained independence in 1966 shortly after Botswana (in the same year), and two years before Swaziland. Lesotho had experienced nearly a century of colonialism and three decades of economic underdevelopment. Due to land alienation by the Boers from the

167

1830s to the 1860s, the Basotho were left to occupy the most mountainous area of southern Africa. The country's altitude ranges between 5000 and 10 000 feet. There are three ecozones: the lowlands, the foothills and the mountains. The majority of people and livestock – including cattle, sheep and goats – occupy the lowlands, which contain most of the arable land. The lowlands area constitutes only fifteen per cent of Lesotho's land area. That is where eighty-five per cent of its human population is located as well as the vast majority of its animal population. Lesotho's current population is approximately 1.7 million.

Since this is a comparative chapter, it has been structured to reflect the themes of Chapters 2 to 5 on Swaziland. The first section will consider Lesotho's political economy from the period of incorporation to the present; the second section, the political economy of fibre production; and the third, the role of cottage industries and factories. The final section will provide my conclusions.

7.2 THE BEGINNING OF COMMODITY PRODUCTION AND LABOUR MIGRATION 1869–84

This period represents the beginning of the incorporation of the Basotho into the regional political economy, with the introduction of mercantile capital and the emergence of the diamond mining industry at Kimberley. Furthermore, missionaries entered the territory and were to play a decisive role in class formation *vis-à-vis* petty-commodity production on mission land, the promotion of labour migration and the usurpation of chiefly power. The British played a major role during this period in negotiating boundaries and eventually incorporating Basutoland (Lesotho's colonial name).

It was King Moshoeshoe I who united the southern Sotho tribe and some disparate Ngunis during the *lifaqane* (a period in the 1820s when warfare and famine were widespread in south-eastern Africa). Unlike the Zulu king, Shaka, who actually precipitated the *lifaqane*, Moshoeshoe responded to the process in an organised fashion. He was a master of diplomacy, negotiating with both Boer and Briton. He viewed missionaries as important advisers and a positive influence on his people.[2]

Moshoeshoe had won many loyal followers through the *mafisa* system. This system was one whereby the chieftaincy leased its excess livestock to less-privileged members of the Basotho social formation. The lessees would have the responsibility for caring for the stock and were required to reciprocate by performing tasks for the chiefly lender. In the event of loss of livestock, lessees would be expected to pay compensation. By the 1870s, non-chiefly homesteads were among the first to engage in sub-subsistence agricultural production, which signalled increasing incorporation.[3]

To focus more fully on the Basotho political economy, Basutoland began to experience incorporation in the 1830s as the *trekboers* and the *voortrekkers* descended on the area occupied by the Southern Sotho near the Orange and Caledon rivers. By the late 1860s, the two groups had expropriated the best land, leaving the Basotho to occupy the most mountainous areas of the region. The boundaries of present-day Lesotho, which were more-or-less delineated in the 1869 Treaty of Aliwal North, left intact only a small portion of the lowland area they had previously occupied.

In the 1870s, the Basotho began to occupy the foothills and mountains because of land shortage in the small area of the lowlands that was left. Because non-lowland areas were not suited to crop cultivation, Basotho occupying those areas relied heavily on sheep- and goat-herding.[4]

Missionaries from the Paris Evangelical Missionary Society arrived in Basutoland in 1833.[5] Thompson indicates that they were the Basothos' advocates in maintaining their land base. Missionaries founded missions on which they set up schools and developed a self-sufficient agricultural component. Those Basotho who were the first to become Christian and had been proletarianised often joined missions and were allocated land there. J. Kimble indicates that, by the 1870s, missionaries were collaborating heavily with the British colonial administration.[6]

Although there was little European settlement in Basutoland, traders followed hard on the heels of missionaries in the mid-1850s.[7] The Paris Evangelical Missionary Society was the first to establish a mission in Basutoland, therefore the first Basotho were converted to Protestantism. It was not until the early 1860s that the Roman Catholic Church began to preach in the territory. However, the process of Christian conversion did not accelerate until the turn of the century. It has been suggested that, in contemporary Lesotho, where there is one ethnic group religion acts as a major divisive element.

By 1854, three of Moshoeshoe's sons were placed in, or appointed to chieftainships in the four original districts of Basutoland, which had previously been under the jurisdiction of local chiefs.[8] But after their father's death, they developed different loyalties, which undermined the unity of the Basotho nation. Basutoland had been annexed to the Cape Colony thereby reinforcing its role as a labour reserve to the diamond mining industry. However, when the Cape Magisterial Government began to impose heavy taxation and to attempt to disarm the Basotho, a rebellion was precipitated, called the Gun War, in 1880–81. Basutoland became a British protectorate in 1884. This new arrangement meant direct governance by the British Crown.

In 1886, towards the end of the period of land alienation in Basutoland, diamonds were discovered at Kimberley. The Basotho were among the first miners to work at the diamond diggings. Kimble suggests that during that period a major motivation for labour migration was for the acquisition of guns to fend off further land alienation.[9] Also, during this period, Basutoland became a producer of the agricultural commodities wheat, sorghum, maize, wool and mohair for Orange Free State farmers. Thus, grain and labour became its two major commodities.

In the period after the Great Trek in 1834, when Boers fled from the Cape Colony because of the abolition of slavery, the British were concerned with impeding Boer expansion and, to some extent, with protecting the rights of indigenous peoples. Thus they were responsible for intervening in land disputes and delineating boundaries. When the extent of South Africa's mineral wealth was determined, they took a keener interest in controlling the Boer republics. In 1884, the British annexed Basutoland and Bechuanaland as protectorates, followed by Swaziland in 1903. This was a strategy to inhibit Boer expansionism into other potentially mineral-rich areas and for purposes of acquiring a seaport.

7.3 BASUTOLAND'S INCORPORATION AS A LABOUR RESERVE 1884–1935

With the inception of British rule, taxation was imposed to generate revenue for the colonial administration and to foster labour migration. Shortly after colonial rule began, gold was discovered on the Witwatersrand. Responding to mining magnates' demand for cheap male labour, the Basotho began to go to the gold mines in large numbers around the time of the First World War. They developed a reputation for their skill in drilling mineshafts.

Just after the turn of the century, the British began to introduce new political structures. Mission-educated Basotho began to found their own political organisations. Furthermore, despite labour migration as an alternative to agricultural production, Basotho began to experience mass sub-subsistence production and underdevelopment. It was women in the rural areas who bore the brunt of sub-subsistence production, having the responsibility of providing for the family in the absence of the miner/husband.

The National Council, composed of 100 members, was formed in 1903. Ninety-five members were appointed by the Paramount Chief and the remaining five by the Resident Commissioner.[10] The first Basotho political organisation, The Progressive Association, was founded in 1907 and a second political organisation, Lekhotla la Bafo, in 1918. The latter eventually gained more popular support.

Lekhotla la Bafo was composed of Basutoland's incipient middle class – teachers, clerks, ministers, journalists and traders – whose concern was with re-establishing the legitimacy of the chieftaincy under British colonial rule.[11] Furthermore, they were opposed to the presence of the white population and to South African overtures for incorporation. One impact of missionary involvement was that Basutoland had one of the highest literacy rates in sub-Saharan Africa, with women having a higher literacy rate than men. However, the movement had already begun to dwindle when the Basutoland African Congress (later Basutoland Congress Party) was formed by young, educated people.

C. Murray considers the underdevelopment process to have begun in the 1930s.[12] Kimble argues that Basutoland was a major producer of grain for the Orange Free State between 1870 and 1885.[13] However, J. P. Hunter suggests that the sale of animal fibres – wool and mohair – had surpassed grain sales by 1904.[14] In the context of animal-fibre production, mohair has been considered to be more lucrative than wool. This created the potential for the further development of fibre production to provide cash for Basotho to purchase foodstuffs.

By the time the Swazis were beginning to be incorporated into the regional political economy in the 1880s, the Basotho incorporation process was fully under way. In the case of Swaziland, land concessions within a territory that had already been a victim of land alienation represented the precipitating factor for incorporation. J. Crush mentions that the Swazi response to incorporation did not involve peasant production for newly-created white settler markets.[15] I am inclined to think that land alienation was such a devastating experience to the Swazi peasantry that they became preoccupied with their own subsistence. Besides, white-owned farms whose networks extended into the eastern Transvaal could cater to emerging urban markets. Trade restrictions inhibited the Basotho's access to Orange Free State markets. Moreover, by this time, the core of industrial development had shifted from Kimberley to Johannesburg.

The land partition in Swaziland actually anticipated the 1913 Land Act in South Africa. When the latter was enacted, it had a direct impact on Basutoland because landless blacks from the Orange Free State migrated to the protectorate.[16]

During British colonial rule, Basutoland's function as a male labour reserve for the South African gold mines became entrenched and incontrovertible. In response to obvious proletarianisation in the three protectorates, the British colonial administration commissioned Sir Alan Pim to assess their economic conditions and to make recommendations for the alleviation of attendent social problems.

South Africa had designs on Basutoland's incorporation throughout the latter's colonial history, but until the early 1930s, the British rejected such overtures. By that time, British and Basotho popular opinion was opposed to annexation, primarily because of the erosion of black political rights in South Africa.[17]

It is obvious that the British undertook the 'protection' of Basutoland with no intention of arresting the underdevelopment process. It had become increasingly clear during this period that Basutoland could not be economically self-sufficient. However, by the end of the period, the British realised it was necessary to make some kind of commitment to maintain the economic status quo. Furthermore, in keeping with their protective function, they resisted Basutoland's incorporation into South Africa, which would have been an easy solution for them.

7.4   INCREASING ECONOMIC STAGNATION AND DEPENDENCE 1935–66

The recommendations of the Pim Report were published in 1935. Prior to that time, colonial rule had been solely supported by revenues generated by the taxation of the Basotho. Although not making a vigorous effort, British colonial officials were willing to acknowledge, fund and implement some of the recommendations. In the report, Pim was critical of the dual political system and suggested that Indirect Rule be implemented.[18] However, Swaziland was the major beneficiary of the report's recommendations for economic aid. In Lesotho, some effort was made to initiate rural development and the control of soil erosion.

The Paramount Chieftaincy retained many of its duties during the period of its protectorate status. However, in 1939, a major dispute arose over succession after the death of Paramount Chief Seeiso Griffith.[19] His disputed successor died after serving in office for one year. He was survived by three wives. His first wife had no male children, his second wife, an infant son; and his third, a son who was older than the second wife's child. Following strict primogeniture, the baby Bereng (the second wife's son) was chosen to be Paramount Chief. The senior wife, 'Mantsebo, was appointed as Regent until he reached the age of majority.

In the post-Second World War period, some significant political changes occurred in Basutoland. The British colonial administration introduced district councils that provided democratic structures at the local level. It is assumed that development of these structures represented a gradual effort to groom Basutoland for eventual independence. Also, the first contemporary political organisation, the Basutoland African Congress (BAC), which later became the Basutoland Congress Party (BCP), was founded in 1952 by Ntsu Mokhehle, a former member of the ANC Youth League. The BCP became a mass party that eventually controlled the district councils and was the most vocal advocate for Basutoland's independence.

As independence approached, other parties began to split off from the BCP. Having realised that Basutoland would be heading for independence rather than incorporation into South Africa, neither the British Government, the South African Government nor the Catholic Church wanted to see an independent Lesotho under the leadership of the Basutoland Congress Party. The former are considered to be the forces behind the formation of the Christian Democratic Party, which later became the Basutoland National Party (BNP), founded in 1958 under the leadership of Leabua Jonathan. Jonathan, a grandson of Moshoeshoe's second house and a chief of Leribe district, had a Standard 6 education (sixth grade) and was a former gold miner.[20]

Yet another break occurred with the formation of the Marematlou Party – which later merged with the Freedom Party to become the Marematlou Freedom Party (MFP) in 1961 – to advocate a central position for the monarchy and the protection of the chieftaincy. In addition, the Basutoland Communist Party was formed in 1962.[21]

However, it was Mokhehle's BCP that went to New York to testify before the United Nations Committee on Colonialism in 1962 in an effort to keep the decolonisation process on track in southern Africa.[22] Nevertheless, in constitutional talks held in London in 1965, the BNP was able to prevail in having its platform for independence recognised, to the chagrin of the other two parties. As proposed, the constitution would make provision for the Paramount Chief to be a constitutional monarch despite the objections of the Marematlou Freedom Party. Although the BCP was anti-chieftaincy, it joined forces with the MFP to oppose the BNP because of Jonathan's pro-South African stance and the view that his party was not supported by the majority of the electorate.

The BNP won the pre-independence elections by two seats.[23] This anticipated the small victory of the INM in Swaziland by a slim majority. In fact, Leabua Jonathan did not win the election in his constituency. Another prominent member of the party became Prime Minister until Jonathan was elected from another constituency in the first by-elections. Just prior to the 1970 elections, the Jonathan Government was becoming increasingly unpopular because of its close collaboration with South Africa.

By the time elections were held, popular opinion was against the BNP. In the 1970 elections, when it was apparent that the BCP would be victorious, the Jonathan government nullified the election results and invoked a State of Emergency for three years. This signalled the end of Westminister-style democracy and the beginning of mass murders, detentions and intimidation.

Many BCP supporters were killed during the State of Emergency and the party was in disarray. However, in 1974, the BCP attempted a coup. In its aftermath, two of its leaders, Ntsu Mokhehle and Koenyama Chakela, fled the country. Nevertheless, a number of BCP leaders remained in Lesotho and continued working for their party. Among the latter group, a small contingent began to collaborate with the Jonathan regime. A few were appointed to the interim parliament. Elsewhere, I have represented these schisms as the BCP-in-residence, the interim-BCP and BCP-in-exile.[24]

Here, I want to return to an issue discussed in Chapter 3 concerning the role of the monarchy in Swaziland and Lesotho. Certainly, the two countries differ in the metamorphosis of the monarchy. Lesotho never really embraced the ideology of traditionalism in the way that Swaziland did. I think that Lesotho's earlier incorporation and the impact of Christian missions have been contributory factors to the secularisation of Basotho society with a chiefly presence in government. The Basotho were educated, Christianised and introduced to Western views about land ownership and new agricultural techniques in the mission context. This, to some extent, undermined the chieftaincy and portended the development of new political institutions and organisations in the first decades of the twentieth century. Furthermore, although the Basotho monarchy has disproportionate access to land and livestock, it has no monopoly on Lesotho's other meagre resources. Therefore, the monarchy was not in a position to fully impose its authority and to monopolise the economy.

Basutoland's high literacy rate, the introduction of district councils and the influence of South African nationalism are all factors that catapulted it to the forefront of the pro-independence struggle in southern Africa. However, its independence would be won without national autonomy for the Lesotho political economy.

7.5 LESOTHO'S INCREASING SEMI-PERIPHERAL AND CORE DEPENDENCY 1966–77

When Lesotho became independent in 1966, it had £1000 sterling in its treasury and two miles of paved road. Virtually no industrialisation had taken place. Gold mining remittances were its major source of revenue. However, as an internationally-recognised independent country, it was eligible for membership in international organisations and to receive donor aid. In its own development planning, Lesotho wanted to achieve economic self-sufficiency but proposed a number of development projects that could not be funded domestically. The Oxbow project – finally started in the late 1980s – a major hydro-electric project to be constructed at the source of the Orange River in the mountains of Lesotho, was first proposed during this period. This project's primary goal was to fulfil the Witwatersrand's hydro-electric needs with those of Lesotho being secondary.

Although Lesotho was eligible for donor aid at independence, it was not until the mid-to-late 1970s that substantial aid allocations were forthcoming. However, a few integrated rural development projects were initiated in the meantime. These include projects such as Senqu, Khomokhoana, Thaba Tseka and Thaba Bosiu. Some of these projects, which catered almost exclusively to males, were total failures, while others achieved very limited success. The one possible exception is the Thaba Tseka project, because its location in the geographic centre of the country has had some impact in reorientating infrastructural development from the lowlands.

In relation to development projects, P. Wellings suggests that the lack of success of these projects has made donors reluctant to make further allocations to rural development projects.[25] A re-emphasis has been made to support urban, capital-intensive projects instead. However, this might in part be reflective of a change in emphasis from rural development to urban, industrial development by the World Bank and other major donor agencies. Nevertheless, there are alternative views on the current development emphasis.

Women in Development projects were implemented in the mid-1970s in an attempt to alleviate rural poverty. Most of these projects are peripheral in that they provide casual employment to enable economically-marginal women and children to survive who have little or no access to migrant remittances. They usually involve performing tasks located in or near the village such as road-, track- and bridge-building, and also provide work for casual labourers on male-orientated development projects. Some projects include a handicraft component. The women taking part are members of the stagnant or latent labour reserve.

Women in Lesotho generally occupy lower- and middle-echelon positions in the public and private sectors. Among professionals, there is a preponderance of teachers and nurses. However, there are a few women doctors and university lecturers. In the civil service, women occupy lower- and middle-echelon positions and, in a few instances, higher-echelon positions such as permanent secretaries and ministers. Furthermore, new governmental structures have been created in the last decade, such as the Women's Bureau, the Commission for Women and a women's affairs ministry.

In the private sector, women rarely occupy managerial positions, instead being banktellers, clerks and secretaries. Obviously, educated men occupy the higher-echelon positions in the public sector and middle- and upper-level management positions in the private sector. Banks in Lesotho tend to be highly localised while newly-investing manufacturing industries usually have white managerial staff and Basotho men at the middle-level.

For the bulk of male employment, Lesotho has continued to function as a labour reserve to the gold mining industry. Its modern sector can only employ about eight per cent of Lesotho's active labour force, about 40 000 people.[26] Lesotho exhibits the highest rate of labour migrancy of any country in the world. Between 1965 and 1977, there was a six per cent increase in the number of Basotho in the South African gold mines.[27]

In the late 1970s, half of Lesotho's able-bodied male labour force was working in the mines at any given time. Furthermore, the government received half of its revenues from migrant remittances. The South African Chamber of Mines' post-Soweto strategy to become less reliant on foreign labour had the potential for reorientating recruiting strategies in Lesotho and Swaziland. In the Lesotho case, the gold mines have employed the core of Basotho working men. Whereas experienced miners were being retained, few novices were being hired. Thus it appeared that there would be a gradual phasing out of Basotho labour. In the Swazi case, the gold mines had only absorbed its surplus labour.

This also coincided with a period when the gold price was high and considerable mechanisation was taking place in the mines. With increased mechanisation, a production speed-up occurred which compromised mine safety. There was considerable labour unrest, in response to which wages were increased. Furthermore, there was the potential for further reduction of the mines' foreign labour supply.

Lesotho's increasingly antagonistic stance towards South Africa and incipient trade union activity by Basotho gold miners persuaded the Lesotho Government that it needed some means of absorbing surplus male labour in the event of mass dismissals from the mines. The World Bank funded the Labour-Intensive Construction Unit (LCU) in the late 1970s. Although more capital-intensive projects have been designed for men, should there be mass dismissals, they would probably perform a similar type of work to that performed by women. The project can absorb a maximum of 10 000 men. Such a project could have only alleviated the initial shock without staving-off the long-term devastation of Lesotho's political economy.

DeBeers invested in a diamond mine at Letseng-le-terai in the mid-1970s only to withdraw in 1982 when the diamond price plummetted. Upon closure, the mine had to dismiss 900 men. Diamonds had temporarily usurped wool and mohair as the highest foreign exchange earner. The mine had generated fifty per cent of export earnings.

When South Africa unilaterally declared the Transkei independent in 1976, Lesotho protested to the international donor community that since it did not recognise the homeland's independence, their common border was, in effect, closed to trade. It was at that point that Lesotho began to experience a substantial donor aid increase from a number of sources. Wellings suggests that the 'border closure' issue played on the guilt of core nations whose governments refused to assault apartheid directly but who perceived themselves as doing so indirectly by allocating donor aid to Lesotho.[28] Thus, donor aid helped to bolster a regime that had begun to become increasingly critical of South Africa while experiencing increasing domestic opposition.

Of course, donor aid usually has certain stipulations about its use, including the number of foreign 'experts' employed; wages paid to local employees; the scale, orientation and duration of the project; and the purchase of equipment and agricultural inputs. There is the feeling that expatriates are highly-paid temporary sojourners in the country who do not have a genuine commitment to Lesotho's development. Expatriate experts often view the Basotho with disdain.

Farmers participating in integrated rural development projects sometimes found themselves heavily in debt after their project ended, because of inputs obtained on credit. Furthermore, Basotho wanted to see development projects have an impact upon a broader spectrum of their society. During the period that Jonathan was in power, a common complaint was that members of the BNP were the principal beneficiaries of these projects. Moreover, the Lesotho Government has not had the funding to continue development projects once foreign donors have withdrawn. In the aftermath of the 1986 coup, the expulsion of Chinese and Koreans led to the cessation of a number of projects.

South Africa benefits from donor-aid allocations to Lesotho. Since core subsidiaries – particularly American and British companies – are located in South Africa, much of the equipment and inputs utilised by donor aid-funded projects are purchased in South Africa. Furthermore, although white South Africans are not generally hired to work on major development projects, they are often subcontracted for building and road construction. Moreover, border towns such as Ladybrand and Ficksburg benefit from purchases made by expatriates and middle-class Basotho.[29]

To summarise the period, it was one in which a number of entities, upon which the Lesotho political economy was buttressed, became more tenuous. The mining industry was considering internalising its labour force. Donor aid was forthcoming but made no appreciable impact on arresting Lesotho's underdevelopment. All these processes were occurring against the backdrop of escalating unrest throughout the region and increasingly in South Africa itself. It has been argued that, because Lesotho's political economy is so dependent on South

Africa, the latter economy's recessionary trends are automatically transferred to the former.

In 1977, in response to these recessionary trends in the South African economy and high black unemployment, the Chamber of Mines restricted the employment of foreign labour. Of the countries of the region, Lesotho was the largest supplier, the most dependent on migrant remittances and therefore the most vulnerable.

Failed integrated rural development projects and prospects of more restricted migratory labour recruitment helped to entrench recessionary trends of greater severity in the Lesotho political economy than in Botswana and Swaziland. Realising Lesotho's increasing vulnerability, major donors decided to reorientate projects to the urban industrial base and to make contingency plans in the event of mass dismissals of miners. Despite a dubious beginning, the Jonathan government was enjoying the height of popularity at the end of this period.

7.6 AN UNCERTAIN FUTURE: 1977–PRESENT

The post-1977 period has been one of increasing uncertainty. Lesotho's role as a supplier of migrant labour to the gold mining industry continued to be in jeopardy. The Jonathan Government became increasingly unstable and repressive. Lesotho emerged as a debtor nation. Furthermore, Lesotho's overt confrontation with South Africa was to become more collaborative on the eve of substantial shifts in the South African political economy.

More recently, Lesotho's political history has been punctuated by a series of coups. In 1986, the military overthrew the Government headed by Leabua Jonathan. In 1991, there was a coup within the military, ousting Major-General Justin Lekhanya; a month after his ousting, Lekhanya made an unsuccessful counter-coup attempt.

Just prior to the Chamber of Mines' implementation of a quota system on foreign labour, Lesotho supplied 125 000 migrants.[30] In the post-1977 period, the figure has continued to hover above 100 000. In 1987, according to the Chamber of Mines, Lesotho had approximately 112 000 migrants in the mines.[31] However, in the first half of 1990, the figure was up to 127 000[32]. Contracts have been lengthened to retain more skilled workers. In addition, re-engagement certificates are offered which require miners to return to work within a limited period of time in order to retain the same job and rate of pay. Less than five per cent of Basotho recruits are novices.

J. Crush argues that those who predicted dire outlooks for the employment of foreign labour in the gold mines have been a bit too hasty in making long-term generalisations about short-term trends.[33] He points out that throughout the gold mining industry's history, the foreign labour supply has not been stable. During periods of foreign labour instability, substitutes from within and outside have been sought. For example, because of an unstable labour supply immediately after the Boer War, Chinese indentured servants were recruited.

From 1886 to 1973, the percentage of foreign labour did not drop below fifty per cent.[34] However, between 1973 and 1977, when social scientists were speculating on the implications of the 'internalisation' policy, the percentage of foreign labour dropped from 79.6 per cent to 39.2 per cent.[35] Although Crush conceded that there is a higher percentage of South African labour in the mines, he suggests that foreign suppliers have maintained the relative percentages that prevailed in the late 1970s, with attrition being the means of lowering the percentage of foreign workers in the long term.[36] Now, attrition does not seem to be taking place.

J. H. Bardill and J. E. Cobbe suggest that as a response to the 'internalisation' policy, Lesotho was almost exclusively a labour reserve for the gold mining industry in the 1980s.[37] Previously, workers had also been recruited for employment on Orange Free State farms as well as in other industries. However, in an article published in 1991, Cobbe suggests the possibility of mass migrations of Basotho to South Africa for employment in the post-apartheid period.

Despite increasing restrictions on Basotho labour migration, both women and men continue to migrate illegally to South Africa.[38] Many Basotho have lived in South Africa at some point during their lives. Businesspeople have often accumulated capital through South African township investments before establishing themselves in Lesotho. Furthermore, with working-class Basotho, illegal migration has become more viable since dompasses (permits designating race, work status and place of employment) were abolished in South Africa in 1986. Lack of influx control has resulted in the overurbanisation of South African townships.

Since its independence, Lesotho has relied heavily on donor aid from various international agencies. As mentioned above, this has been particularly the case since 1976. Earlier, most of Lesotho's donor aid was allocated in the form of grants. However, as the Government became a more successful donor-aid entrepreneur, it began to receive larger loans. Therefore, it is now paying a substantial amount of debt service and has become a debtor nation. Its percentage of debt service rose from 7.5 per cent of government revenue in 1980/81 to twenty-seven per cent in 1984/85.[39]

Subsequently, Lesotho debt service has become more manageable: foreign debt peaked at $18 million in 1988 but was expected to decrease to $15 million in 1989.[40] In addition, by 1989, Lesotho's balance of payments had improved due to increased investment by export-processing industry, primarily in clothing and footwear.[41] This is occurring in response to Lesotho's IMF structural adjustment programme.[42]

Popular support for Prime Minister Jonathan, which was never very high, began to wane during this period. As the tenth anniversary of the 1970 'coup' approached, the Mokhehle faction of the BCP-in-exile organised the Lesotho Liberation Army (LLA) in Botswana. In 1979, they began to infiltrate the country to engage in acts of sabotage, assassinations and guerrilla warfare in an attempt to topple the Jonathan regime. The regime alleged South African collusion with the LLA to enable guerrillas to enter South African-surrounded Lesotho. The LLA claimed that they infiltrated Lesotho through the Sotho-speaking homelands. There was considerable popular support for Mokhehle, who was viewed as a charismatic leader. The high probability of South African collusion was generally ignored by his supporters. The Government responded to BCP/LLA support with political repression.

After the Soweto riots in 1976, Lesotho had a steady flow of young refugees who, once in the country, usually joined one of the major liberation organisations. However, Lesotho did not have guerrilla-training facilities for these refugees, despite repeated South African allegations. South African Special Branch agents were regularly sent to Lesotho for surveillance of refugees and, in some instances, to kidnap them. At that time, some high-ranking African National Congress members lived in Maseru, including Chris Hani, chief of staff of Umkonto We Sizwe, and Thomazile Botha, a prominent trade-unionist from Port Elizabeth.

With the inception of the Reagan Administration in the United States, the Carter Administration's policy of constructive disengagement with South Africa was reversed, to become 'unconstructive engagement'. There were high-level consultations between the two governments on security-related issues. The South African Defence Force began to invade independent countries in the region, on the pretext that they had allowed themselves to be springboards for acts of sabotage against South Africa. A raid occurred in Lesotho in December 1982 in which forty-two people were killed, including some Basotho nationals.

In late 1985, domestic tensions began to mount against the Jonathan regime as the BNP's Youth League went on a rampage in which they fired civil servants from their jobs, extorted money from business-people and raped women. To worsen matters, the South African Government implemented an economic blockade against Lesotho. By January, the people were on the brink of starvation. As tensions mounted and people began to become restless, the military took over the government of Lesotho in a relatively bloodless coup.

Even though some scholars have argued that South Africa had no involvement in the coup, I think it is implicit, because South Africa implemented an economic embargo contributing to the coup and, in the aftermath, pressured the military government to expel ANC members. Most were sent to countries that were more distant from South Africa's borders. This placed Lesotho's military government on bad terms with the ANC.

Another order of business to which the South African government wanted Lesotho to attend was the signing of the Highlands Water Scheme Agreement, as water seems to be the country's most exploitable resource. The former dropped negotiations on the original Oxbow project when it decided to build a dam across the border from Lesotho. However, the dam proved to have low velocity because of its distance downstream from the source of the Orange River. Negotiations were concluded in 1988, with substantial funding from the World Bank (IBRD) in addition to that of the South African government. Now the World Bank is implementing a structural adjustment programme in Lesotho as a condition of its loan. The Lesotho government has had to streamline its civil service, increase existing taxes on basic services and commodities, and introduce new taxes. For a country that is among the world's poorest, this is quite a burden, because the populace is already experiencing high unemployment and inflation. Structural adjustment affects most segments of society differentially. Working- and lower-class people in urban areas, and single mothers in urban and rural areas, would find survival more of a struggle. University students have protested against the adjustment programme because of its economic austerity.

With the military coup of 1986, Lesotho became the first country in southern Africa to have a military government. Elated in the aftermath of the coup, or 'change of government' that the Jonathan regime had been overthrown, the Basotho quickly became disillusioned with Justin Lethanya's military government as it attempted to entrench itself rather than hand over power to a civilian government.

Whereas King Moshoeshoe II had been at loggerheads with the Jonathan regime and had remained in exile for an extended period of time, he was asked to become head of state in the military government. Two of his cousins were members of the six-person Military Council and one of his brothers was Minister of Interior.

The king had some conflicting tendencies. On the one hand, he was an ANC supporter; on the other, he had a vision of Lesotho as a more traditional society rather like King Sobhuza's Swaziland. Village-level democratic structures were to be introduced, to the exclusion of national ones. The king's dabbling in politics tarnished his benevolent image among urban Basotho. By the middle of 1989, people had become so dissatisfied with his political manoeuvring that they wanted to see him step down. He was perceived – and was later so accused by Lekhanya – to be the major obstacle to the return to civilian rule. The King went into exile in England early in 1990 from where he is said to have denied the allegations. Lekhanya dethroned him later that year and replaced him with his son, who has assumed the title King Letsie III.

With King Moshoeshoe II's departure, Lekhanya's own opposition to elections was illuminated. Furthermore, his collaboration with South Africa and his implication in the murder of a young man continued to haunt him. In fact, it was the King's two cousins on the Military Council who revealed that Lekhanya had committed the murder, and not a junior officer accompanying him. The King ran into difficulty with Lekhanya because he refused to approve their removal from the Military Council. Lekhanya was acquitted of murder charges but accused the Letsies, the King's cousins, of having killed two ministers in the Jonathan regime and their wives. In addition, he was implicated in some corrupt business deals. Although there was speculation that South Africa wanted Lesotho to return to civilian rule, the 1991 coup within the military that replaced Lekhanya pre-empted South African demands. Military wages were cited as the reason for the coup.[43]

With the apparent objective of making land more available to the Basotho, the 1979 Land Act was passed, to privatise land ownership in Lesotho. Previously, the chiefs had controlled land allocation. Whereas this was an impediment to European land ownership during the colonial period, the Government began to view it as an impediment to foreign investment in the 1970s. Furthermore, it would allow for the consolidation of plots of land which in the past had been quite scattered. Plot consolidation would facilitate farm mechanisation and thereby increase production.

The privatisation of land did confer some benefits on to members of the Basotho peasantry who could not afford to buy land, because it was theirs to pass down from generation to generation.[44] Before, it was only theirs by usufruct. Unused land could be expropriated by the chief and plots could not be inherited by succeeding generations. It has been noted that there is an increasing land shortage among Lesotho's peasantry. It is thought that the Land Act is portending greater differentiation of the peasantry, exacerbated by the fact that fewer rural men have access to mining employment.

Tourism has been an area of considerable joint investment by the Lesotho National Development Corporation (LNDC) and foreign investors. In the late 1970s, there were three major hotels – Hotel Victoria, the Holiday Inn and the Lesotho Hilton. The Holiday Inn had one casino and the newly-opened Hilton added another. However, the Hilton's opening coincided with the opening of Sun City in the South African homeland of Bophuthatswana. With the assistance of the South African media, Sun City was successful in syphoning off tourists from Lesotho. One South African newspaper ran headlines about 'The Lesotho War' for several days prior to Christmas 1979, and the Lesotho hotel industry never recovered. In the meantime, the Sun Hotel group bought the Hilton and the Holiday Inn franchise in southern Africa, which included the hotels in Lesotho. Now, Lesotho has two Sun hotels and only one casino.[45] Thus, tourism has dropped precipitously since the late 1970s, due to hotel monopolisation and bantustan competition.

After a brief period from the mid-1970s to the early 1980s, wool and mohair were returned to their previously-held position as the major foreign exchange earners after the closing of Letseng-le-terai diamond mine. The two animal fibres are processed and marketed through the South African Wool Board and the South African Mohair Board. Basotho wool is shipped to Durban, East London and Port Elizabeth; mohair, to Port Elizabeth only. A number of unsuccessful efforts have been made to seek foreign investment to provide wool- and mohair-processing facilities in Lesotho, of which there will be some discussion in the following section, on fibre production.

Returning to the issue of Lesotho's uncertain future, one wonders if a scheduled return to civilian rule in 1992 will be compatible with anticipated changes in South Africa. There is considerable concern by Lesotho's middle class that their country will be left out in the cold when a post-apartheid state emerges in the area. People attribute this view to the fact that Lesotho did not treat ANC refugees well and removed them to other countries after the military coup. Furthermore, they are worried that they will be denied substantial donor aid because they will no longer be surrounded by a hostile government. Disturbed by the military's wait-and-see attitude, some members of the middle class would like to see Lesotho devise a plan for functioning within a post-apartheid southern Africa. In fact, this should probably be SADCC's role. Lesotho's reluctance may stem from the fact that it has been reincorporated into the South African political economy and as a consequence does not have such strong ties with SADCC.

Donor aid has been channelled into sectors of Lesotho's economy differentially. In response to sectoral differentiation in the 1980s, Basotho women have responded by mobilising the masses to provide grassroots social services in the larger towns.[46] Urbanisation generates new social problems as well as heightening pre-existing ones. The social services formed have usually been multipurpose with a day-care component. Secondary components include women's agricultural and handicraft co-operatives and services for the handicapped and elderly. These self-help organisations are usually started with funds provided by the community, but may receive some support from the smaller funding agencies once they become viable.

Throughout this period, there has been intense stress on the Lesotho political economy. For the first time, Lesotho has a large foreign debt. Germany and the EC have made substantial inroads into the Lesotho political economy as the 1992 integration of the latter approaches. Despite the fact that 'internalisation' of mine labour is not proceeding at a pace that represents an immediate threat to Lesotho's domestic economy, it is virtually impossible for it to absorb all its workers domestically. Furthermore, Lesotho's 'war of words' with South Africa has led to increasingly repressive measures by the latter. Having alienated the ANC, which will probably control the post-apartheid government, Lesotho's future continues to be riddled with uncertainty.

7.7 FIBRE PRODUCTION

Since the introduction of merino sheep and angora goats in the 1860s, the sale of wool and mohair has had great impact on the Lesotho political economy:[47] the two fibres surpassed grain in export value by the turn of the century. However, fibre prices fell heavily after 1928.[48] Since 1931, there has been a decline in the number of sheep and a rise in the number of goats.[49]

Traditionally, it was taboo for women to herd cattle. Since cattle were often herded with sheep and goats, men and boys were often the herders. However, J. P. Hunter indicates that recently more women are becoming flock managers.[50] Female flock managers tend to be older than males and to manage smaller flocks. J. Gay proposes that female participants in Lesotho Handspun Mohair's primary production units should raise their angora goats collectively to improve their quality.[51]

It is well documented that migrant labourers go to the mines to enable them to engage in capital accumulation at home. Although it has frequently been argued that labour migration has resulted in the decline of agricultural production in peripheral areas of southern Africa, it is usually migrant households that are the most prosperous. Migrant remittances are used to purchase ploughs, cattle, sheep and goats. Hunter observes that the larger the migrant household, the larger the flock.[52] Furthermore, cash from fibre sales can be used to purchase food.

Until the post-independence period, European traders had a virtual monopoly on mohair and wool sales. Unlike the Swazi case, in which concessionaires were allowed free rein in obtaining farming, mining and grazing rights, King Moshoeshoe restricted traders to temporary residence in the country under a customary law called Moshoeshoe I's Law of Trade of 1859.[53] Notwithstanding the law, many traders left the territory during the Gun War, at which time Fraser's bought a number of abandoned trading stations. In 1958, twenty-one per cent of trading stations were owned by Fraser's. At present, over a third of these are licensed for private mohair and wool trading.[54]

A major problem with wool and mohair trading is that the price can fluctuate wildly between the time of purchase by the trader and time of sale in South Africa.[55] Payment in advance could lead to the trader's loss, while payment after the sale could lead to the farmer's loss. After the Second World War, the British colonial government introduced co-operative societies for the sale of mohair and wool, which met with little success.[56] In 1972, the Lesotho Government introduced the advance- and post-payment system whereby the farmer would get a percentage of his/her payment at the time of the sale and receive the remainder after the fibre's auction in South Africa.[57] The Government introduced its own marketing system in 1978 to provide an alternative for traders. Of course, smugglers have operated as alternative sellers for some farmers for years.[58]

Lesotho's mohair and wool have proved to be of inferior quality to South Africa's, due to communal grazing. South African farms are highly-capitalised and -rationalised to prepare sheep and goats for the best possible production outcome. In addition to wool selling well on the South African market, Lesotho's mohair has found its own niche because it is requested by buyers from other parts of southern Africa as well as from Britain.

In its efforts to make forward linkages to mohair and wool production, the Lesotho Government has made a number of attempts to attract investors to build a wool- and mohair-processing facility in the country. The first unsuccessful negotiations were made with a South African firm. More recently, negotiations have taken place with a firm from the People's Republic of China: the China Shanghai Corporation for Foreign Economic and Technological Co-operation. In the three phases proposed in the second deal for the wool and mohair scouring plant and topmaking factory, the projected employment was 3000 workers.[59] This venture, too, fell through in 1989.

Topmaking is a high-risk operation because of price fluctuations from the time of purchase to the time of processing. Because of the volume that South African processors handle, they can offset the risk to a certain extent. In the case of Lesotho, it would need to process some wool and mohair from elsewhere to make its operation profitable.

7.8 COTTAGE INDUSTRIES AND FACTORIES

Cottage industries and factories were introduced into Lesotho at different times. Cottage industries were introduced as early as the 1930s (but did not become fully entrenched until the early 1970s), whereas textile factories only began to migrate into the country in sizeable numbers in the early 1980s.

There is a paucity of research on rural handicraft production. C. M. Rogerson's research on handicraft production considers initiatives made in the 1930s to revitalise traditional handicrafts or to introduce new ones as a way of reducing rural poverty in the South African periphery and the British protectorates.[60] I conducted a survey of Basotho cottage industries in 1986, which serves as the basis for their description below.

In the late 1960s and early 1970s, a number of tapestry-weaving industries were started in Lesotho. Some were co-operatives while others were privately-owned. Cottage industries of both types are located in rural and urban areas. The cost structure of the mohair industry has been conducive to a heavy turnover in capital and labour. Several cottage industries have been unsuccessful, a few have changed ownership, and new industries have merged with old ones sometimes across international boundaries. For example, Setsoto Designs in Lesotho is a sister industry to Mantenga Crafts in Swaziland. Monopolisation makes cottage industries more competitive with factories.

The location of cottage industries in Swaziland and Lesotho reflect differences in the pattern of industrialisation and land tenure. In the Swazi case, there is a clear delineation between cottage industries and other industries in that the former tend to be located near Swazi Nation Land and the latter, Title Deed Land or industrial estates in urban areas. In Lesotho, due to delayed industrialisation, cottage industries have penetrated into areas ordinarily occupied by factories.

Most cottage industries are enclosed by fences in areas of high unemployment because large numbers of women line up outside to await a call to work. Nevertheless, in areas where there are other employment options, cottage industries experience a high labour turnover. Owners and managers are disturbed by this trend because of the time spent on training women to spin and weave.

Expatriate designers have developed a distinctive weaving style with depictions of women, *rondavels* (traditional huts), aloe trees and village animals. As mentioned in Chapter 3, Setsoto Designs encouraged women to do *litema*, traditional geometric patterns, as their weaving designs during the mid-1980s. Whereas some of their weavings were marketed locally to tourists and in South Africa, cottage industries producing higher-quality weavings were able to market them in Europe and North America.

In developing its mohair industry, I suspect that Lesotho viewed itself as being in a unique position to produce mohair tapestries in the early 1970s. However, mohair tapestry-weaving industries have been formed subsequently in Swaziland, Botswana and a few of the South African homelands. These are international competitors to Lesotho's industry, who recruit from similar labour pools and sell to limited speciality markets thereby competing more keenly with each other. Lesotho's tapestry-weaving industries will have to be more innovative in order to compete successfully.

The most comprehensive mohair project is Lesotho Handspun Mohair (LHM), a CARE-sponsored co-operative project started in the mid-1970s. Headquartered in Maseru, LHM had nine primary production units (PPUs) in rural areas of Lesotho, with 1900 participants.[61] When the project was started, women were sold spinning wheels made from bicycle tyres. On a monthly basis, CARE would send field staff to PPCs to 'put out' raw mohair, the price of which was deducted from the sale of handspun yarn.

Spun mohair was taken back to Maseru after being sorted, graded and weighed. There, it was dyed and packaged for sale, or used to knit and crochet jerseys, dresses, mittens and household items. Orders were processed and shipped to other countries. There was an outlet store on the premises. The project began to encounter production problems with rural spinners in the mid-1980s, when they began to complain about the quality of raw mohair. Its poor quality made hand-processing difficult. To address this problem, LHM decided to purchase tops from Port Elizabeth thereby eliminating washing, carding and combing.[62] Spinning was then the only aspect of the labour process left to be executed in the village.

Thus it is clear that the labour-intensive process employed by Basotho women was paralleled by the capital-intensive process undertaken at the Port Elizabeth scouring and topmaking plant. LHM fragmented the labour process by substituting and recombining the labour- and capital-intensive features and thereby compromised the self-sufficiency of the project. Tops are expensive. Since utilising tops made spinning faster, LHM found that it was stockpiling yarn and losing profits.

Because LHM failed to become self-supporting after several years of funding by CARE, the agency conducted a feasibility study in 1985 and decided after its completion to leave the PPCs intact while selling LHM to a private company.[63] Village spinning was suspended in January 1986 and resumed in June 1989. The new company – Hilton Lesotho Weavers – is renting the Maseru facility from the village co-operatives and has resumed the putting-out of tops to PPCs and the purchase of handspun mohair. At the time of my field research, the last of the stockpiled yarn was being sold. This is but one more example of the growing trend towards privatisation and monopolisation of the tapestry-weaving industry in the region.

Turning now to textile factories, Lesotho has two designated growth points – Maseru and Maputsoe – where industrial estates have been established. In the 1980s, South African textile industries began to relocate to these estates. Gallant, a clothing factory, is based in Maputsoe. The factory manufactures garments for retail outlets such as Berger's, Edgar's and Foshini in South Africa that have branches in the southern African periphery. Other textile factories are located in Maseru.

Because of the lack of backward linkages in Lesotho, these factories import their raw materials from South Africa. In 1984, former Prime Minister Leabua Jonathan indicated at the opening ceremony of the Lesotho Knitwear Factory, a Hong Kong-owned firm, that it was his wish that Lesotho have wool-processing facilities in the near future to provide a means of integrating wool produced by Basotho farmers into the country's textile industry.[64] (Wool and mohair processing are virtually identical.)

Lesotho emphasises import-substitution in its investment policy. However, the variety of small clothing firms investing there engage in limited production for the local market, with the bulk of production for export. However, they have provided a substantial number of jobs in recent years. By 1985, at least twenty-five per cent of jobs created by LNDC-affiliated companies were textile-related. This represented the creation of approximately 900 jobs.[65] According to LNDC, nine textile projects were established in 1987 alone.[66] The former textile industries manufactured knitted jerseys and cardigans, woven tapestries and rugs; men's ties; men's, women's and children's apparel; and embroidered items. The 1987 additions are clearly orientated to markets in North America and Europe, to which they export jeans and other garments. Thus, import-substitution is only one small component in shaping investment goals. Of course, export-orientated production is in keeping with World Bank/IMF conditions.

When compared to Swaziland, Lesotho exhibits a distorted development more typical of the South African homelands. It has not developed backward and forward linkages that provide an attractive industrial base for long-term industrial relocation. With considerable capital turnover, it will be difficult to develop a skilled textile labour force. Swaziland, by contrast, has achieved industrial integration in a number of sectors of its economy, although these linkages perpetuate semi-peripheral and core dependency. This comparison indicates gradations in economic stratification within the periphery that are often obscured by the emphasis on incorporation in world-system theory.

Despite substantial investment in Lesotho's manufacturing sector, miners' remittances still remain the single most important source of government revenue. In 1986, total earnings were (in maloti) M240 109 132 and remittances M135 770 415.[67] The former represents a fifteen per cent increase over the previous year and the latter a seventeen per cent increase. Thus, Lesotho's basic dependency relationship on the South African gold mining industry remains intact.

The most successful rural households tend to be those that receive migrant remittances, which are used to buy agricultural inputs. However, with fewer novices being recruited and little employment being generated within the country, it is very difficult for young adult males to start their own households.

Although census data do not provide a statistical breakdown of female-headed households, the works of E. Gordon and C. Murray indicate a growing tendency towards female-headed households, as documented in Swaziland and Botswana.[68] However, both studies were conducted in the context of the migratory labour system. Gordon's study represents a sample of the forty to sixty per cent of Basotho wives whose husbands are away in the mines most of the year.[69] She characterises these women as experiencing loneliness, helplessness and poverty.[70] However, Gordon's study ignores the fact that the wives of miners are not the poorest women in Lesotho. There are many others, because of the decreasing number of male mining recruits and lack of marriage opportunities, who are forced to seek wage labour. In many cases, these women – like their counterparts throughout the southern African periphery – are attempting to support not only themselves but also their young children. Murray found that a third of households in his research village in northern Lesotho were headed by females.[71]

7.9 CONCLUSION

Undertaking an inter-peripheral comparison of Lesotho and Swaziland, it is clear that, although they are both former British protectorates, there are a number of factors by which they differ. The incorporation process began half a century earlier in the case of Lesotho and the two countries have different resource levels, racial compositions, political economies, patterns of industrialisation and articulations into the South African political economy. Whereas Swaziland is more articulated into the regional political economies of Natal and the eastern Transvaal, Lesotho is more articulated into those of the Orange Free State and the Witwatersrand.

In relation to incorporation, the pattern of land expropriation in Lesotho was one in which much of the lowlands was granted to the Boers, forcing the Basotho to live in the more mountainous areas. This and early dependency on labour migration initiated incorporation and entrenched underdevelopment. In the case of Swaziland, European concessionaires expropriated two-thirds of the land. However, what land remained for the peasants was more fertile than Lesotho's. Nevertheless, most Swazi peasants are producing at the sub-subsistence level, although at higher rates of production than Basotho peasants.

Lesotho's resources include mohair, wool, water and a few diamonds, and Swaziland's, sugar cane, citrus fruit, cotton, forestry products, coal and asbestos. The former has only recently been successful in achieving forward linkages for its water resources, at a tremendous price. The other areas have not been integrated. Swaziland, despite its economic dependency, is in a better position to negotiate donor aid and investment as well as forward and backward linkages to industries.

Swaziland's European population has set the tone for its industrialisation to the extent that only the monarchy has made inroads into European investment. Nevertheless, as mentioned above, most peasants are producing at the sub-subsistence level. Until the 1979 Land Act, the Lesotho Government had managed to fend off substantial land alienation by white South African investors. However, implementation of the Act has the potential to escalate Basotho proletarianisation. There are few white settlers in Lesotho.

In general, the conjunctures in the Lesotho and Swaziland political economies do not fully coincide. However, within the three-year period 1970–73, both governments rejected Westminister-style constitutions. Yet the Basotho situation has been marked by repeated waves of domestic repression as well as confrontation with South Africa. Swaziland's repression has been more subtle, in part because of the central role of the monarchy. With the notable exception of labour disputes, the Swazi monarchy tends to project an image of benevolence.

The pattern of industrialisation differs between the two countries. Lesotho's industrialisation has got under way in the 1980s in such a way that it does not compete with mining employment. Swaziland, although having experienced incorporation later, began to industrialise just after the Second World War. It has used gold mining employment to syphon off surplus male labour. Despite the fact that both countries pay low wages, Swaziland has had the most volatile labour disputes.

Women in both countries – as is the case in the rest of the southern African periphery – experience extreme labour segmentation, thereby forming separate reserve armies of labour from men. However, I would speculate that if I conducted a similar survey in Lesotho to the one conducted in Swaziland, I would find that Basotho women workers have less access to livestock and crops than do Swazi women. Textile industrialisation, which is resulting in greater female employment in both countries, is affecting Lesotho and Swaziland differently. In Lesotho, it is women who do not have access to migrant remittances that are seeking textile employment, but in Swaziland the pace of textile industrialisation *vis-à-vis* increasing male unemployment seems to be inverting male and female labour segmentation.

The South African political economy is highly regionalised. Lesotho is more orientated to the Orange Free State highveld, which is a major producer of its staple crop, maize. Furthermore, the centrality of migratory labour to the gold mines binds Lesotho to the gold fields of the Witwatersrand and the Orange Free State. Swaziland, as a producer of sugar-cane and cotton, has linkages with contiguous ecozones producing similar crops in the eastern Transvaal and in northern Natal. Infrastructure such as cotton spinning mills and sugar-mills have been centrally located in those areas of South Africa, with a few extensions into Swaziland. That country has positioned itself well to receive donor aid and private investment regardless of the post-apartheid situation in South Africa.

8   A SADCC Comparison: Regionalism and Industrial Development

Having begun with an analysis of secondary industrialisation in South Africa to provide a context for women and textile industrialisation in Swaziland, it is only fitting to conclude with an analysis of the major alternative to South African economic hegemony in the southern African periphery. That alternative is the Southern African Development Coordination Conference (SADCC) founded in 1980. Since its formation, an ideology of regional economic integration has emerged that involves individual economies both detaching from South Africa and linking with each other.[1]

SADCC was originally – and until recently – composed of nine countries in the southern African region including Angola, Botswana, Lesotho, Malawi, Mozambique, Swaziland, Tanzania, Zambia and Zimbabwe. Namibia became its tenth member after its independence in 1990. Each country has a different historical and politico-economic relationship to South Africa. Furthermore, because of different resource bases, there are substantial politico-economic gradations among SADCC nations. Many resources are being exploited and/or processed and marketed by the South African semi-periphery or by various core nations. Thus, the SADCC region *per se* has not been able to gain access to the resource bases of member states.

An alternative view of SADCC's function in the region is to serve as a funnel for donor aid that can be utilised for regional projects. D. Mbilima views SADCC's formation as a function of the region receiving less donor aid as a direct result of global recessions.[2] However, projects funded through SADCC tend to be based nationally rather than regionally.[3] Only a fraction of aid allocated to member-states enters SADCC's coffers.

Most assuredly, South Africa represents the centre of capitalist development in the region. As a direct consequence, much of the industrialisation that has taken place in the southern African periphery – which includes some SADCC countries (for example, BLS) has been

194

South African-inspired.[4] The imposition of international economic sanctions against South Africa has illuminated the extent of economic dependency, the status of the de-linking process and the contradictions in continued linkages between SADCC nations and South Africa.

SADCC is at a crossroads in its development because attempts to implement its strategies are occurring against the backdrop of negotiations between the South African Government and the African National Congress. As I see it, the outcome could occur in one or a combination of the following scenarios:

1. A right-wing coup initiated by the military, police, farmers and various right-wing organisations;
2. Uncontrollable urban unrest initiated by young radicals, who perceive ANC negotiations with the South African Government as 'selling out', so disrupting the negotiation process; or
3. Continued evolutionary change by the South African Government in collaboration with the ANC with the maintenance of the existing economic order devoid of overt racial discrimination. Other black groups possibly having input include the Pan-Africanist Congress and Inkatha.

SADCC must be prepared to react according to the emerging situation because foreign policy could vary significantly with each single or combined scenario.

With regard to textile industrialisation, SADCC must acknowledge the oppression of black South African textile workers, on the one hand. On the other, SADCC countries must exhibit a united front against national and regional exploitation by these industries, by preventing profit from being repatriated and reinvested elsewhere.

In the southern African context, there is a dichotomy between development and industrialisation. Development represents the reorganisation of relations of production through donor-aid-supported projects. These projects have as their expressed objectives increased production and economic self-sufficiency for project participants. What is unexpressed is that these projects often fail, leaving participants more proletarianised than they had been prior to project participation. They thus become candidates for wage employment provided by relocating industries.

Industrialisation refers to an international process initiated in Europe, whereby technological innovations are incorporated into the labour process to allow more precision and rapidity – and less expense

– in production. This process has occurred at different times and under varying circumstances. Whereas South African industrialisation began in the second half of the nineteenth century, industrialisation in the SADCC region began after the Second World War. Most member countries have been recipients of donor aid since independence, thereby positing slightly different relationships between industrialisation and development.

In considering this dichotomy, South Africa – because of its high degree of industrialisation and its symbolic isolation from the international community since the early 1960s – has been primarily involved. After giving the homelands more definition and autonomy, it has attempted to act as their donor for development – and industrialisation. However, for the SADCC region, it has primarily been involved in industrialisation, particularly in mining and forestry.

The dichotomy between industrialisation and development is reflective of the gender dichotomy in southern Africa. In the colonial period, men became very active in the industrialisation process, often necessitating that they migrate for long distances to pursue jobs in mines, foundries and factories. Women were much less mobile, often remaining in rural areas. Men remaining in rural areas were either prosperous peasants or too young, too infirm or too elderly to pursue industrial employment. In the post-colonial period, women and prosperous peasants were more likely to be beneficiaries of rural development projects. The industrial employment made available to women necessitated their more circumscribed migration to urban centres for light manufacturing jobs. However, throughout most of the SADCC region, the majority of the population still resides in rural areas. Clearly, if SADCC is to achieve its objectives, it must become a mediator between development and industrialisation.

Can SADCC wrest itself from South Africa's tentacles? What are the best strategies for achieving that end? Would donor dependency actually improve its economic position *vis-à-vis* South Africa? Is SADCC reconciling industrialisation and development? How will SADCC fare in the post-apartheid period? Can SADCC formulate a policy to reconcile gender relations so that southern Africans can re-form viable family units?

This chapter is divided into several sections. The topics to be considered are SADCC's founding; the characteristics of the SADCC region; its relationship with South Africa and with the West; SADCC's strategies for utilising its resources; its bureaucratic structure; constraints on its development; and its role in textile industrialisation.

8.1 THE FOUNDING OF SADCC

The ten member-states in SADCC are quite diverse in terms of their
national political economies. Social scientists analysing SADCC have
used different typologies to classify them. Some use a capitalist/
socialist dichotomy; others emphasise the Frontline State/non-Front-
line State dichotomy; still others dichotomise SADCC countries
according to independence in the 1960s and independence subsequently; and, finally, a few view Zimbabwe (and, possibly Namibia) as being
the core of SADCC.

Just over half of the SADCC member-states have economies that
are, for the most part, capitalistic. At the opposite end of the political
spectrum, Angola and Mozambique have exhibited the most socialistic
orientation, with Zimbabwe, Zambia and Tanzania exhibiting some
socialistic elements.[5] The BLS countries and Malawi are at the more
capitalistic end of the spectrum. Thus far, no attempt has been made to
rearticulate SADCC economies so as to provide a socialist alternative
to South African capitalism. In fact, established socialistic elements are
being undermined. World Bank/International Monetary Fund structural adjustment programmes and changes in global politico-economic
relations are forcing more of those countries to shift to the middle
politically and to the right economically.

One could argue that British and Portuguese colonialism in the
region led to varying degrees of incorporation into the South African
political economy which served as the centre for British colonialism
and imperialism. As W. Minter has argued, Portugal maintained a
stranglehold on its colonies because it was a peripheral European
country.[6] The British controlled the Portuguese banks, which gave the
former more leverage in influencing Portuguese rule in southern
Africa. Angola, Mozambique and Zimbabwe, as three original
members of SADCC, fought protracted wars of liberation against
their colonial masters. This gave them the potential to escape from the
tentacles of incorporation in order to pursue a different course of
development.

Initially, Angola and Mozambique were steadfast in their adherence
to a socialist alternative. However, South Africa has backed guerrilla
organisations in both countries, has resorted to repeated invasion of
the two countries by the South African Defence Force and has secured
non-aggression pacts from both governments. The masses in both
countries have become victims of, as well as refugees from, maiming
and genocide. The economy of Mozambique, in particular, has become

severely disrupted as a result of guerrilla activity. Angola, because of revenues from oil production, has cushioned its economy against the former's devastation, although peasants have suffered equally in the two countries.

There is considerable stratification among SADCC countries. As mentioned earlier, Zimbabwe is the most developed country in the region. It generates forty-five per cent of the manufacturing value-added in SADCC.[7] Zimbabwe manufactures footwear, clothing, soap, detergents, furniture, paper, beer, wine, cigarettes, tea, coffee, pins and needles.[8] There is some concern that Zimbabwe's membership of SADCC could bolster its own economy, due to the polarisation effect.[9] Also, it has been the major recipient of donor aid in the SADCC region since its independence.

Of course, the BLS countries have experienced a negative polarisation effect in the context of the Southern African Customs Union. In the SADCC context, the BLS countries and Malawi are on its periphery. Angola and Mozambique have suffered more severe underdevelopment and mass impoverishment, of course, due to wars of destabilisation waged against them. However, Lesotho is the least endowed in natural resources and probably the most impoverished. Tanzania – and possibly Angola – provide the only exceptions to the unique asymmetrical dyadic relationship that each SADCC country has with South Africa.

I would argue that despite the fact that South Africa was unable to formalise its Constellation of Southern African States (CONSAS), the Government has been able to serve as a disruptive force to SADCC's viability by increasing militarism. This strategy put a brake on SADCC countries' assistance to the South African liberation struggle. At its 1989 FRELIMO Party Congress, the Mozambican Government announced that it was revamping its domestic economic policy to allow free enterprise in certain sectors of the economy. Of course, many investors will be South African. Although Mozambique has always supplied a substantial number of migrants to the South African gold mining industry, I would suggest that FRELIMO's adoption of a mixed economy model is a step towards reincorporation into the South African semi-periphery. Angola, which has few economic ties to South Africa, has had its hands tied so that it can no longer be instrumental in the South African liberation struggle. Under the terms of the negotiated settlement for Namibian independence, the ANC could no longer base any military operations in that country.

A sizeable literature has been produced on SADCC's conception from the perspective of member states, potential donors and South Africa. One oft-repeated view is that the Front Line States, having ushered Zimbabwe to its independence, sought to continue the process by including Lesotho, Swaziland and Malawi.[10] Another view is that Henry Kissinger, in his capacity as US Secretary of State, proposed a Marshall Plan for southern Africa to be initiated after the independence of war-torn Zimbabwe. Yet another is that SADCC emerged as a counter-strategy to South African Prime Minister Pieter Botha's proposed Constellation of Southern African States.[11]

Botha's CONSAS proposal made in late 1979, assumed a victory by Abel Muzorewa in the forthcoming Zimbabwe pre-independence elections and a closer alliance between that country and South Africa.[12] Such a victory was viewed as completing an alliance that would have included the BLS countries and the 'independent' South African homelands. The victory by Robert Mugabe presented quite an upset to CONSAS. SADCC was formed at Lusaka in April 1980, about two weeks before Zimbabwe's independence with Prime Minister-elect Mugabe in attendance.

The above represent alternative historical views, all of which may have been elements contributing to SADCC's founding. However, I think SADCC's *raison d'être* has to be viewed in broader politico-economic perspective. What was the conjuncture at which its formation occurred? Since the mid-1970s, the global economic system has been plagued by repeated recessions. Whereas core industrial nations experienced some degree of economic recovery from each recession, peripheral nations have experienced lingering negative trends always exacerbated by subsequent recessions. It was at this conjuncture that IMF and World Bank were formulating their structural adjustment programmes to create new labour and consumer markets in the periphery, for the core.

8.2 CHARACTERISTICS OF THE SADCC REGION

The SADCC region has a population of seventy-four million and occupies an area the size of the United States, excluding Alaska.[13] The countries of the region have an abundance of mineral resources including iron ore, zinc, tungsten, nickel, manganese, magnetite, cobalt, chromium, vanadium, titanium, beryllium, copper, lead, antimony, tantalite, soda ash, platinum, fluorite, sulphur, phosphates, gypsum, potash, limestone, silica, sodium, sulphate, mica, alabaster, kaolin, feldspar, gold, silver, diamonds, emeralds and agate.[14] Adding its abundant water and coal supplies, one can characterise the region as being rich in energy resources. However, forests are rapidly being depleted because most of the inhabitants of the SADCC region utilise wood as a major energy source.

Cash crops produced in the region include tobacco, sugar, cashew nuts, cotton, tea, pineapples, oranges, sisal, palm oil, beef cattle and coffee.[15] Major subsistence crops include maize, rice, cassava, sweet potatoes and sorghum.

Each country's articulation in the world-system is both determined and characterised by the minerals and/or crops produced. Most engage in mono-mineral or mono-crop production, thereby making their economies more vulnerable to fluctuations in world market prices over which they have no control. Commodities that have suffered from low markets prices include Zambian copper, Zimbabwean iron and steel, Malawian tea, Botswana diamonds, Tanzanian coffee, Mozambican cashew nuts, Swazi sugar and Angolan oil.[16] Furthermore, since 1974, oil has been a major foreign exchange expenditure for all these countries, with the exception of Angola. Due to recessionary trends, Western donors have been more reluctant to provide adequate aid at a time when developing nations experience a greater need for it.

The SADCC region can be compared to other areas in relation to its industrial characteristics. It is slightly more industrialised than other developing countries, or Africa as a whole.[17] Industry throughout the region grew more slowly than average during the 1970s. However, this reduction can be accounted for, in part, by the fact that industry was destroyed in war-torn Angola and Mozambique. Industry is generally characterised by the processing of minerals and agricultural raw materials. Only Zimbabwe, Zambia and Tanzania have relatively diversified manufacturing bases.

8.3 SADCC AND SOUTH AFRICA

In my opinion, the timetable for South African liberation was built into the SADCC timetable for development. In some of the literature on the subject, it was assumed that the liberation of South Africa itself was decades away, but that Namibian independence was more imminent.[18] Many of these articles were written in the early-to-mid-1980s, several years before Namibian independence. No one entertained the idea that South African 'liberation' might follow so quickly. Thus, Namibian independence was significantly delayed and has probably come about in 1990 because South Africa could no longer maintain it as its last buffer.

SACU binds Botswana, Lesotho and Swaziland more closely in terms of trade relations, making it more difficult for these countries to extricate themselves to form viable trade ties with other SADCC countries. SACU and migratory labour serve as bargaining chips whenever South Africa wants to discipline the BLS countries.

South Africa has succeeded in placing a wedge between SADCC and the liberation movements. D. G. Anglin states that in 1984 SADCC ceased to give the liberation movements observer status at its summits.[19] By that time, the South African Defence Force had invaded a number of SADCC member countries. Furthermore, a few countries had signed non-aggression pacts with South Africa. The most infamous was the Nkomati Accord with Mozambique. Angola had already signed a similar accord, and Swaziland had done so in secret two years previously. During this period, Lesotho also signed an accord. The destablisation of Angola and Mozambique continued after these accords were signed. Anglin considers the Nkomati Accord to be a major setback for SADCC.

Actually, the protracted negotiations taking place between the South African Government and the ANC are providing an opportunity for the implementation of South Africa's structural adjustment programme. Strategic industries, many of which have fixed points of production, will remain within the confines of South Africa. Low-wage industries, such as clothing and textile industries, are relocating into SADCC countries to tap sources of cheap female labour.[20] In addition, J. Isaksen predicts that there will be a mini-brain-drain of managerial staff from SADCC countries to South Africa in the post-apartheid period. I see SADCC responding to politio-economic processes after they have been initiated rather than forcibly changing relations of production, which S. Amin views as a necessity for the post-apartheid transformation of the South African economy.[21] This issue will be discussed more fully in the section on textile industrialisation.

South Africa views SADCC countries as natural markets for its capital and consumer goods, as labour reserves in the case of the BLS countries, and as reserves of natural resources. A high priority for South Africa is the satisfaction of its energy needs, particularly for hydro-electric power. Cunene dam in southern Angola, Kariba in Zambia/Zimbabwe and Cabora Bassa in Mozambique all contribute towards South Africa's hydro-electric needs.

The Witwatersrand, the area of highest industrial concentration, has had increasing hydro-electric demands. Casting about more deeply in the southern African interior, the South African Government viewed the source of the Orange River in the mountains of Lesotho as providing the greatest potential for satisfying that country's hydro-electric needs. SADCC has no role in this project whatsoever. The dam is being constructed with Lesotho's hydro-electric needs being second-ary and no provision of hydro-electric power to any other SADCC country. Considering the World Bank's partial funding of the project, structural adjustment is an overarching paradigm for Lesotho, South Africa and SADCC to contend with.

There is some concern that Nelson Mandela has made few visits to the BLS countries since his release from prison. His perceived snub is attributed to the fact that those countries were not as supportive of the liberation struggle in the second half of the 1980s. This is evidenced by Lesotho's ousting of ANC refugees after the military coup of 1986, Mozambique's signing of the Nkomati Accord and the governments of Botswana and Swaziland's reputed co-operation with South African authorities in refugee kidnappings and assassinations.

With the exception of the countries that have minimal economic ties with South Africa in SADCC, none of the others actually implemen-ted economic sanctions against South Africa. Countries such as Zimbabwe were instrumental in lobbying for the imposition of sanctions by the United States, the Commonwealth and the Eur-opean Community. However, at both regional and national levels, sanctions were viewed as being potentially damaging to most SADCC economies.

Thus the post-apartheid South Africa that the ANC may inherit will have more rigid relations of production, due to the conditions of the World Bank's structural adjustment programme. The ANC may not even have the option of nationalising the mining and banking industries. However, female workers will be exploited by South African industries operating in SADCC countries. Conversely, skilled personnel will be attracted to the South African core. SADCC may not be prepared for this turn of events in South Africa, and the attendant uneven development.

8.4 SADCC AND DONOR AID

From the Western perspective, it has been argued that SADCC functions as a vehicle for deflecting member countries' concerns away from South Africa. In other words, the organisation is viewed as being 'counter-revolutionary' because it is preoccupied with its own priorities. Furthermore, there has been concern that SADCC member states were just exchanging one colonial master for another in their attempts to circumvent semi-peripheral ties with South Africa and to establish direct relations with core nations.

Direct periphery–core relations have had their problems. The International Monetary Fund (IMF) and the World Bank are key actors in the SADCC region in this regard. The IMF provides loans to countries experiencing balance-of-payments difficulties, while the World Bank finances major infrastructural projects. The IMF usually requires that a country agrees to undergo a structural adjustment programme as a condition for the loan. In the 1980s, the World Bank followed suit with a similar policy in situations in which a country's borrowing exceeds its quota.[22]

In the SADCC region, a number of countries are heavily-indebted to the IMF or the World Bank, whose influence on the agencies' policies are minimal.[23] Structural adjustment programmes are designed to increase government austerity; to promote free enterprise; to freeze wages; to facilitate foreign investment and profit remittance; to raise interest rates; to curb inflation; and to devalue the country's currency.[24] From a global perspective, the World Bank's approach to development is in the areas of transportation, manpower training and education.[25] Simultaneously, the United States' Government proposed to allocate $100 million to Sudan alone, $30 million to Somalia and $35 million to Kenya. In comparison, SADCC's request for nine nations was a pittance. E. Brown suggests that Ronald Reagan's Administration viewed South Africa as the colonial and historical regional centre and was tacitly reinforcing that country's position by minimising its aid to SADCC.[26]

South Africa, a signatory of the Bretton Woods Agreement forming the IMF and World Bank, assumed a central position as a major gold-producing country. However, after the lifting of the gold standard in 1971, the oil-deficient South African economy experienced major inflationary (and recessionary) trends. Despite its apartheid policy, which had become increasingly abhorrent to the international community, South Africa received two IMF loans in 1976–77. This period coincided with the establishment of a Cuban presence in Angola and the Soweto riots.[27] This was followed by a $1.1 billion loan in 1982. The former loans were larger than those granted to all African countries combined over the same period.[28] Internationally, only Mexico and Britain were granted higher individual loans.

In relation to the 1982 loan, which was the most controversial, the IMF discussed a number of issues, summarised as follows:

- that South Africa received eighty per cent of the loan without any conditions being specified;
- that no budget restraint was recommended despite heavy defence spending;
- that there was insufficient monetary control, for example, subsidies to white farmers;
- that due to apartheid hiring policies there was a lack of full utilisation of manpower; and
- that no banking policy was being implemented to reverse a decline in the interest rate.[29]

V. Padayachee suggested that South Africa was becoming a liability to the core, both politically and economically, and would eventually have to be dealt with sternly.[30] He predicted that the US and the IMF would play a substantial role in shaping a post-apartheid South Africa.[31] I find it interesting that the ban on IMF loans to South Africa was not lifted, along with other sanctions, by the Bush Administration.

Structural adjustment programmes are being (or have been) implemented in a number of SADCC countries including Lesotho, Mozambique, Zimbabwe, Zambia and Tanzania. Since all SADCC countries are members of the IMF and World Bank, if they are not already responding to an explicit structural adjustment programme, they may be preparing themselves for such a loan or responding to the structural adjustment programmes of their neighbours.

The EC has made considerable inroads in establishing post-colonial ties with the developing world in general and in Africa in particular. The twelve-member Community, composed of a number of decolonising European countries, was organised to facilitate trade and to gain access to raw materials unavailable in Europe. It formulated the series of Lome Conventions, to which most African, Caribbean and Pacific countries are signatories, for that very purpose.

For sub-Saharan African countries, the Bank recommended specialisation in the production of agricultural commodities partly for local consumption but mainly for international markets.[32] It originally predicted that the implementation of such a policy would lead to an accelerated growth rate in the South.[33] Later, the Bank revised its policy after it had assessed the difficulties for agricultural economies in their attempts to become more export-orientated.

The US Government, having had tremendous input into the formulation of World Bank policy, also has more direct contact with developing countries through its own programmes. Brown, in analysing American foreign policy in southern Africa, contrasts the Reagan Administration's policy towards Africa as being 'geostrategic' as compared to the previous Administration's (President Carter's) 'Africanist' or 'regionalist' policy.[34] In characterising aid allocations to Africa under the former, he suggests that there was an emphasis on security with the Horn countries (Sudan, Somalia and Kenya) receiving military assistance, and Liberia and Zaire receiving economic assistance; an emphasis on bilateral aid instead of multilateral; aid and the promotion of indigenous private enterprise.[35] Because aid is ideological, Angola and Mozambique are often excluded. In 1983, SADCC made a request for $30 million to support regional projects as a core organisation assisting a peripheral region. In the 1990s, US policy could be characterised as being bipolar.

The EC is not a monolithic organisation. Although there are some 'Third Worldist' politicians working with it, the majority of its functionaries are conservative businessmen.[36] It was given a further conservative twist by US pressure during Richard Nixon's and Gerald Ford's Administrations, suggesting that Third World countries should not be granted too many concessions. Third-World governments, particularly those in Africa, viewed the EC's initial overtures with caution, but later began to organise collectively for the free access of their commodities to EC markets.[37] The EC is one of SADCC's largest contributors. In terms of image, the EC's relationship with SADCC can be viewed as one in which it seeks to perpetuate an international division of labour in which Africa engages in agriculture and mining, and Asia in agriculture and manufacturing, to complement a heavy emphasis on industrial development in the West.[38]

The EC is moving towards becoming a more integrated monetary and commercial entity in 1992. This militates against a New International Economic Order in which the South collectively negotiates with the North, instead facilitating greater incorporation of the South by the North. The EC's policies are compatible with those of the World Bank.

Eastern bloc nations had been reticent about funding SADCC projects. Since the Communist parties of most Eastern bloc countries are no longer dominant, it is likely that even less donor aid will be allocated by members of that grouping: they will probably channel funds into their own economic development efforts. Thus, the European Community, the United States and Japan will be the major economic actors in the southern African region in the future.

Clearly, donor nations and agencies have their own agendas, which have the potential for relegating SADCC to a more dependent position than its current one. The Eastern bloc has not provided an alternative in the past and will probably not provide one in future. In the circumstances, the only alternative for SADCC seems to be a balancing act between the core and the semi-periphery: that is, the West and South Africa.

8.5 STRATEGIES FOR UTILISING SADCC'S RESOURCES

There are a number of strategies for SADCC's development proposed by SADCC officials and social scientists from different disciplines. D. B. Ndlela suggests that to make SADCC viable, transformation must occur on three levels – first, at the level of individual economies; second, in the internal relationships between SADCC states; and third, between member states and the outside world.[39]

At the Lusaka Summit in 1980, emphasis was placed on migration, and education and training. In the early 1980s, approximately half a million Africans from SADCC countries held jobs in South Africa and Zimbabwe, representing one in six of all employed Africans in the region.[40] Observing that the South African Chamber of Mines was the largest single group of employers, there was growing concern about the threat of mine labour localisation. The proceedings suggest that supplier states would have to find a way to absorb their migrant labour.[41] It is also suggested that the international community compensate supplier nations for their added employment burden.[42]

In the proceedings, concern was expressed that in the 1960s, when a number of SADCC countries gained independence, there were not enough Africans with secondary school education and very few who were university-educated. However, by the 1970s, many who had completed secondary school were unemployed. Nevertheless, the SADCC countries have found it necessary to establish regional training facilities for areas such as teaching, management, the professions and applied fields.[43] At all educational levels, there is concern that there should be a strong emphasis on science.[44]

R. Peet cites Ann Seidman, who, in formulating her position on the development of the SADCC region, takes an opposing view to that of the World Bank. She considers the formation of cottage industry as a vehicle for industrialisation in her emphasis on development for the masses.[45] The types of cottage industries she proposes would include those producing both capital and consumer goods. Thus, nations would build their economies from the bottom up to address their economic needs, thereby reconciling industrialisation and development.

Tractor production is the focus of a study by T. Ostergaard, who views joint activities in production as the most difficult areas for SADCC. He identifies various institutional constraints that inhibit co-operation *vis-à-vis* transnational corporations, banks, national institutions and donor policies which will be discussed below (see page 210).[46] He considers agricultural production to be the basis for industrialisation.[47] Tractors, as capital goods, are regarded as the key to the initiation of this process and to the goal of economic development.

Tanzania, Zimbabwe and Swaziland all engage in some form of tractor production. All three import tractor kits which they assemble for sale. Zimbabwe is the only country that engages in total production of some types of tractor. However, most tractor manufacturers cater to the demands of the commercial market rather than the needs of the smallholder. As a result, the vast majority of tractors produced or assembled are over 50hp. Yet tractors below 50hp are actually more appropriate. To compound the problem of the availability of appropriate tractors, a number of different brands requiring different spare parts are available. Ostergaard considers the standardisation of tractors in the SADCC region to be a top priority.

In Swaziland, Massey-Ferguson revived the failing Tinkhabi project in 1988.[48] The latter had been suffering a slow demise since 1986. When the original project was started by the United Nations Industrial Development Organisation (UNIDO), it was quite successful because tractor purchases were subsidised. However, as production continued, tractors became larger and more expensive. According to an article in the *Swazi Sunday Mirror*, the Massey-Ferguson operation was quite successful in making sales throughout the region, including South

Africa. The company sells nearly half its stock which includes ploughs, planters, cultivators and harrows to the Swazi rural market. It sells expensive tractors to the sugar, timber and citrus plantations. This provides yet another instance in which the revived tractor company does not cater to peasant needs by producing tractors of an appropriate size and price.

E. Friedland, in comparing the development potential of the SADCC region with the NICs in Asia, suggests that SADCC governments should implement policies such as protective tariffs and/or import controls to protect those industries from international competition.[49] With other areas designated for transnational corporation (TNC) investment, the TNCs would engage in the production of some goods for the domestic market in order to avoid alienating indigenous support. In the smaller countries in the SADCC region, indigenous people do not have capital to invest in major industrial ventures. In many instances, parastatals engage in joint ventures with indigenous entrepreneurs or foreign multinationals.

Friedland also suggests strategies for development in the SADCC region. Of key concern are land reform and the taxation of the wealthiest inhabitants of the region – whether indigenous or expatriate – for income redistribution in the form of provision of social services.[50] She also places considerable emphasis on education.[51] In the case of the latter, she sees a concerted effort by countries such as the United States, Britain, Germany and Japan to put pressure on developing countries, to eliminate free public services and to make their economies more *laissez-faire*. This is also the case with the IMF and the World Bank in implementing their structural adjustment programmes in individual countries.

Since the move towards democratisation in Eastern Europe, Western donor nations are beginning to make this a requirement to qualify for aid. In truth, however, by pressuring developing countries into eliminating free public services and calling for democracy, they are sending conflicting messages. In Western nations, the provision of free public services has given their economies more stability. Developing nations eliminating such services would be forced to resort to increased repression in order to maintain such stability.

Some interesting starting points and development alternatives have been presented above. Clearly, the theorists are concerned about SADCC's dependency on the West and on South Africa and are seeking ways in which it can develop its own resources with a minimum of dependency.

8.6 THE BUREAUCRATIC STRUCTURE OF SADCC

Given the ideological, politico-economic and ethnic differences in various SADCC nations and the experiences of the East African Community, SADCC was formed with a rather amorphous bureaucratic structure with no established policy on economic and political structure. A Council of Ministers engages in high-level decision-making. A secretariat was established in Gaborone, Botswana, which has been expanded recently.

At SADCC's inception, transportation and communication were deemed to be major areas for the allocation of donor aid. The Commission for Transportation and Communication was set up in Maputo in 1980. It was not until 1986, however, that an emphasis on industry and trade was actually initiated. A number of co-ordination units were set up, with Dar es Salaam being assigned Industry and Trade; Maseru, Soil and Water Conservation, and Land Utilisation and Tourism; Mbabane, Manpower Training; Luanda, Energy Conservation and Development; and Lilongwe, Fisheries, Wildlife and Forestry.[52] R. Weisfelder has noted that co-ordination units are not necessarily assigned to areas which possess relevant expertise.[53] They may in fact be assignments to problem areas. In the case of Lesotho, one of its most pressing land utilisation problems is soil erosion. However, in the case of Angola, that country has the potential to supply all of SADCC's oil needs twice over.[54]

Anglin suggests that SADCC's voluntaristic approach encourages the synchronisation of each member country's five-year development plan.[55] I had an opportunity to observe the workings of the Soil and Water Conservation and Land Utilisation Unit. Based in the Ministry of Agriculture in Maseru, SADCC personnel – including citizens of SADCC nations and expatriates – plan conferences and co-ordinate projects that include a research component. Depending on the conservation problem, civil servants in appropriate ministries throughout the region undertake feasibility studies to determine how best to implement each project according to the country's economic circumstances. Academics in local universities are selected as consultants. They run workshops for civil servants, training them to conduct social science research.

Ongoing development projects are encouraged to incorporate a conservation component. In a few cases, member countries have continued to fund projects in which conservation was emphasised, even after donor aid has been exhausted in which conservation was emphasised. When members of one SADCC unit visit another country, they have an unwritten policy that they pay a courtesy call on its unit. If they need access to an office while there, they can rely on the host unit's services. This promotes more informal communication among co-ordination units.

8.7 INSTITUTIONAL CONSTRAINTS ON SADCC'S DEVELOPMENT

In so far as institutional constraints are concerned, T. Ostergaard enumerates the ways in which TNCs perpetuate underdevelopment in peripheral countries. They drain away investable surplus; oppose the emergence of capital goods industries; promote capital-intensive technologies; oppose corrective types of integration; aggravate uneven development; increase the brain-drain; and divide participants in integration schemes.[56] Banks usually have economic ties with the colonial metropole,[57] often facilitate transfer pricing in which TNCs transfer profits outside the country in which the industry is located[58] and treat TNCs as preferred borrowers for commercial loans.[59] The latter often creates a situation in which capital investment is concentrated in urban industrial areas.[60]

Considering national institutions, Ostergaard suggests that nationalism and decision-making structures are geared towards the national goals of a particular country.[61] He discusses the difficulty in formulating a regional strategy that is dependent upon a series of donor-aid allocations. In general, regional bureaucracies often do not have a strong power base and adequate financial resources. In the case of SADCC, co-ordination units are housed in appropriate ministries in designated countries.

The political economy of donor aid has a significant impact on developing economies.[62] It creates the potential for a recipient's structural dependency on the donor. Furthermore, the recipient may become more complacent because of the presumed reliability of donor aid. *Vis-à-vis* the donor, aid may be tied to the purchase of certain types of equipment or inputs. Moreover, a country or regional entity may have a different agenda from that of the donor agency, which does not allow for full implementation of the former's goals.

With regard to international donors, the hitherto socialist countries of Angola and Mozambique have often been excluded from aid agreements.[63] For example, in 1980, at the SADCC conference in

Maputo, the EC restricted its $100 million allocation to Lome signatories. Prior to the recent reunification of Germany, the EC stipulated that Angola and Mozambique had to recognise West Berlin as the capital of Germany. Since reunification, this has ceased to be a problem. Furthermore, the IMF has an impact on donor aid flows because if its conditions for a loan are refused a country usually has recourse to no other lender.[64]

Returning to banking in the SADCC region, Ostergaard examines the extent to which state regulation of banks can redirect the surplus into its coffers. In Angola, Mozambique and Tanzania, commercial banks are nationalised. Swaziland, Malawi, Zambia and Zimbabwe have varying degrees of state regulation.[65] However, Botswana and Lesotho engage in no state regulation of commercial banking.

Commercial banks have generated substantial profits despite the fact that currencies in most SADCC countries were devalued between 1980 and 1985.[66] However, many SADCC currencies are tremendously overvalued.[67] The IMF often espouses the devaluation of currency as a part of its structural adjustment programmes. This forces countries unaffected by structural adjustment to also devalue their currencies to facilitate trade.

There is no extensive intra-SADCC formal trade.[68] Recorded trade flows tend to have the following configurations:

Botswana–Lesotho–Swaziland
Botswana–Zimbabwe
Botswana–Malawi
Tanzania–Mozambique

SACU countries have to seek permission to enter into any other trade agreement.[69] To facilitate trade, Ostergaard recommends the EC model, in which the SADCC countries would have a common currency, an area monetary policy, and common fiscal and tax policies.[70] However, R. Leys and A. Tostensen argue that the European model of integration is not applicable to SADCC. They consider post-colonial African integration as not being strictly a function of market forces.[71] Tostensen elaborates: 'In Africa. . .the effect has been the opposite (to Europe) mainly because the point of departure of regional co-operative ventures has been wide disparities between partners, disarticulated economies, external dependencies and generally a low level of development. Therefore, the hidden hand of the market cannot be relied upon as an integrative mechanism.'[72]

With the exception of Swaziland, according to Ostergaard, all other SADCC countries have increased the share of commercial loans to their trade sectors.[73] He further suggests that despite the fact that Swaziland's commercial structure has become more prominent in the regional context it is still characterised by first-stage assembly processing of export crops. This does not accurately represent processing in the sugar, citrus or cotton industries at present, however, in which there are forward linkages.

The illumination of intra-regional constraints indicates the need for more comprehensive policies to be formulated to facilitate industrialisation and trade. However, these policies should not be too integrative, given the stratification of the region's economies.

8.8   SADCC AND TEXTILE INDUSTRIALISATION

This chapter cannot be concluded without some consideration of SADCC's role in textile industrialisation and industrial relocation, the subject of this book. In some of the documents prepared by the Industry and Trade Coordination Unit in Dar es Salaam, one can discern the SADCC's official approach to textile production. In the parlance of major donor agencies, the unit has chosen to focus on industrial development that fulfils the basic needs of the population. The basic needs identified fall under the categories of food, clothing and apparel, housing, health, water supply and power, transport and education. By couching clothing and apparel in terms of basic needs, there is the implication that such goods be manufactured for domestic consumption.[74] To implement its objectives, the Industry and Trade Coordination Unit planned to seek funding for the revitalisation of failing industries and to organise investment and promotion conferences. Neither of these strategies would preclude foreign investment. However, S. Sassen suggests that currently more core foreign investment centres on export-processing than on import-substitution.[75]

In order to have a viable textile industry, there have to be backward linkages to agriculture and forward linkages to the textile and clothing industries. Cotton farmers – whether commercial or smallholder – require comprehensive extension services that provide them with the necessary information on soil conservation as well as the most appropriate agricultural inputs. Cotton cultivation has a tendency to quickly exhaust the soil. Cotton farmers in many areas of southern Africa need irrigation to produce high yields because of unreliable rainfall. Furthermore, they must tailor their production to the industrial needs of ginneries and spinning mills.

Prior to the establishment of a cotton-spinning mill in Swaziland, Zimbabwe and Tanzania had fully-integrated textile industries. Other countries in the region produce textiles on a smaller scale. Does the SADCC region need another fully-integrated textile industry? One should bear in mind that most of the existing industries produce for export outside the region, as is the plan for Swaziland. However, Swaziland's industry seems more closely articulated with South Africa's with regard to processing and marketing.

As Mbilima has suggested, SADCC did emerge at a time of global economic recession.[76] Most of the countries of the region, including South Africa, have suffered some recessionary trends over the last decade. SADCC's hopes of becoming a repository of donor aid for regional projects has not been realised because it has not been able to establish a solid structural position between the machinations of the apartheid political economy and that of core political economies. The countries that are most dependent on South Africa will find themselves in its grip regardless of what moves they make towards forward linkages of industries and self-sufficiency. It is South African investment, raw and processed materials imported for production, and South African control of the marketing apparatus for major resources that perpetuate dependence. With regard to manufacturing, Swaziland is being transformed into a vertically-integrated export-processing zone, and Lesotho an undiscriminating host of a hodge-podge of runaway shops.

If the textile industry is indeed a permanent sector in the SADCC regional economy, then textile employers must make a greater effort to socialise workers into viewing themselves as possessing marketable skills. This must occur in conjunction with management being more localised and having a more receptive view of trade unionism.

The isolation of the apartheid state has also led to the isolation of progressive forces within South Africa from their counterparts elsewhere. Thus there is minimal interaction between trade unions in South Africa and those in SADCC. As a consequence, the latter are deprived of an important aspect of their political consciousness because there is no attempt to articulate trade unionism and capital mobility in South Africa with peripheral capitalist manifestations in neighbouring countries. Should progressive forces implement the transformation of the South African political economy more rapidly than anticipated, SADCC could represent a regressive force *vis-à-vis*

the post-apartheid political economy. It is imperative at this juncture
to initiate dialogue with black South African trade unions to avoid one
group being manipulated against the other.

Ndlela discusses the lack of capital goods production in the SADCC
region.[77] His argument is primarily based on steel production and
manufacture, thereby overlooking other forms of capital goods
production. For highly-mechanised spinning mills, steel-based, computerised equipment would be quite suitable. For clothing factories,
sewing machines should be manufactured on a regional basis. For
labour-intensive cottage industries, more appropriate technologies
need to be manufactured on a larger scale than is the case at
present. Among the capital goods to be considered are spinning
wheels, looms of various types, and carding and combing devices for
processing raw fibre. At present, Lesotho and Swaziland only produce
spinning wheels. G. N. Mudenda suggests the formation of a coordination unit for local technologies which would potentially address
these issues.[78]

The Soil and Water Conservation and Land Utilisation Unit, the
Energy Unit and the Industry and Trade Unit should all have some
input in co-ordinating textile industrialisation. But is it possible for
these units, located in different countries, to co-ordinate their efforts
for one SADCC country, let alone for the whole region? The Soil and
Water Conservation and Land Utilisation Coordination Unit would
have an impact on cotton- and mohair-producers as well as on the
disposal of industrial wastes. The Southern African Trade Union
Coordination Council (SATUCC) probably has the best potential
for dealing with the issue because it is encouraging women's trade
union activism in the region. In addition, a women's affairs coordination unit would be useful since most of the workers involved
in textile industrialisation are female.

This chapter would not be complete without some recommendations
for curbing textile industry relocation. It is essential that the Industry
and Trade Coordination Unit formulate investment guidelines for the
textile industry – as well as other industries – that emphasise the
following:

- the elimination of tax holidays in the SADCC region;
- the requirement of submission of a localisation plan for the managerial staff by individual industries;
- the implementation of regular on-the-job training for unskilled
  workers;

- the phasing-in of dependence on indigenous or locally-produced raw materials, as opposed to South African raw materials;
- the promotion of the trade of textile resources within the SADCC region;
- active support of unionisation efforts in the industry;
- consultation with textile union leadership in South Africa to determine the status of retrenched workers as a consequence of industrial relocation in a SADCC country;
- fostering the enactment of legislation in SADCC countries requiring that industries give at least ninety days' notice of their plans to relocate, with provisions made for workers' compensation and the option of having the jointly investing parastatal purchase the industry; and
- establishing a committee to monitor the implementation of the above on an annual basis.

These recommendations are being made whilst acknowledging the reality of South African industrial relocation in SADCC countries. On the one hand, SADCC, in separating from the South African economy and linking to member economies, must not tacitly approve of the oppression of black South African textile workers. On the other, SADCC countries must exhibit a united front against national and regional exploitation by these industries, by allowing profit to be exported and reinvested elsewhere rather than being utilised toward the development effort of the SADCC region.

Along these lines, SADCC must consider forming its own cotton marketing board. It should also assist Lesotho in establishing wool and mohair processing facilities. Furthermore, it should support the development of plants producing polyester and other synthetic fibres in the region since synthetics are often used in clothing manufacture. SADCC should also promote the manufacture of the most 'appropriate' capital goods as well as the more highly-mechanised capital goods for the industry.

All of the above should be executed with some provisions made for the possibility of re-linking with South Africa in the post-apartheid era. It is hoped by that time that SADCC will have reconciled the relationship between industrialisation and development. Then there will be an entire SADCC region that engages in planned economic development without having to make unprofitable concessions to opportunistic industries. SADCC member states should bear in mind that South African runaway shops have a much more limited trajectory of relocation than do American and European textile industries, because of South Africa's limited diplomatic ties and economic sanctions.

8.9 CONCLUSION

The founding of SADCC provided a forum for resisting apartheid at the regional level. Despite the goal of splitting from South Africa and linking with each other, however, SADCC from its inception was defined *vis-à-vis* the apartheid political economy. Thus this regional organisation was founded to provide a temporary basis for restructuring until the apartheid political economy undergoes transformation. As events unfold, it appears that such a transformation may not be as profound as earlier anticipated. It is occurring before the 'delinking' process becomes routine.

The problem emerges in part from global recessionary trends which may have influenced SADCC's founding, as well as the central position of South Africa in the region as the conduit for core capital investment. Thus whereas the core has assisted in South African industrialisation, it has been content to provide donor aid for the development of individual peripheral countries, and thus to maintain existing economic ties with the semi-periphery. As a consequence, in SADCC's peripheral status, it is being isolated by the periphery and the core. Although the EC is its major donor, the World Bank and IMF are playing major roles in restructuring SADCC and South Africa to fulfil the economic imperatives of the core.

SADCC has also provided the peripheral nations in the region with some basis for regional integration despite a less-than-enthusiastic response by the international community. It might be that the South African transformation is so incomplete that SADCC may decide to continue the splitting-off process or, in the event of a complete transformation, invite the post-apartheid South African state to become a member. That is why it is crucial to observe and anticipate the economic and foreign policies formulated by the ANC.

At the inter-governmental level, SADCC is having an impact on the region. It has led to greater communication, regional planning, and inter-governmental and inter-ministerial interaction. This is a model from which post-apartheid South Africa could benefit.

In relation to textile industrialisation, SADCC has neither the policy nor the power to regulate capital migration from South Africa to

SADCC countries. However, just because the IMF and the World Bank have a master plan for the region, it does not follow that it will be fully implemented. Different forms of resistance will continue to emerge. If the post-apartheid government is a truly progressive one, SADCC should try to work out an industrial decentralisation plan for the region from which all member states can benefit. In the meantime, however, despite the early 1990s' global recession, it is business-as-usual for SADCC.

9 Conclusion: Cottage Industries, Factories and Female Wage Labour

Industrialisation in southern Africa, as elsewhere, has been a complex process in its transformation from core to semi-periphery to periphery. It has initiated the formation of a hierarchy of political economies which have considerable complementarity. To analyse the periphery, the core and semi-peripheral contexts must be established.

In the case of *Swaziland*, its political economy has emerged through a variety of direct relationships with the core and semi-periphery as well as some indirect relationships with the core mediated through the semi-periphery. Industrialisation within Swaziland has sexually-segmented the reserve army of labour in Swaziland – as has been the case in South Africa and Europe. This has profound implications for gender relations within these societies.

European industrialisation began more than a century before South African industrialisation, which was ushered in by *mining*. Although Swaziland's incorporation was partially influenced by this mining, it was a much smaller territory with fewer resources – enough to provide some revenue to the entrepreneurs and the Swazi monarchy, and domestic employment for some Swazi men. However, a substantial number of Swazi men worked in the South African gold mines for higher wages.

Textile industrialisation began in urban areas of South Africa after mining production got under way, and employed a labour force of varying racial and gender composition in each province. It included a predominantly coloured female labour force in the Cape with white and Malay tailors; a predominantly Afrikaner female labour force in the Transvaal; and a predominantly Indian and black male labour force in Natal. By the 1950s, white females were moving into clerical jobs and those that remained in the textile industry had supervisory positions as participants in the family consumer economy. South African labour legislation led to the standardisation of working conditions, thereby eliminating the role of the tailor.

In the 1930s, the proletarianisation of the reserves had become evident. As a stop-gap measure, an attempt was made to introduce semi-industrialised industries into these areas to provide a means of subsistence for women and children. This strategy was also followed in the British protectorates. Although similar efforts were made subsequently, it was not until the 1970s that they became more established in peripheral areas of southern Africa.

Because of South Africa's Industrial Decentralisation Policy, *manufacturing* industries were provided with incentives for relocation outside the Witwatersrand to less developed areas of South Africa, including cities such as Durban and the bantustans. Although some manufacturing industries had relocated into the BLS countries in the late 1960s and 1970s, it was not until the 1980s that the pace began to increase. Economic sanctions in 1986 merely reinforced the pre-existing process.

Whereas manufacturing industries had initially been slow to respond to Industrial Decentralisation incentives, the pace of relocation increased as South Africa began to experience extreme recessionary trends in the 1970s. These trends were accompanied by high black unemployment, urban unrest and labour disputes. The textile industries were facing mounting labour costs and saw the need to range more widely for cheap female labour.

Swaziland's industrialisation process began shortly after gold mining on the Rand with more heightened industrialisation after the Second World War. Since the turn of the century, that country has sent substantial numbers of able-bodied men to the South African gold mines. However, after the Second World War, domestic migration began to surpass foreign migration. Gold mining employment then functioned to absorb Swaziland's male labour surplus.

Swaziland's monarchy has emerged in the post-independence period, buttressed by the reinvestment of its mineral trusts in the monopoly sectors of the Swazi economy. This gives the monarchy a number of functions including those of major ideologue, land allocator and employer within the Swaziland political economy. Thus the monarchy, in collaboration with multinational interests, is an active participant in Swaziland's incorporation and monopolisation, and the resulting proletarianisation of Swazi peasants and the exploitation of its working class.

Swazi women have faced increasing restrictions on foreign migration culminating in its prohibition by South Africa in 1963. Those who had little or no access to migrant remittances had to resort to farm labour and some petty commodity production. Whereas a decade and a half ago most women lived in rural areas, the sex ratios in towns are now nearly equal. Swazi women have become a burgeoning labour reserve which is being tapped by manufacturing industries, particularly textiles and clothing.

Countries such as Swaziland have not formulated comprehensive industrial legislation and have not developed the level of trade union militancy that has been prevalent in South Africa. Furthermore, Swaziland was willing to offer a number of attractive incentives that would minimise the industrialists' cost of relocating there. For the most part, textile industries have relocated in Matsapha Industrial Estate. Despite the fact that they recruit widely, they have not tapped into the labour reserves that cottage industries rely upon. They tend to recruit younger, more educated women.

Because of gender-based employment differentials, men and women have a tendency to migrate to different areas of the country or, in the case of men, to South Africa. Furthermore, although female rates of employment are considerably lower than those of men, the creation of female-orientated jobs is occurring at a higher rate than male-orientated jobs. As H.I. Safa has observed, such conditions are conducive to significant changes in family structure.[1] As has been the case in other countries where a concentration of textile relocation has occurred, more female-headed households have emerged thereby exacerbating a pre-existing trend precipitated by the migratory labour system. While female-headed households in and of themselves are not aberrant, their concentration at the lowest socio-economic levels is a major social welfare issue. As single mothers of young children, these women do not participate in a *family wage economy*.

Although *Swazi working class women* would not identify themselves as 'feminists' in the Western sense, they find themselves in a position where they have to fight for their own and their children's survival. Because they are relatively autonomous, the intent of their class-based actions is essentially feminist. They will have to modify the industrial outlook to accommodate their needs for a living wage, safe working conditions, adequate health care benefits for themselves and their children, day-care centres and adequate pensions upon retirement from the labour force.

Because Swaziland has more exploitable resources, it has depended more heavily on *private enterprise* for development. Thus cottage industries tend to be privatised. The relationship between expatriate female employers and Swazi employees is reflective of the dichotomy between core white, middle-class women and lower-class women of colour in the periphery. The former are often feminists but in relation to their employees there is some manifestation of class and global hierarchies. As feminists, expatriate handicraft-industry owners and managers must make an effort to identify, encourage and support talented Swazi women, who might start their own cottage industries and co-operatives.

In the future, Swaziland will probably become a major textile centre in southern Africa, given its position as a cotton producer, its access to foreign and local capital, its proximity to South Africa and its traditionalist ideology that suppresses women. Strengthened forward linkages with the cotton industry will make it difficult for newly-investing textile industries to relocate elsewhere in southern Africa. If this becomes the case, then textile industrialists may face increasing confrontation with its cheap female labour force.

SACU has served as an obstacle to the independent development of the BLS countries and a conduit for South African investment. SACU effectively eliminated the possibility of import-substitution industries being established in the BLS countries because of its role in protecting South African industrialists and farmers and its tariff structure. This has made it difficult for BLS countries to form alternative economic linkages, even among themselves.

In this book, some comparisons have been drawn between Lesotho and Swaziland. Lesotho has clearly undergone a longer period of incorporation and underdevelopment and exhibited a higher degree of economic dependency on South Africa. However, despite Swaziland's ability to develop forward linkages for its resources, it still exhibits considerable dependency on South Africa and on core economies via South Africa. For example, its sugar industry was initiated by the Commonwealth Development Corporation and now has investments from Tate & Lyle and Lonrho, two British multinationals, and investments from the monarchy's trust, Tibiyo Taka Ngwane.

Swaziland's political economy is articulated into the regional political economy that includes Natal and part of the eastern Transvaal in which sugar and cotton are the major commodities. Due to the pattern of investment in the region, I consider them to be co-commodities. Tate & Lyle, having been involved in the development of Simunye Sugar Mill (Swaziland's third), has more recently invested in the National Textile Corporation, the country's only cotton spinning mill. In South Africa, Tongaat has investments in the cotton and sugar industries. However, there is evidence in South Africa that the major mining houses are attempting to monopolise both industries. Swaziland has already experienced Anglo American's monopolisation of its forestry industry.

By contrast, *Lesotho* has few exploitable resources and is heavily dependent upon male labour migration to the South African gold mines. Thus, gold mining employment serves as a contingency for most development planning. Diamonds were only mined for a brief period by the Anglo American Corporation. Lesotho's other resource is water which, in the context of the Highlands Water Agreement funded by the World Bank, will be used primarily to satisfy the hydro-electric needs of the Witwatersrand.

Manufacturing industrialisation became more pronounced in the 1980s. Many of the relocating industries were textile industries which employ Basotho women. However, since Lesotho provides no backward linkages for wool and mohair, and produces no cotton, its textile industry lacks vertical integration. Clothing factories are producing a variety of items for sale in international markets.

Given Lesotho's paucity of natural resources, its role as a male migrant labour supplier and its geographical encapsulation by South Africa, it has been a recipient of considerable donor aid. Some of the smaller donor agencies have initiated cottage industries that are unprivatised. Thus, Basotho women are exposed to co-operative alternatives to fill in the many gaps unexploited by capitalism.[2]

SADCC was formed in 1980 as an organisation to promote regional integration in southern Africa and to provide an economic alternative to South Africa. SADCC has not been very successful, for a number of reasons, in separating member economies from the South African economy and linking them with each other. Member states, both individually and collectively, have unique relationships with the South African political economy. Furthermore, South Africa has been disruptive of SADCC's planning in its invasions and acts of sabotage against those SADCC countries harbouring ANC members, and its Nkomati-like pacts. Moreover, core countries, the major contributors of donor aid, are not enthusiastic about supporting regional development projects. After all, core donors have a primary relationship with the South African semi-periphery and would act in a self-interested fashion to maintain the periphery in a secondary relationship.

The *European Community* has been SADCC's largest contributor. However, *vis-à-vis* the periphery, the EC members are collectively forming new economic relationships in the Community's quest for raw materials and consumer markets. Despite the fact that the EC and

SADCC have similar goals, the core–periphery dichotomy makes this a highly exploitative relationship. A close economic relationship with the EC would compromise SADCC aspirations for some degree of economic autonomy through trade.

However, the *South African factor* must be taken into consideration. Even if it might be responding to regional circumstances, South Africa is undergoing domestic changes that may undermine SADCC's *raison d'être*. SADCC has had to take a back seat in the very delicate negotiations between the De Klerk Government and the African National Congress. However, it is unclear what a military solution to the South African situation would have yielded for SADCC countries in terms of greater regional integration.

In analysing industrialisation in Europe *vis-à-vis* that of South Africa and the southern African periphery, I would argue that the latter are quite configurational in that the components of industrialisation are selected and arranged according to the exigencies of those peripheral contexts, rather than according to a more spontaneous politico-historical ordering of those components. This represents the master plan of the IMF and World Bank for South Africa and the SADCC region. Thus we find cottage industries and textile factories operating simultaneously and successfully in Swaziland and Lesotho. Popular demand in South Africa and the SADCC region require that these components be reconfigured in the future on national and regional bases respectively, to incorporate race, class and gender equity.

Appendix I

Table A1 Textile Industries Surveyed*

	Name	No. of Employees	No. of Women	Product
1.	Swaziland Tapestries Ngwenya	47	30	Mohair tapestries
2.	Imbuti Ngwenya	13	13	Mohair curtains, tapestries
3.	Coral Stephens Piggs Peak	68	38	Mohair shawls, etc.
4.	Shiba Bethany	26	16	Cotton rugs
5.	Rosecraft Shiselweni	40	40	Mohair tapestries, shawls, etc.
6.	Mantenga Craft Ezulwini	51	24	Mohair tapestries, pottery
7.	Knitwit Knitwear Designs Manzini	5	5	Synthetic jerseys (sweaters)
8.	Bombshell Spinning and Weaving Manzini	12	5	Cotton tapestries
9.	Tishweshwe Malkerns	7	7	Mohair jerseys, household accessories, clothing
10.	Tongotongo Hlatikulu	6	6	Cotton yarn, mohair tapestries
11.	National Textile Corporation Matsapha	500	300	Cotton/polyester blend fabric
12.	Injobo Matsapha	800	?	Flannel shirts, polo shirts, etc.

Note: *Figures from 1989.

Appendix II

A mini-survey was conducted that included fifteen enterprises in Matsapha Industrial Estate. Nine of these enterprises had a labour force that was more than fifty per cent female; six of the nine industries – African Sun Knitting, Francois Fashions, Matsapha Knitwear, Oriental, Pan-African Clothing and YKK – were textile industries and three others included factories manufacturing footwear, furniture and chemical products. Of the six industries that employed a low percentage of women, the only textile-related industry was a cotton ginnery, Cotona Cotton. Interestingly, the enterprises with the highest concentration of women had a tendency towards paying the lowest monthly wages. Table A2 describes the number of employees, the percentage who are female and the average monthly income of women employed at each enterprise.

Table A2   Mini-survey Data

Enterprise	No. of Workers	Female (%)	Average Monthly Wage (emalangeni)
African Sun Knitting	200	100	149
Cotona Cotton	173	8	N/Avail.
Dulux Swaziland	15	27	500
Francois Fashions	120	99	195
Hartwood Industries	175	66	116
I & E Industries	153	31	98
Matsapha Knitwear	360	99	230
Oceanic Fruit Co.	121	73	50
Oriental	306	98	208
Pan African Clothing	900	98	72
Sikanye Footwear	483	95	N/Avail.
Steel & Wire Intl.	38	0	N/Avail.
Swaziland Bottling Co.	214	2	725
Swaziland Chemical	23	65	160
YKK	120	52	238

In comparing the wages for women in the major survey with those of the mini-survey, it is obvious that textile industries pay some of the lowest wages, with a few exceptions. Industries with heavier concentrations of male workers generally pay substantially higher wages.

Notes

CHAPTER 1: INTRODUCTION

1. D. Innes, *Anglo American and the Rise of Modern South Africa* (New York: Monthly Review Press, 1984).
2. T. M. Shaw, 'International Stratification in Africa: Sub-Imperialism in Southern and Eastern Africa', *Journal of Southern African Affairs*, (April 1977) pp. 145–165.
3. H. I. Safa, 'Runaway Shops and Female Employment: The Search for Cheap Labour', *Signs*, 712 (1981) pp. 418–33.
4. J. Nash (ed.), *Women, Men and the International Division of Labour* (Albany: State University of New York Press, 1983).
5. Letter to Head of Research, Central Bank of Swaziland from J. W. Olivier, Manager, The Employment Bureau of Africa Limited, 7 February 1989.
6. P. McFadden, 'Women in Wage-Labour in Swaziland: A Focus on Agriculture', *South African Labour Bulletin*, VII (1982) pp. 140–66.
7. H. Braverman, *Labour and Monopoly Capital* (New York: Monthly Review Press, 1974) pp. 386–8.
8. P. Thompson, The Nature of Work: An Introduction to Debates on the Labour Process, 2nd edn (London: Macmillan, 1989) pp. 192–5.
9. Government of Swaziland, *The Fourth National Development Plan 1983/4–1987/8* (Mbabane: Swaziland Printing & Publishing Company, n. d.) p. 80.

CHAPTER 2: SECONDARY INDUSTRIALISATION IN SOUTH AFRICA

1. L. Tilly and J. Scott, *Women, Work and Family*, 2nd edn (Boston: Routledge & Hall, 1989).
2. G. Gullickson, *Spinners and Weavers of Auffay* (Cambridge University Press, 1986) p. 69.
3. Ibid., p. 107.
4. A. Stadler, *The Political Economy of Modern South Africa* (New York: St. Martin's Press, 1987) p. 30.
5. D. Innes, *Anglo American and the Rise of Modern South Africa* (Johannesburg: Ravan Press, 1984) pp. 47–9.
6. J. A. Schmiechen, *Sweated Industries and Sweated Labour* (Urbana and Chicago: University of Illinois Press, 1984) p. 27.
7. D. Kayongo-Male and P. Onyango, *The Sociology of the African Family* 2nd edn (London and New York: Longman, 1986) p. 24.
8. Stadler, p. 129.

9. M. Nicol, 'A History of Garment and Tailoring Workers in Cape Town 1900–1939' (unpublished Ph.D. dissertation, University of Cape Town, 1984) pp. 13–144.
10. B. Freund, 'The Social Character of Secondary Industry in South Africa: 1915–1945', ch. 5 in A. Mabin (ed.), *Organisation and Economic Change* (Johannesburg: Ravan Press, 1989) p. 81.
11. Nicol, p. 80; A. B. Bozzoli, 'The Origins, Development and Ideology of Local Manufacturing in South Africa', *Journal of Southern African Studies*, 1, 2 (1975) p. 196.
12. Bozzoli, p. 202.
13. Ibid., p. 201–2.
14. Ibid., p. 202.
15. Ibid., pp. 196–7.
16. Ibid., p. 200.
17. Nicol, pp. 81–2.
18. Ibid., p. 95.
19. Ibid., p. 99.
20. Ibid., p. 119.
21. Bozzoli, p. 197.
22. Nicol, p. 25.
23. Bozzoli, p. 203.
24. Ibid., p. 204.
25. Nicol, p. 16.
26. Ibid., pp. 28–9.
27. Ibid., p. 29.
28. Ibid., p. 30.
29. Ibid., p. 44.
30. Ibid., p. 43.
31. Ibid., p. 30.
32. Ibid., p. 43.
33. A. Hirsch, 'An Introduction to Textile Worker Organisation in Natal', *South African Labour Bulletin*, 4, 8 (1976) p. 4.
34. S. J. Ettinger, 'The Economics of the Customs Union between Botswana, Lesotho, Swaziland and South Africa' (unpublished Ph.D. dissertation, University of Michigan, 1974) p. 60.
35. Ibid., p. 65.
36. Stadler, p. 48.
37. Ibid., p. 50.
38. Ibid., p. 41.
39. J. Mawbey, 'Afrikaner Women of the Garment Union during the Thirties and Forties', in Eddie Webster (ed.), *Essays in South African Labour History* (Johannesburg: Ravan Press, 1978) p. 192.
40. Freund, p. 100.
41. Nicol, p. 91.
42. E. Webster, 'Introduction', Section 2, *Essays in Southern African Labour History* (Johannesburg: Ravan Press, 1978) p. 68; Nicol, p. 105.
43. Nicol, p. 107.
44. Ibid., p. 123.
45. Ibid., p. 124.

46. Ibid., p. 126.
47. Ibid., p. 170.
48. Ibid., p. 220.
49. Ibid., p. 40.
50. Freund, p. 81.
51. Ibid., p. 84.
52. Nicol, p. 15.
53. Ibid., p. 119.
54. Ibid., p. 51.
55. Ibid., p. 196.
56. Ibid., p. 52.
57. Ibid., p. 54.
58. Ibid., p. 75.
59. Ibid., p. 77.
60. J. Lewis, 'Solly Sachs and the Garment Workers' Union' in Eddie Webster (ed.), *Essays in Southern African Labour History*, (Johannesburg: Ravan Press, 1978) p. 182–4.
61. Lewis, p. 188–9.
62. Ibid., p. 184.
63. E. Brink, '"Maar 'n klomp 'factory' meide": Afrikaner Family and Community on the Witwatersrand during the 1920s' in Belinda Bozzoli (ed.), *Class, Community and Conflict: South African Perspectives* (Johannesburg: Ravan Press, 1987) p. 191.
64. H. P. Pollak, 'An Analysis of the Contributions to Family Support of Women Industrial Workers on the Witwatersrand', *South African Journal of Science*, 28 (1931) p. 573.
65. Brink, p. 184.
66. Pollak, p. 575.
67. I. Berger, 'Solidarity Fragmented: Garment Workers of the Transvaal, 1930–1960' in Shula Marks and Stanley Trapido (eds), *The Politics of Race, Class and Nationalism in Twentieth Century South Africa* (London and New York: Longman, 1987) p. 129.
68. Pollak, p. 582.
69. Brink, p. 179.
70. Ibid., p. 180.
71. Ibid., p. 179–80.
72. Ibid., p. 183 and 185.
73. Ibid., p. 182.
74. Ibid., p. 185.
75. Berger, p. 135.
76. Ibid., p. 138.
77. Freund, p. 83.
78. Berger, p. 133.
79. Freund, p. 83.
80. Ibid., p. 84.
81. Berger, p. 141.
82. Freund, p. 92.
83. Berger, p. 146.
84. Ibid., p. 148.

85. Ibid., p. 128–9.
86. Ibid., p. 143.
87. A. Hirsch, p. 3.
88. Ibid., p. 4.
89. Ibid., p. 6.
90. Ibid., p. 18.
91. Ibid., p. 20.
92. Ibid., p. 21.
93. Ibid., p. 4.
94. Ibid., p. 5.
95. Ibid., p. 15.
96. Ibid., p. 19.
97. A. J. Norval, *A Quarter of a Century of Industrial Progress in South Africa* (Cape Town: Juta & Co. Ltd, 1962) pp. 13–19.
98. Norval, p. 135.
99. Ettinger, p. 67.
100. Ibid., p. 69.
101. Ibid., p. 66.
102. Ibid., pp. 77–8.
103. Ibid., p. 78.
104. Ibid., p. 80.
105. Ibid., p. 87.
106. Ibid., p. 64.
107. P. M. Landell-Mills, 'The 1969 Southern African Customs Union Agreement', *The Journal of Modern African Studies*, 9, 2 (1971) p. 273.
108. B. Turner, 'A Fresh Start for the Southern African Customs Union', *African Affairs*, 70, 280 (1971) pp. 270–1.
109. Stadler, p. 14.
110. Ibid., p. 135.
111. Ibid., p. 57.
112. Ibid., p. 59.
113. Ibid., p. 50.
114. Ibid., p. 30.
115. Freund, p. 104.
116. D. Posel, '"Providing for the Legitimate Labour Requirements of Employers": Secondary Industry, Commerce and the State in South Africa during the 1950s and Early 1960s' in Alan Mabin (ed.), *Organisation and Economic Change, Volume 5* (Johannesburg: Ravan Press, 1989) p. 200.
117. Posel, p. 203.
118. Ibid., pp. 201–2.
119. Hirsch, p. 5.
120. Ibid., p. 19.
121. Ibid., p. 135.
122. Ibid., pp. 7–9.
123. Ibid., p. 15.
124. F. R. Tomlinson, *Summary of the Report of the Commission for the Socio-Economic Development of the Bantu Areas within the Union of South Africa* (Pretoria: The Government Printer, 1955) p. 35.

125. Tomlinson, pp. 122–9.
126. Norval, p. 70.
127. Ibid., p. 99.
128. Ibid., p. 31.
129. Tomlinson, p. 134.
130. Ibid., p. 199.
131. Ibid., p. 134.
132. Ibid., p. 133.
133. Ibid., p. 132.
134. Ibid., p. 189.
135. Ibid., p. 190.
136. Posel, p. 203.
137. Ibid., p. 205–6.
138. Ibid., p. 209.
139. Ibid., p. 207.
140. Ibid., p. 206.
141. Berger, p. 135.
142. Ibid., p. 134.
143. Ibid., p. 136.
144. Ibid., p. 139.
145. Ibid., p. 124.
146. Ibid., p. 141.
147. P. Wellings and A. Black, 'Industrial Decentralisation under Apartheid: The Relocation of Industry to the South Africa Periphery', *World Development*, 14, 1 (1986) p. 2.
148. Turner, p. 272.
149. Ibid., p. 274.
150. Landell-Mills, p. 267.
151. Ibid., p. 265.
152. Ibid., p. 280.
153. Ettinger, p. 101.
154. Turner, p. 275.
155. Ibid., pp. 275–6.
156. Ettinger, p. 215.
157. Turner, p. 274.
158. Landell-Mills, pp. 278–9.
159. Ibid., p. 270.
160. Ettinger, p. 227.
161. Ibid., pp. 246–7.
162. Ibid., p. 250.
163. Ibid., pp. 27–8.
164. Ibid., p. 273.
165. Ibid., p. 274.
166. Ibid., p. 223.
167. Ibid., p. 253.
168. Ibid., pp. 260–1.
169. Stadler, p. 161.
170. Ibid., p. 66.
171. Ibid., p. 15.

172. Ibid., p. 167.
173. Ibid., p. 85.
174. J. Yawitch, 'The Incorporation of African Women into Wage Labour 1950–80', *South African Labour Bulletin*, 10, 3 (1983) pp. 83–7.
175. D. Innis and D. O'Meara, 'Class Formation and Ideology: The Transkei Region', *Review of African Political Economy*, 7 (1976) pp. 69–86.
176. Wellings and Black, p. 4.
177. Ibid., p. 2.
178. Ibid., p. 6.
179. Ibid., p. 3.
180. Ibid., p. 24.
181. Ibid., p. 6.
182. Ibid., p. 3.
183. Ibid., p. 17.
184. Ibid., p. 11.
185. Ibid., p. 12.
186. Ibid., p. 17.
187. Ibid., p. 18.
188. Ibid., p. 6.
189. Ibid., p. 12.
190. Ibid., p. 23.
191. Ibid., p. 20.
192. Ibid., pp. 24–5.
193. Ibid., p. 20.
194. T. Bell, 'International Competition and Industrial Decentralisation in South Africa', *World Development*, 13, 10/11 (1987) p. 1291.
195. Ibid., pp. 1293–4.
196. Ibid., p. 1294.
197. Ibid., p. 1297.
198. Ibid., p. 1295.
199. Ibid., p. 1302.
200. Ibid., p. 1301.
201. J. Pickles and J. Woods, 'Taiwanese Investment in South Africa', *African Affairs*, 88, 353 (1989) p. 508.
202. Ibid., p. 518.
203. Ibid., p. 522.
204. Ibid., p. 517.
205. Ibid., p. 523.
206. Ibid., p. 528.
207. *Weekly Mail*, 'South Africa and the Soviets: From Cold War to Hot Peace', 3–9 March 1989, p. 15.
208. *Sechaba*, 'ANC Mission in USSR' (March 1989) p. 12.
209. *Weekly Mail*, 'ANC Campaigns to Stop Debt Rescheduling', 21–27 July 1989, p. 15.

CHAPTER 3:   INDUSTRIALISATION IN SWAZILAND

  1. P. Bonner, *Kings, Commoners and Concessionaires* (Johannesburg: Ravan Press, 1983) p. 212.

2. Bonner, p. 190.
3. Ibid., p. 79.
4. Ibid., p. 128.
5. J. Crush, *The Struggle for Swazi Labour 1890–1920* (Kingston and Montreal: McGill–Queen's University Press, 1987) p. 34.
6. Bonner, p. 184.
7. C. P. Youe, 'Imperial Land Policy in Swaziland and the African Response', *Journal of Imperial and Commonwealth History*, 7 (1978) p. 58.
8. Crush, p. 34.
9. Ibid., p. 36.
10. Ibid., p. 39.
11. Ibid., p. 41.
12. A. R. Booth, *Tradition and Change in a Southern African Kingdom* (Boulder, Col.: Westview Press, 1983) p. 23; Crush, p. 54.
13. Crush, p. 204.
14. Booth, p. 23.
15. Crush, p. 39.
16. Ibid., p. 42.
17. Ibid., p. 44.
18. Ibid., pp. 44–5.
19. Ibid., p. 46.
20. Ibid., p. 83.
21. Ibid., p. 89.
22. L. Callinicos, *A People's History of South Africa: Gold and Workers 1886–1924, Vol. 1* (Johannesburg: Ravan Press, 1985) p. 57.
23. Crush, p. 47.
24. Ibid., p. 66.
25. Ibid., pp. 66–7.
26. Ibid., p. 94.
27. Youe, p. 58.
28. Crush, p. 212.
29. H. Macmillan, 'Swaziland: Decolonisation and the Triumph of "Tradition"', *The Journal of Modern African Studies*, 23, 4 (1985) p. 646.
30. F. de Vletter, 'Labour Migration in Swaziland: Recent Trends and Implications', *South African Labour Bulletin*, 7, 6/7 (1982) p. 115.
31. Crush, p. 149.
32. Ibid., pp. 150–1.
33. Booth, p. 20.
34. J. S. M. Matsebula, *History of Swaziland* (Cape Town: Longman, 1976) p. 184.
35. Booth, pp. 21–2.
36. Crush, p. 145.
37. K. Matthews, '"Squatters" on Private Tenure Farms in Swaziland: A Preliminary Investigation', in M. Neocosmos (ed.), *Social Relations in Rural Swaziland: Critical Analyses* (Kwaluseni: Social Science Research Unit, University of Swaziland, 1987) p. 196.
38. Matthews, p. 197.

39. H. Ngubane, 'The Swazi Homestead, ' in F. de Vletter (ed.), *The Swazi Rural Homestead* (Kwaluseni: Social Science Research Unit, University of Swaziland, 1983) p. 103.
40. Ngubane, pp. 104–5.
41. Ibid., p. 98.
42. Ibid., pp. 99–100.
43. Ibid., p. 101.
44. Ibid., p. 114.
45. Ibid., p. 111.
46. Matthews, p. 198.
47. Crush, pp. 178–9.
48. Booth, p. 23; Youe, p. 64.
49. Macmillan, p. 645.
50. Crush, p. 161.
51. Ibid., p. 94.
52. Booth, p. 90.
53. Crush, p. 93.
54. Ibid., p. 194.
55. Ibid., p. 99.
56. Ibid., pp. 112–3.
57. Ibid., p. 116.
58. Ibid., p. 120.
59. Ibid., p. 142.
60. Ibid., p. 172.
61. Ibid., p. 169.
62. Ibid., p. 141.
63. Youe, p. 65.
64. Booth, p. 31.
65. Youe, p. 67.
66. Crush, p. 211.
67. Booth, p. 24; Crush, p. 134.
68. Booth, p. 24; Crush, p. 167.
69. Booth, p. 26.
70. Ibid., p. 27.
71. Macmillan, p. 647; Libandla is a lower but larger council than Liqoqo, composed of chiefs, leading councillors and headmen.
72. Ibid., p. 651.
73. Ibid., p. 649.
74. Ibid., p. 654.
75. Ibid., pp. 651–2.
76. Ibid., p. 643.
77. Ibid., p. 644.
78. Ibid., p. 643.
79. B.M. Khaketla, *Lesotho 1970: An African Coup under the Microscope* (Berkeley and Los Angeles, Calif.: University of California Press, 1972) p. 162.
80. I. Winter, 'The Post-Colonial State and the Forces and Relations of Production: Swaziland', *Review of African Political Economy*, 9 (1974) p. 42.

81. Crush, p. 201.
82. Ibid., p. 204.
83. Ibid., p. 27.
84. Booth, p. 55.
85. Ibid., p. 31.
86. R. H. Davies, D. O'Meara and S. Dlamini, *The Kingdom of Swaziland: A Profile* (London: Zed Books, 1985) pp. 2–3.
87. Hunting Technical Services Ltd, *Review of Rural Development Areas: Interim Report* (Mbabane: Government of Swaziland, 1983) p. 4.
88. M. Fransman, 'Labour, Capital and the State in Swaziland, 1962–1977', *South African Labour Bulletin*, 7, 6/7 (1982) p. 61.
89. Fransman, p. 66.
90. Ibid., p. 68–9.
91. Ibid., p. 70.
92. Booth, p. 32.
93. De Vletter, p. 118.
94. Booth, p. 75.
95. Booth, p. 75; Matsebula, p. 263.
96. De Vletter, p. 118.
97. Ibid., p. 119.
98. P.-H. Bischoff, 'Why Swaziland is Different: An Explanation of the Kingdom's Political Position in Southern Africa', *The Journal of Modern African Studies*, 26, 3 (1988) p. 480.
99. Macmillan, p. 660.
100. Ibid., p. 658.
101. H. Kuper, *The Swazi: A Southern African Kingdom*, 2nd edn (New York: Holt, Rhinehart and Winston, 1986) pp. 107–10.
102. Davies, O'Meara and Dlamini, p. 16.
103. Winter, p. 40.
104. Ibid., p. 32.
105. Booth, p. 70.
106. Macmillan, p. 657.
107. Ibid., p. 652.
108. Ibid., p. 653.
109. Booth, pp. 70–1.
110. Hunting Technical Services, p. 6.
111. Ibid., p. 21.
112. Winter, p. 40.
113. Booth, p. 71; Winter, pp. 41–2.
114. Winter, p. 40.
115. Booth, pp. 72–4.
116. Ibid., p. 76.
117. De Vletter, p. 117.
118. Ibid., p. 115.
119. Ibid., p. 128.
120. Ibid., p. 120.
121. Ibid., p. 130–1.
122. Ibid., p. 127.
123. Booth, p. 37.

124. Ibid., p. 50.
125. Davies, O'Meara and Dlamini, pp. 11–2.
126. Booth, p. 105.
127. Davies, O'Meara and Dlamini, p. 11.
128. Ibid., p. 21.
129. Ibid., p. 22.
130. Ibid., p. 23.
131. Ibid., p. 28.
132. Booth, p. 105.
133. Davies, O'Meara and Dlamini, p. 12.
134. Ibid., p. 14.
135. Ibid., p. 15.
136. Ibid., p. 22.
137. Winter, p. 42.
138. Booth, p. 102.
139. Davies, O'Meara and Dlamini, p. 29.
140. Bischoff, p. 462.
141. B. J. Harris, 'Foreign Aid, Capital Investment and Migrant Labour' (paper presented at African Studies Association meeting, New Orleans, Louisiana, November 1985).
142. Davies, O'Meara and Dlamini, p. 30.
143. J. R. A. Ayee, 'Swaziland and the Southern African Customs Union', *Journal of African Studies*, 3/4 (1988) p. 64.
144. Ibid., p. 66.
145. M. Matsebula, 'Academic View of Withdrawal from Customs Union', *The Swazi Sunday Mirror*, 30 October 1988, p. 1. The Preferential Trade Area for Eastern and Southern Africa has 15 member states and includes six SADCC countries. Member states are Burundi, Comoros, Djibouti, Ethiopia, Kenya, Lesotho, Malawi, Mauritius, Rwanda, Somalia, Swaziland, Tanzania, Uganda, Zambia and Zimbabwe. Three additional SADCC countries have observer status. The PTA is orientated towards the development of free-trade linkages among member states on selected commodities.
146. Booth, p. 91.
147. Davies, O'Meara and Dlamini, p. 25.
148. Ibid., p. 15.
149. Ibid., p. 17.
150. Ibid., p. 18.
151. Ibid., p. 19.
152. Booth, p. 106.
153. Winter, p. 42.
154. Ibid., p. 35.
155. Bischoff, p. 464.
156. Winter, p. 38.
157. Booth, p. 75.
158. Bischoff, p. 465.
159. J. S. M. Matsebula, pp. 278–98.
160. Davies, O'Meara and Dlamini, p. 62.
161. Macmillan, p. 665.

162. Ibid., p. 470.
163. Booth, p. 77.
164. Davies, O'Meara and Dlamini, p. 31.
165. Economic Intelligence Quarterly, *Lesotho Country Report*, 1 (London: EIU, 1988) p. 40.
166. Booth, p. 117.
167. Bischoff, p. 463.
168. Ibid., p. 468.
169. A. R. Booth, 'South Africa's Hinterland: Swaziland's Role in Strategies for Sanctions-Breaking', *Africa Today*, 26, 1 (1989) pp. 41–50.
170. Bischoff, p. 469.
171. 'Where Tinkundla Needs Change', *The Times of Swaziland*, 7 February 1989. p. 8.
172. 'Nine Thrown in Jail for 60 Days', *The Times of Swaziland*, 13 March 1989, p. 1.
173. 'Fear of the Death Threats', *The Times of Swaziland*, 14 March 1989, p. 1.
174. 'Jail Bust "Tools Found"', *The Times of Swaziland*, 20 March 1989, p. 1.
175. 'Zwane Pamphlets Probe', *The Times of Swaziland*, 11 March 1989, p. 1.
176. 'Banks Strike is Off', *The Times of Swaziland*, 20 June 1989, p. 1.
177. 'Bayethe!' is a salutation to the king.
178. 'Banks Crisis is Over', *The Times of Swaziland*, 27 July 1989, p. 1.

CHAPTER 4: AGRICULTURAL PRODUCTION IN SWAZILAND

1. Government of Swaziland, *Fourth National Development Plan 1983/84–1987/88* (Mbabane: Swaziland Printing and Publishing Company, 1983) p. 20.
2. Government of Swaziland, p. 21.
3. Ibid., p. 22.
4. Food and Agriculture Organisation, *Cotton Development in Swaziland* (Rome: Food and Agriculture Organisation, 1981) p. 30.
5. Food and Agriculture Organisation, p. 29.
6. 'Harvest Joy for Hhohho', *The Times of Swaziland*, 27 April 1989, p. 1.
7. H. Standing, 'Gender Relations and Social Transformation in Swaziland', in M. Neocosmos (ed.), *Social Relations in Rural Swaziland: Critical Analyses* (Kwaluseni: Social Science Research Unit, University of Swaziland, 1987) p. 136.
8. Standing, p. 129.
9. Ibid., p. 136.
10. Food and Agriculture Organisation, p. 27.
11. A. Graves and P. Richardson, 'Plantations in the Political Economy of Colonial Sugar Production: Natal and Queensland, 1860–1914', *Journal of Southern African Studies*, 6, 2 (1980) p. 214.
12. Graves and Richardson, p. 221.
13. Ibid., p. 225.
14. Ibid., p. 226.
15. D. Lincoln, 'South African Sugar Mill Labour during the 1970s', *South African Labour Bulletin*, 6, 6 (1981) p. 40.

16. B. Dinham and C. Hines, *Agribusiness in Africa* (Trenton: Africa World Press, 1984) p. 172.
17. Lincoln, p. 41.
18. Dinham and Hines, p. 170.
19. Ibid., p. 171.
20. Ibid., p. 172.
21. Ibid., pp. 172–3.
22. Ibid., p. 178.
23. Ibid., p. 180.
24. Ibid., p. 179.
25. Ibid., p. 180.
26. R. Levin, 'Uneven Development in Swaziland: Tibiyo, Sugar Production and Rural Development Strategy', *Geoforum*, 12, 2 (1986) p. 239.
27. Levin, p. 242.
28. Ibid., p. 243.
29. Ibid., p. 244.
30. Ibid., p. 249.
31. Ibid., p. 244.
32. 'Massive Rise in Local Sugar Sales', *The Times of Swaziland*, 16 November 1988, p. 7.
33. Levin, p. 245.
34. 'Citrus at Ubombo?', *The Times of Swaziland*, 8 May 1989, p. 6.
35. The lilangeni (plural emalangeni – represented by the letter E) is the official currency of Swaziland. It is tied to the South African rand. During the period of my research, its value fluctuated between US$.35 and US$.45.
36. R. Levin, 'Contract Farming in Swaziland', *Social Relations in Rural Swaziland: Critical Analyses* (Kwaluseni: Social Science Research Unit, University of Swaziland, 1987) pp. 180–1.
37. Norval, p. 71.
38. Ministry of Agriculture, *Cotton Breeding in Swaziland* (Mbabane: Ministry of Agriculture, 1968) p. 1.
39. T.J. Kliest, 'The Smallholder Cotton Sector in Swaziland', Research paper No. 2 (Kwaluseni: Social Science Research Unit, University of Swaziland, 1982) p. 6.
40. Kliest, p. 3.
41. Ibid., p. 7.
42. Food and Agriculture Organisation, p. 4.
43. Kliest, p. 22.
44. Ibid., p. 15.
45. Ibid., p. 28.
46. Ibid., p. 22.
47. Ibid., p. 11.
48. Ibid., p. 12.
49. Ibid., p. 20.
50. Ibid., pp. 24–5.
51. Ibid., p. 27.
52. Ibid., p. 26.
53. Food and Agriculture Organisation, p. 1.

54. Swaziland Cotton Board, *Annual Report and Accounts* (Manzini, Swaziland Cotton Board, 1988) p. 6.
55. '1988: A Record Year for Swazi Cotton', *The Times of Swaziland*, 22 November 1988, pp. 10–11.
56. Swaziland Cotton Board, p. 7.
57. Kliest, p. 8.
58. Food and Agriculture Organisation, p. 27.
59. Ibid., p. 52.
60. Ibid., pp. 47–8.
61. Food and Agriculture Organisation, p. 45.
62. Ibid., p. 2.
63. Ibid., p. 3.
64. Ibid., p. 4.
65. Ibid., p. 11.
66. Ibid., p. 2.
67. 'E7 Civil Works on EEC Dams', *The Times of Swaziland*, 30 September 1988, p. 7.
68. 'Irrigation: Expansion Headache', *The Times of Swaziland*, 15 August 1989, p. 9.
69. Food and Agriculture Organisation, p. 18.
70. Ibid., p. 12.
71. Ibid., p. 7.
72. 'Truck Kills 11 Men', *The Times of Swaziland*, 25 March 1989, p. 1.
73. Food and Agriculture Organisation, p. 15.
74. 'Cotton's Best Season', *The Times of Swaziland*, 13 October 1988, p. 7.
75. 'Cotton Heading for Another Record', *The Times of Swaziland*, 15 August 1989, p. 9.
76. 'Cotton: What Collapse', *The Times of Swaziland*, 12 April 1989, p. 7.
77. 'Cotton Warning: No Polypropylene', *The Times of Swaziland*, 23 May 1989, p. 7.
78. '1988: A Record Year for Swazi Cotton', *The Times of Swaziland*, 22 November 1988, p. 11.
79. W. A. Pringle and J. A. Dockel, 'The South African Angora Goat and Mohair Industry', *South African Journal of Economics*, 57, 3 (1989) pp. 215–17.
80. Pringle and Dockel, p. 221.
81. Ibid., p. 228.
82. Wayne Durdle, *Tibiyo Goat Project Reports* (Malkerns: Tibiyo Agricultural Projects, 1981–85).
83. 'Tongaat-Hulett Earnings Are Up', *The Times of Swaziland*, 17 November 1988, p. 7.

CHAPTER 5: TEXTILE MANAGEMENT

1. P. Selwyn, *Industries in the Southern African Periphery* (Boulder, Col.: Westview Press, 1975) p. 13.
2. Selwyn, p. 34.
3. Ibid., p. 41.

4. Ibid., pp. 55–6.
5. Ibid., pp. 56–7.
6. Ibid., p. 67.
7. Ibid., p. 75.
8. Ibid., p. 87.
9. Ibid., p. 92.
10. Ibid., p. 99.
11. Ibid., p. 106.
12. Ibid., p. 111.
13. Ibid., p. 117.
14. Ibid., p. 133.
15. Ibid., p. 135.
16. C. M. Rogerson, 'Reviving Old Technology?: Rural Handicraft Production in Southern Africa', *Geoforum*, 17, 2 (1986) p. 177.
17. Rogerson, p. 178.
18. Ibid., p. 173.
19. H. I. Safa, 'Runaway Shops and Female Employment: The Search for Cheap Labour', *Signs*, 7, 3 (1981) p. 418.
20. Safa, p. 419.
21. Ibid., p. 421.
22. Ibid., p. 424.
23. Ibid., pp. 427–8.
24. J. Nash, 'Introduction' in J. Nash and P. Fernandez-Kelly (eds), *Women, Men and the International Division of Labour*, (Albany, NY: State University of New York Press, 1983) pp. vii–xv.
25. A. Robert, 'The Effects of the International Division of Labour of Female Workers in the Textile and Clothing Industries', *Development and Change*, 14, 1 (1983) p. 20.
26. Robert, p. 22.
27. Ibid., p. 23.
28. Ibid., p. 22.
29. K. Ward, 'Introduction and Overview' in K. Ward (ed.), *Women Workers and Global Restructuring* (Ithaca, NY: Cornell University Press, 1990) p. 5.
30. H. P. Gray, 'The Multi-Fibre Arrangement and the Least Developed Countries', *Industry and Development*, 26 (1989) p. 89.
31. S. Burne and M. Hardingham, 'Textiles: Options for a Viable Future', *Appropriate Technology*, 15, 2 (1988) p. 4.
32. H. Kuper, 'Colour, Categories and Colonialism: The Swazi Case' in V. Turner (ed.), *Colonialism in Africa 1870–1960*, vol. 3 (Cambridge University Press, 1971) p. 304.
33. Kuper, p. 305.
34. Burne and Hardingham, p. 3.
35. Ibid., p. 1.
36. P. Teal, 'Unravelling the Cottage Problems', *Appropriate Technology*, 15, 2 (1988) p. 23.
37. F. de Vletter, 'Footloose Foreign Investment in Swaziland' in A. Whiteside (ed.), *Industrialisation and Investment Incentives in Southern Africa* (London: James Currey Publishers, 1989) pp. 160–1.

38. L. Loughran and J. Argo, *Assessment of Handicraft Training Needs for Rural Women in Swaziland*, 1 (Mbabane: TransCentury Corporation, 1986) p. 7.
39. Loughran and Argo, p. 38.
40. E. Boserup, *Women's Role in Economic Development* (New York: St. Martin's Press, 1970).
41. Loughran and Argo, p. 8.
42. Ibid., pp. 9–10.
43. Ibid., p. 10.
44. M. Russell, P. Dlamini and F. Simelane, *Report on a Sample Survey of Women in Women in Development Project, Entfonjeni, Swaziland* (Kwaluseni: Social Science Research Unit, University of Swaziland for United Nations Children's Fund, 1984) p. 24.
45. Loughran and Argo, p. 23.
46. M. Russell, 'The Production and Marketing of Swazi Women's Handicrafts', *Interim Report for ILO/DANIDA Project* (University of Swaziland: January–June 1983).
47. Russell, p. 7.
48. Selwyn, p. 44.
49. De Vletter, p. 146.
50. Ibid., p. 144.
51. Ibid., p. 145.
52. A. Booth, 'South Africa's Hinterland: . . .' p. 49.
53. A. Doran and G. Wheller, *Swazi Textile Corporation (SWATEX) Ltd Swaziland: Appraisal Report* (London: Commonwealth Development Corporation, 1984) p. 7.
54. 'Tycoon Kirsh Under Fire From SFTU', *The Swazi Observer*, 3 May 1989, p. 1.
55. 'Kirsh Plans E 1 Billion Textile Plants', *The Times of Swaziland*, 4 August 1989, p. 1.
56. Natal Labour Research Group, 'Control Over a Workforce – The Case of Frame', *South African Labour Bulletin*, 8, 5 (1980) pp. 17–47.

CHAPTER 6: FEMALE WORKERS IN COTTAGE INDUSTRIES AND FACTORIES

1. C. Murray, 'Migrant Labour and Changing Family Structure', *Journal of Southern African Studies*, 6, 2 (1980).
2. Murray, p. 143.
3. B. B. Brown, 'The Impact of Male Labour Migration on Women in Botswana', *African Affairs*, 82, 328 (1983) p. 368.
4. Brown, p. 371.
5. Ibid., p. 373.
6. Ibid., p. 370.
7. Ibid., p. 372.
8. Ibid., pp. 375–6.
9. Ibid., p. 383.
10. Ibid., p. 384.

11. B. Rosen-Prinz and F. Prinz, *Migrant Labour and Rural Homesteads: An Investigation into the Sociological Dimensions of the Migrant Labour System in Swaziland*, World Employment Programme Working Paper (Geneva: International Labour Organisation, 1978); H. Ngubane, 'The Swazi Homestead', in F. de Vletter (ed.), *The Swazi Rural Homestead* (Kwaluseni: Social Science Research Unit, University of Swaziland, 1983).
12. Rosen-Prinz and Prinz, p. 3.
13. Ibid., p. 26.
14. Ngubane, p. 113.
15. Rosen-Prinz and Prinz, pp. 11–13.
16. Ibid., p. 12.
17. Ibid., p. 32.
18. Ibid., p. 20.
19. Ibid., p. 23.
20. Ngubane, p. 117.
21. Rosen-Prinz and Prinz, p.20.
22. M. Neocosmos, 'Homogeneity and Differences on Swazi Nation Land', in M. Neocosmos (ed.), *Social Relations in Rural Swaziland: Critical Analyses* (Kwaluseni: Social Science Research Unit, University of Swaziland, 1987) pp. 46–7.
23. Neocosmos, p. 47.
24. P. McFadden, 'Women in Wage Labour in Swaziland: A Focus on Agriculture', *South African Labour Bulletin*, 7, 6 (1982) p. 146.
25. McFadden, p. 147.
26. Ibid., p. 148.
27. Ibid., p. 158.
28. Ibid., pp. 154–5.
29. Ibid., p. 159.
30. Ibid., p. 153.
31. Ibid., p. 148.
32. Ibid., p. 162.
33. A. Armstrong, *A Sample Survey of Women in Wage Employment in Swaziland* (Kwaluseni: Social Science Research Unit, University of Swaziland, 1985) pp. 5–6.
34. Armstrong, p. 9.
35. Ibid., p. 16.
36. Ibid., p. 39.
37. Ibid., p. 16.
38. Ibid., p. 37.
39. Government of Swaziland, *The Regulations of Wages (Manufacturing and Processing Industry) Order*, Legal Notice No. 33 (Mbabane: Government Printing Office, 1988) pp. 18–9.
40. Armstrong, p. 20.
41. 'Swaziland's Birth Rate "Highest in the World"', *The Swazi Observer*, 24 February 1989, p. 1.
42. Armstrong, p. 24.
43. A. Armstrong and R. T. Nhlapo, *Law and the Other Sex: The Legal Position of Women in Swaziland* (Mbabane: Webster Print, n.d.).

44. Central Statistical Office, *Report on the 1986 Swaziland Population Census* (Mbabane: Apollo Printers, n.d.) p. 216.
45. Armstrong, *A Sample Survey. . .*, p. 11.
46. 'Swaziland's Birth Rate "Highest in the World"', *The Swazi Observer*, 24 February 1989, p. 1.
47. A. Rwomire, *The Family Life Association of Swaziland: An Evaluation of Selected Programmes* (Manzini: The Family Life Association, 1989) p. 37.
48. Ibid., p. 82.
49. Ibid., p. 81.
50. Armstrong, *A Sample Survey . . .*, p. 16.
51. Armstrong, *A Sample Survey . . .*, p. 22.

CHAPTER 7: A LESOTHO COMPARISON

1. A. R. Booth, *Swaziland: Tradition and Change in a Southern African Kingdom* (Boulder, Col.: Westview Press, 1983) p. 124; R. H. Davies, D. O'Meara and S. Dlamini, *The Kingdom of Swaziland: A Profile* (London: Zed Books, 1985) p. 1.
2. L. Thompson, *Survival in Two Worlds: Moshoeshoe of Lesotho 1786–1870* (London: Oxford University Press, 1975) p. 120.
3. J. Kimble, 'Labour Migration in Basutoland c. 1870–1885' in S. Marks and R. Rathbone (eds), *Industrialisation and Social Change in South Africa: African Class Formation, Culture and Consciousness* (London: Longman, 1982) p. 135.
4. J. P. Hunter, *The Economics of Wool and Mohair Production and Marketing in Lesotho*, ISAS Research Report No. 16 (Roma: Institute of Southern African Studies, 1987) p. 76.
5. Thompson, p. 72.
6. Kimble, p. 134.
7. Hunter, p. 124.
8. Thompson, p. 177.
9. Kimble, p. 121.
10. W. J. Breytenbach, *Crocodiles and Commoners in Lesotho: Continuity and Change in the Rulemaking System of the Kingdom of Lesotho*, No. 24 (Pretoria: Communications of the Africa Institute, 1975) p. 50.
11. R. Edgar, *Prophets with Honour: A Documentary History of Lekhotla la Bafo* (Johannesburg: Ravan Press, 1987) p. 26.
12. C. Murray, 'From Granary to Labour Reserve: An Economic History of Lesotho, *South African Labour Bulletin*, 6, 4 (1980) pp. 3–20.
13. Kimble, p. 119.
14. Hunter, p. 37.
15. J. Crush, *The Struggle for Swazi Labour 1890–1920* (Kingston and Montreal: McGill–Queen's University Press, 1987) p. 203.
16. R. Hyam, *The Failure of South African Expansion 1908–1948* (New York: African Publishing Corporation, 1972) p. 82.
17. Hyam, pp. 130–42.
18. Breytenbach, p. 52.

19. B. M. Khaketla, *Lesotho 1970: An African Coup under the Microscope* (Berkeley and Los Angeles, Cal.: University of California Press, 1972) pp. 63–4.

20. Khaketla, p. 16.

21. J. E. Bardill and J. H. Cobbe, *Lesotho: Dilemmas of Dependence in Southern Africa* (Boulder, Col.: Westview Press, 1985).

22. Khaketla, p. 54.

23. Ibid., p. 12.

24. B. J. Harris, 'Nationalism and Development in Southern Africa: The Case of Lesotho' (unpublished Ph.D. dissertation, Brown University, 1982) p. 127.

25. P. Wellings, 'The "Relative Autonomy" of the Basotho State: Internal and External Determinants of Lesotho's Political Economy', *Political Geography Quarterly*, 4, 3 (1985) p. 197.

26. P. A. Wellings, 'Lesotho: Crisis and Development in the Rural Sector', *Geoforum*, 17, 2 (1986) p. 219.

27. P. A. Wellings, 'Lesotho: Crisis. . .', p. 221.

28. P. Wellings, 'The "Relative Autonomy". . .', p. 196.

29. Ibid., p. 195.

30. Bardill and Cobbe, pp. 63–4.

31. Chamber of Mines of South Africa, *The South African Mining Industry: Facts and Figures* (Johannesburg: Chamber of Mines of South Africa, 1988) p. 11.

32. J. Cobbe, 'Lesotho: What Will Happen after Apartheid Goes?' *Africa Today*, 38, 1 (1991) p. 19.

33. J. Crush, 'The Extrusion of Foreign Labour from the South Africa Gold Mining Industry', *Geoforum*, 17, 2 (1986). pp. 162–3.

34. Ibid., p. 162.

35. Ibid., p. 164.

36. Ibid., p. 169.

37. Bardill and Cobbe, p. 80.

38. J. Cobbe, 'Lesotho: What Will Happen . . .', p. 27.

39. Economic Intelligence Quarterly, *Lesotho Country Report*, 1 (London: 1988) p. 45.

40. Economic Intelligence Quarterly, *Lesotho Country Report*, 1 (London: 1990) p. 40.

41. Ibid., p. 41.

42. Bardill and Cobbe, p. 63.

43. 'Lesotho's Military Leader Ousted by Army Officers', *New York Times*, 1 May 1991, p. 7.

44. P. A. Wellings, 'Lesotho: Crisis. . .', p. 219.

45. Ibid., p. 221.

46. B. J. Harris, 'Providing Grassroots Social Services to Women and Children in Rural Southern Africa: A Roundtable Discussion', *Frontiers*, 10, 1 (1988) pp. 83–7.

47. Hunter, p. 1.

48. Ibid., p. 42.

49. Ibid., p. 69.

50. Ibid., p. 98.

51. John Gay, *Report on a Survey of Spinners and Spinning Cooperatives for CARE and Lesotho Handspun Mohair* (Maseru, Lesotho: CARE, 1985) p. 40.
52. Hunter, p. 102.
53. Ibid., p. 124.
54. Ibid., pp. 124–5.
55. Ibid., p. 127.
56. Ibid., p. 126.
57. Ibid., p. 153.
58. Ibid., p. 169.
59. J. Molefi, 'Final Agreement Signed between LNDC and Shanghai Corporation on Wool and Mohair Scouring Project', *LNDC Newsletter*, IV (1987) pp. 2–3.
60. C. M. Rogerson, 'Reviving Old Technology?: Rural Handicraft Production in Southern Africa', *Geoforum*, 17, 2 (1986) pp. 176–7.
61. Judith Gay, *Women and Development in Lesotho* (Maseru: USAID, 1982) p. 47.
62. John Gay, p. 2.
63. Ibid., p. 44.
64. J. Molefi, 'Prime Minister Assures Potential Investors Healthy Labour Climate in Lesotho', *LNDC Newsletter*, IV (1984) pp. 4–5.
65. J. Molefi, 'Existing Large Investments in Lesotho', *LNDC Newsletter*, IV (1985) pp. 4–5.
66. J. Molefi, '1987 Was a Year of Action for LNDC', *LNDC Newsletter*, I (1988) pp. 6–7.
67. J. Molefi, 'Upward Trend in Basotho Miners' Remittances from Gold Mines', *LNDC Newsletter*, I (1987) p. 11.
68. E. Gordon, 'An Analysis of the Impact of Labour Migration on the Lives of Women in Lesotho' in N. Nelson (ed.) *African Women in the Development Process* (Totowa: Frank Cass, 1981); C. Murray, 'Migrant Labour and Changing Family Structure', *Journal of Southern African Studies*, 6, 2 (1980).
69. Gordon, pp. 57–76.
70. Ibid., p. 61.
71. C. Murray, *Families Divided* (Cambridge University Press, 1981) p. 154.

CHAPTER 8: A SADCC COMPARISON

1. S. Amin, 'Preface' in S. Amin, D. Chitala and I. Mandaza (eds), *SADCC: Prospects for Disengagement and Development in Southern Africa* (London: Zed Books, 1987) p. 1.
2. D. Mbilima, 'Regional Organisations in Southern Africa' in A. Whiteside (ed.), *Industrialisation and Investment Incentives in Southern Africa* (London: James Currey Publishers, 1989) p. 33.
3. D. B. Ndlela, 'The Manufacturing Sector in the Southern African Subregion, with Emphasis on SADCC', in S. Amin, D. Chitala and I. Mandaza (eds), *SADCC: Prospects for Disengagement and Development in Southern Africa* (London: Zed Books, 1987) pp. 37–41.

4. P. Selwyn, *Industries in the Southern African Periphery* (Boulder, Col.: Westview Press, 1975).

5. D. Chitala, 'The Political Economy of SADCC and Imperialism's Response' in S. Amin, D. Chitala and I. Mandaza (eds), *SADCC: Prospects for Disengagement and Development in Southern Africa* (London: Zed Books, 1987) p. 35.

6. W. Minter, *Portuguese Africa and the West* (New York: Monthly Review Press, 1974).

7. T. Ostergaard, *SADCC Beyond Transportation: The Challenge to Industrial Cooperation* (Uppsala: Scandinavian Institute of African Studies, 1989) p. 14.

8. R. Peet, *Manufacturing Industry and Economic Development in the SADCC Countries* (Stockholm and Uppsala: The Beijer Institute and The Scandinavian Institute of African Studies, 1984) p. 38.

9. Ostergaard, p. 23.

10. R. F. Weisfelder, 'The Southern African Development Coordination Conference: A New Factor in the Liberation Process' in Thomas M. Callaghy (ed.) *South Africa in Southern Africa* (New York: Praeger, 1983) p. 241; R. Leys and A. Tostensen, 'Regional Cooperation in Southern Africa: The Southern African Development Coordination Conference', *Review of Africa Political Economy*, 23 (1982) p. 52.

11. Weisfelder, p. 238; J. Matthews, 'Economic Integration in Southern Africa: Progress or Decline?', *South African Journal of Economics*, 52, 3 (1984) p. 260.

12. Ibid., p. 240; C. R. Hill, 'Regional Cooperation in Southern Africa', *African Affairs*, 82, 327 (1983) p. 215.

13. Ostergaard, p. 13.

14. E. A. Friedland, 'The Southern African Development Coordination Conference and the West: Cooperation or Conflict?' *The Journal of Modern African Studies*, 23, 2 (1985) p. 288.

15. Peet, p. 34.

16. J. Edlin, 'Key to Southern Africa's Economic Independence', *Africa Report* (1983) p. 45.

17. Peet, p. 28.

18. Hill, p. 223; Weisfelder, p. 262.

19. D. G. Anglin, 'SADCC After Nkomati', *African Affairs*, 84, 335 (1985) p. 179.

20. J. Isaksen, 'Industrial Development in Post-Apartheid Southern Africa. Some Issues for Further Research in a SADRA/Nordic Context' in B, Oden and H. Othman (eds), *Regional Cooperation in Southern Africa: A Post-Apartheid Perspective* (Uppsala: The Scandinavian Institute of African Studies, 1989) p. 208.

21. S. Amin, 'Introduction' in S. Amin, D. Chitala and I. Mandaza (eds), *SADCC: Prospects for Disengagement and Development in Southern Africa* (London: Zed Books, 1987) p. 3.

22. Ostergaard, pp. 53–4.

23. Ibid., p. 55.

24. Ibid., p. 54.

25. Peet, p. 75.

26. E. Brown, 'Foreign Aid to SADCC: An Analysis of the Reagan Administration's Foreign Policy, *Issue*, 12, 3/4 (1982) pp. 33–4.
27. V. Padaychee, 'Apartheid South Africa and the International Monetary Fund', *Transformation*, 3 (1987) pp. 43–5.
28. Padaychee, p. 46.
29. Ibid., p. 48.
30. Ibid., pp. 51–2.
31. Ibid., pp. 52–3.
32. Ibid., p. 71.
33. Ibid., pp. 71 and 74.
34. Brown, p. 30.
35. Ibid., p. 31.
36. E. Frey-Wouters, *The European Community and the Third World: The Lome Convention and Its Impact* (New York: Praeger, 1980) p. 22.
37. Frey-Wouters, pp. 26–30.
38. Peet, p. 71–4.
39. Ndlela, p. 40.
40. A. J. Nsekela (ed.), *Southern Africa: Toward Economic Liberation* (London: Rex Collings, 1981) pp. 194–7.
41. Nsekela, pp. 200–1.
42. Ibid., p. 205.
43. Ibid., pp. 206–7.
44. Ibid., p. 202.
45. Peet, p. 64.
46. Ostergaard, p. 7.
47. Ibid., p. 17.
48. 'Swaziland Mechanised Farming Revives Tinkhabi Project', *The Swazi Sunday Mirror*, 16 October 1988, p. 8.
49. Friedland, p. 308.
50. Ibid., p. 311.
51. Ibid., p. 313.
52. *Southern African Development Coordination Conference: A Handbook* (Gaberone: SADCC Secretariat, 1984).
53. Weisfelder, p. 247.
54. Peet, p. v.
55. Anglin, p. 173.
56. Ostergaard, p. 40.
57. Ibid., p. 44.
58. Ibid., p. 41.
59. Ibid., p. 45.
60. Ibid., p. 46.
61. Ibid., p. 50.
62. Ibid., p. 52–3.
63. Ibid., p. 98.
64. Ibid., p. 99.
65. Ibid., p. 80.
66. Ibid., p. 81.
67. Ibid., p. 95.
68. Ibid., p. 92.

69. Ibid., p. 90.
70. Ibid., p. 107.
71. Leys and Tostensen, p. 56.
72. A. Tostensen, *Dependence and Collective Self-Reliance in Southern Africa: The Case of the Southern African Development Coordination Conference* (Uppsala: Scandinavian Institute of African Studies, 1982) p. 112.
73. Ostergaard, 84.
74. SADCC, 'SADCC Industrial Development Activity' (Dar es Salaam: SADCC Industry and Trade Coordination Unit, 1984).
75. S. Sassen, *The Mobility of Labour and Capital* (Cambridge: Cambridge University Press, 1988) pp. 102–3.
76. Mbilima, p. 31.
77. Ndlela, pp. 52–4.
78. G. N. Mudenda, 'The Development of a Local Technological Capacity in the SADCC Region' S. Amin, D. Chitala and I. Mandaza (eds), *SADCC: Prospects for Disengagement and Development in Southern Africa* (London: Zed Books, 1987) pp. 128–46.

CHAPTER 9: CONCLUSION: COTTAGE INDUSTRIES, FACTORIES AND FEMALE WAGE LABOUR

1. H. I. Safa, 'Runaway Shops and Female Employment: The Search for Cheap Labour', *Signs*, 37, 2 (1981) pp. 427–8.
2. B. J. Harris, 'Ethnicity and Gender in the Global Periphery: A Comparison of Basotho and Navajo Women', *American Indian Culture and Research Journal*, 14, 4 (1990) p. 25.

References

ARTICLES

ANGLIN, D. G., 'SADCC After Nkomati', *African Affairs*, 84, 335 (1985) pp. 163–81.
AYEE, J. R. A., 'Swaziland and the Southern African Customs Union', *Journal of African Studies*, 3/4 (1988) pp. 61–70.
BELL, T., 'International Competition and Industrial Decentralisation in South Africa', *World Development*, 13, 10/11 (1987) pp. 1291–1307.
BISCHOFF, P.-H., 'Why Swaziland is Different: An Explanation of the Kingdom's Political Position in Southern Africa', *The Journal of Modern African Studies*, 26, 3 (1988) pp. 457-71.
BOOTH, A. R., 'South Africa's Hinterland: Swaziland's Role in Strategies for Sanctions-Breaking', *Africa Today*, 26, 1 (1989) pp. 41–50.
BOZZOLI, A. B., 'The Origins, Development and Ideology of Local Manufacturing in South Africa', *Journal of Southern African Studies*, 1, 2 (1975) pp. 194–214.
BROWN, B. B., 'The Impact of Male Labour Migration on Women in Botswana', *African Affairs*, 82, 328 (1983) pp. 367–88.
BROWN, E., 'Foreign Aid to SADCC: An Analysis of the Reagan Administration's Foreign Policy', *Issue*, 12, 3/4 (1982) pp. 27–36.
BURNE, S. and M. HARDINGHAM, 'Textiles: Options for a Viable Future', *Appropriate Technology*, 15, 2 (1988) pp. 1–4.
COBBE, J., 'Lesotho: What Will Happen after Apartheid Goes?' *Africa Today*, 38, 1 (1991).
CRUSH, J., 'The Extrusion of Foreign Labour from the South Africa Gold Mining Industry', *Geoforum*, 17, 2 (1986) pp. 161–72.
DE VLETTER, F., 'Labour Migration in Swaziland: Recent Trends and Implications', *South African Labour Bulletin*, 7, 6/7 (1982) pp. 114–37.
EDLIN, J., 'Key to Southern Africa's Economic Independence', *Africa Report* (1983) pp. 43–6.
FRANSMAN, M., 'Labour, Capital and the State in Swaziland, 1962–1977', *South African Labour Bulletin*, 7, 6/7 (1982) pp. 58–89.
FRIEDLAND, E. A., 'The Southern African Development Coordination Conference and the West: Cooperation or Conflict?' *The Journal of Modern African Studies*, 23, 2 (1985) pp. 287–314.
GORDON, E., 'An Analysis of the Impact of Labour Migration on the Lives of Women in Lesotho' in N. Nelson (ed.), *African Women in the Development Process*, (Totowa: Frank Cass, 1981) pp. 57–76.
GRAVES, A. and P. RICHARDSON, 'Plantations in the Political Economy of Colonial Sugar Production: Natal and Queensland, 1860–1914, *Journal of Southern African Studies*, 6, 2 (1980) pp. 214–29.
GRAY, H. P., 'The Multi-Fibre Arrangement and the Least Developed Countries', *Industry and Development*, 26 (1989) pp. 89–96.

HARRIS, B.J., 'Providing Grassroots Social Services to Women and Children in Rural Southern Africa: A Roundtable Discussion', *Frontiers*, 10, 1 (1988) pp. 83–7.

HARRIS, B.J., 'Ethnicity and Gender in the Southern African Periphery: A Comparison of Basotho and Navajo Women', *American Indian Culture and Research Journal*, 14, 4 (1990) pp. 15–38.

HILL, C.R., 'Regional Co-operation in Southern Africa', *African Affairs*, 82, 327 (1983) pp. 215–39.

HIRSCH, A., 'An Introduction to Textile Worker Organisation in Natal', *South African Labour Bulletin*, 4, 8 (1976) pp. 1–10.

INNIS, D. and D. O'MEARA, 'Class Formation and Ideology: The Transkei Region', *Review of African Political Economy*, 7 (1976) pp. 69–86.

LANDELL-MILLS, P.M., 'The 1969 Southern African Customs Union Agreement', *The Journal of Modern African Studies*, 9, 2 (1971) pp. 263–81.

LEVIN, R., 'Uneven Development in Swaziland: Tibiyo, Sugar Production and Rural Development Strategy', *Geoforum*, 12, 2 (1986) pp. 239–50.

LEYS, R. and A. TOSTENSEN, 'Regional Cooperation in Southern Africa: The Southern African Development Coordination Conference', *Review of African Political Economy*, 23, (1982) pp. 52–71.

LINCOLN, D., 'South African Sugar Mill Labour during the 1970s', *South African Labour Bulletin*, 6, 6 (1981) pp. 37–48.

MACMILLAN, H., 'Swaziland: Decolonisation and the Triumph of "Tradition"', *The Journal of Modern African Studies*, 23, 4 (1985) pp. 643–66.

MATTHEWS, J., 'Economic Integration in Southern Africa: Progress or Decline?', *South African Journal of Economics*, 52, 3 (1984) pp. 256–65.

McFADDEN, P., 'Women in Wage-Labour in Swaziland: A Focus on Agriculture', *South African Labour Bulletin*, VII (1982) pp. 140–66.

MURRAY, C., 'From Granary to Labour Reserve: An Economic History of Lesotho', *South African Labour Bulletin*, 6, 4 (1980) pp. 3–20.

MURRAY, C., 'Migrant Labour and Changing Family Structure', *Journal of Southern African Studies*, 6, 2 (1980) pp. 139–156.

Natal Labour Research Group, 'Control Over a Workforce – The Case of Frame', *South African Labour Bulletin*, 8, 5 (1980) pp. 17–47.

PADAYCHEE, V., 'Apartheid South Africa and the International Monetary Fund', *Transformation*, 3 (1987).

PICKLES, J. and J. WOODS, 'Taiwanese Investment in South Africa', *African Affairs*, 88, 353 (1989) pp. 507–28.

POLLAK, H.P., 'An Analysis of the Contributions to Family Support of Women Industrial Workers on the Witwatersrand', *South African Journal of Science*, 28 (1931) pp. 572–82.

PRINGLE, W.A. and J.A. DOCKEL, 'The South African Angora Goat and Mohair Industry', *South African Journal of Economics*, 57, 3 (1989) pp. 215–30.

ROBERT, A., 'The Effects of the International Division of Labour of Female Workers in the Textile and Clothing Industries', *Development and Change*, 14, 1 (1983) pp. 19–37.

ROGERSON, C.M., 'Reviving Old Technology?: Rural Handicraft Production in Southern Africa', *Geoforum*, 17, 2 (1986) pp. 173–85.

SAFA, H.I., 'Runaway Shops and Female Employment: The Search for Cheap Labour', *Signs*, 7, 2 (1981) pp. 418–33.

SHAW, T.M., 'International Stratification in Africa: Sub-Imperialism in Southern and Eastern Africa', *Journal of Southern African Affairs*, (April 1977) pp. 145–63.

TEAL, P., 'Unravelling the Cottage Problems', *Appropriate Technology*, 15, 2 (1988) pp. 23–5.

TURNER, M., 'A Fresh Start for the Southern African Customs Union', *African Affairs*, 70, 280 (1971) pp. 269–76.

WELLINGS, P.A., 'Lesotho: Crisis and Development in the Rural Sector', *Geoforum*, 17, 2 (1986) pp. 217–37.

WELLINGS, P., 'The "Relative Autonomy" of the Basotho State: Internal and External Determinants of Lesotho's Political Economy', *Political Geography Quarterly*, 4, 3 (1985) pp. 191–218.

WELLINGS, P. and A. BLACK, 'Industrial Decentralisation under Apartheid: The Relocation of Industry to the South Africa Periphery', *World Development*, 14, 1 (1986) pp. 1–38.

WINTER, I., 'The Post-Colonial State and the Forces and Relations of Production: Swaziland', *Review of African Political Economy*, 9 (1974) pp. 27–43.

YAWITCH, J., 'The Incorporation of African Women into Wage Labour 1950–80', *South African Labour Bulletin*, 10, 3 (1983) pp. 82–93.

YOUE, C.P., 'Imperial Land Policy in Swaziland and the African Response', *Journal of Imperial and Commonwealth History*, 7 (1978) pp. 56–70.

BOOKS

ARMSTRONG, A. and R.T. NHLAPO, *Law and the Other Sex: The Legal Position of Women in Swaziland* (Mbabane: Webster Print, n.d.).

BARDILL, J.E. and J.H. COBBE, *Lesotho: Dilemmas of Dependence in Southern Africa* (Boulder, Col.: Westview Press, 1985).

BONNER, P., *Kings, Commoners and Concessionaries* (Johannesburg: Ravan Press, 1983).

BOOTH A.R., *Swaziland: Tradition and Change in a Southern African Kingdom* (Boulder, Col.: Westview Press, 1983).

BOOTH, A.R., *Tradition and Change in a Southern African Kingdom* (Boulder, Col.: Westview Press, 1983).

BOSERUP, E., *Women's Role in Economic Development* (New York: St. Martin's Press, 1970).

BRAVERMAN, H., *Labour and Monopoly Capital* (New York: Monthly Review Press, 1974).

BREYTENBACH, W.J., *Crocodiles and Commoners in Lesotho: Continuity and Change in the Rulemaking System of the Kingdom of Lesotho*, No. 24 (Pretoria: Communications of the Africa Institute, 1975).

CALLINICOS, L., *A People's History of South Africa: Gold and Workers 1886–1924, Vol. 1* (Johannesburg: Ravan Press, 1985).

CRUSH, J., *The Struggle for Swazi Labour 1890–1920* (Kingston and Montreal: McGill–Queen's University Press, 1987).

DAVIES, R. H., D. O'MEARA and S. DLAMINI, *The Kingdom of Swaziland: A Profile* (London: Zed Books, 1985).

DINHAM B., and C. HINES, *Agribusiness in Africa* (Trenton: Africa World Press, 1984).

EDGAR, R., *Prophets with Honour: A Documentary History of Lekhotla la Bafo* (Johannesburg: Ravan Press, 1987).

FREY-WOUTERS, E., *The European Community and the Third World: The Lome Convention and Its Impact* (New York: Praeger, 1980).

GULLICKSON, G., *Spinners and Weavers of Auffay* (Cambridge University Press, 1986).

HYAM, R., *The Failure of South African Expansion 1908–1948* (New York: African Publishing Corporation, 1972).

INNES, D., *Anglo American and the Rise of Modern South Africa* (New York: Monthly Review Press, 1984).

KAYONGO-MALE, D. and P. ONYANGO, *The Sociology of the African Family*, 2nd edn (London and New York: Longman, 1986).

KHAKETLA, B. M., *Lesotho 1970: An African Coup under the Microscope* (Berkeley and Los Angeles, Calif.: University of California Press, 1972).

KUPER, H., *The Swazi: A Southern African Kingdom*, 2nd edn (New York: Holt, Rhinehart and Winston, 1986).

MATSEBULA, J. S. M., *History of Swaziland* (Cape Town: Longman, 1976).

MINTER, W. *Portuguese Africa and the West* (New York: Monthly Review Press, 1974).

MURRAY, C., *Families Divided* (Cambridge University Press, 1981).

NASH, J. (ed.), *Women, Men and the International Division of Labour* (Albany, New York; State University of New York Press, 1983).

NKESELA, A. J. (ed.), *Southern Africa: Toward Economic Liberation* (London: Rex Collings, 1981).

NORVAL, A. J., *A Quarter of a Century of Industrial Progress in South Africa* (Cape Town: Juta & Co. Ltd, 1962).

OSTERGAARD, T., *SADCC Beyond Transportation: The Challenge to Industrial Cooperation* (Uppsala: Scandinavian Institute of African Studies, 1989).

PEET, R., *Manufacturing Industry and Economic Development in the SADCC Countries* (Stockholm and Uppsala: The Beijer Institute and The Scandinavian Institute of African Studies, 1984).

SASSEN, S., *The Mobility of Labour and Capital* (Cambridge University Press, 1988).

SCHMIECHEN, J. A., *Sweated Industries and Sweated Labour* (Urbana and Chicago, Ill.: University of Illinois Press, 1984).

SELWYN, P., *Industries in the Southern African Periphery* (Boulder, Col.: Westview Press, 1975).

STADLER, A. *The Political Economy of Modern South Africa* (New York: St. Martin's Press, 1987).

THOMPSON, L., *Survival in Two Worlds: Moshoeshoe of Lesotho 1786–1870* (London: Oxford University Press, 1975).

THOMPSON, P., *The Nature of Work: An Introduction to Debates on the Labour Process*, 2nd edn (London: Macmillan, 1989).

TILLY, L. and J. SCOTT, *Women, Work and Family*, 2nd edn (Boston, Mass.: Routledge & Hall, 1989).

TOSTENSEN, A., *Dependence and Collective Self-Reliance in Southern Africa: The Case of the Southern African Development Coordination Conference* (Uppsala: Scandinavian Institute of African Studies, 1982).

CHAPTERS

AMIN, S., 'Introduction' in S. Amin, D. Chitala and I. Mandaza (eds), *SADCC: Prospects for Disengagement and Development in Southern Africa* (London: Zed Books, 1987) pp. 8–12.

AMIN, S., 'Preface' in S. Amin, D. Chitala and I. Mandaza (eds) *SADCC: Prospects for Disengagement and Development in Southern Africa* (London: Zed Books, 1987) pp. 1–7.

BERGER, I., 'Solidary Fragmented: Garment Workers of the Transvaal, 1930–1960' in Shula Marks and Stanley Trapido (eds), *The Politics of Race, Class and Nationalism in Twentieth Century South Africa* (London and New York: Longman, 1987) pp. 124–55.

BRINK, E., '"Maar 'n klomp 'factory' meide": Afrikaner Family and Community on the Witwatersrand during the 1920s' in Belinda Bozzoli (ed.), *Class, Community and Conflict: South African Perspectives* (Johannesburg: Ravan Press, 1987) pp. 177–208.

CHITALA, D., 'The Political Economy of SADCC and Imperialism's Response' in S. Amin, D. Chitala and I. Mandaza (eds), *SADCC: Prospects for Disengagement and Development in Southern Africa* (London: Zed Books, 1987) pp. 13–36.

DE VLETTER, F., 'Footloose Foreign Investment in Swaziland' in A. Whiteside (ed.), *Industrialisation and Investment Incentives in Southern Africa* (London: James Currey Publishers, 1989) pp. 143–66.

FREUND, B., 'The Social Character of Secondary Industry in South Africa: 1915–1945', ch. 5 in A. Mabin (ed.), *Organisation and Economic Change* (Johannesburg: Ravan Press, 1898) pp. 78–119.

GORDON, E., 'An Analysis of the Impact of Labour Migration on the Lives of Women in Lesotho' in N. Nelson (ed.), *African Women in the Development Process* (Totowa: Frank Cass, 1981).

ISAKSEN, J., 'Industrial Development in Post-Apartheid Southern Africa. Some Issues for Further Research in a SADRA/Nordic Context' in B. Oden and H. Othman (eds), *Regional Cooperation in Southern Africa: A Post-Apartheid Perspective* (Uppsala: The Scandinavian Institute of African Studies, 1989) pp. 199–218.

KIMBLE, J., 'Labour Migration in Basutoland c. 1870–1885' in S. Marks and R. Rathbone (eds), *Industrialisation and Social Change in South Africa: African Class Formation, Culture and Consciousness* (London: Longman, 1982) pp. 119–41.

KUPER, H., 'Colour, Categories and Colonialism: The Swazi Case' in V. Turner (ed.), *Colonialism in Africa 1870–1960*, vol. 3 (Cambridge University Press, 1971) pp. 286–309.

LEVIN, R., 'Contract Farming in Swaziland', *Social Relations in Rural Swaziland: Critical Analyses* (Kwaluseni: Social Science Research Unit, University of Swaziland, 1987) pp. 180–1.

LEWIS, J., 'Solly Sachs and the Garment Workers' Union' in Eddie Webster (ed.), *Essays in Southern African Labour History* (Johannesburg: Ravan Press, 1978) p. 182–4.

MATTHEWS, K., '"Squatters" on Private Tenure Farms in Swaziland: A Preliminary Investigation' in M. Neocosmos (ed.), *Social Relations in Rural Swaziland: Critical Analyses* (Kwaluseni: Social Science Research Unit, University of Swaziland, 1987) pp. 191–216.

MAWBEY, J., 'Afrikaner Women of the Garment Union during the Thirties and Forties' in Eddie Webster (ed.), *Essays in South African Labour History* (Johannesburg: Ravan Press, 1978) pp. 192–206.

MBILIMA, D., 'Regional Organisations in Southern Africa' in A. Whiteside (ed.), *Industrialisation and Investment Incentives in Southern Africa* (London: James Currey Publishers, 1989) pp. 31–44.

MUDENDA, G. N., 'The Development of a Local Technological Capacity in the SADCC Region' in S. Amin, D, Chitala and I. Mandaza (eds), *SADCC: Prospects for Disengagement and Development in Southern Africa* (London: Zed Books, 1987) pp. 128–46.

NASH, J., 'Introduction' in J. Nash and P. Fernandez-Kelly (eds), *Women, Men and the International Division of Labour* (Albany: State University of New York Press, 1983) pp. vii–xv.

NDLELA, D. B., 'The Manufacturing Sector in the Southern African Sub-region, with Emphasis on SADCC' in S. Amin, D. Chitala and I. Mandaza (eds), *SADCC: Prospects for Disengagement and Development in Southern Africa* (London: Zed Books, 1987) pp. 37–61.

NEOCOSMOS, M., 'Homogeneity and Differences on Swazi Nation Land' in M. Neocosmos (ed.), *Social Relations in Rural Swaziland: Critical Analyses* (Kwaluseni: Social Science Research Unit, University of Swaziland, 1987) pp. 17–79.

POSEL, D., '"Providing for the Legitimate Labour Requirements of Employers": Secondary Industry, Commerce and the State in South Africa during the 1950s and Early 1960s' in Alan Mabin (ed.), *Organisation and Economic Change*, vol. 5 (Johannesburg: Ravan Press, 1989) pp. 199–220.

STANDING, H., 'Gender Relations and Social Transformation in Swaziland' in M. Neocosmos (ed.), *Social Relations in Rural Swaziland: Critical Analyses* (Kwaluseni: Social Science Research Unit, University of Swaziland, 1987) pp. 127–49.

WARD, K., 'Introduction and Overview' in K. Ward (ed.), *Women Workers and Global Restructuring* (Ithaca, NY: Cornell University Press, 1990) pp. 1–22.

WEBSTER, E., 'Introduction', Section 2, *Essays in Southern African Labour History* (Johannesburg: Ravan Press, 1978) p. 68.

WEISFELDER, R. F., 'The Southern African Development Coordination Conference: A New Factor in the Liberation Process' in Thomas M. Callaghy (ed.), *South Africa in Southern Africa* (New York: Praeger, 1983) pp. 237–66.

NEWSPAPER ARTICLES, NEWSLETTERS AND OTHER
PERIODICALS

ECONOMIC INTELLIGENCE QUARTERLY, Lesotho Country Report, 1
(London, 1988).
ECONOMIC INTELLIGENCE QUARTERLY, Lesotho Country Report, 1
(London, 1990).
M. MATSEBULA, 'Academic View of Withdrawal from Customs Union',
The Swazi Sunday Mirror, 30 October 1988, p. 1.
MOLEFI, J., 'Prime Minister Assures Potential Investors Healthy Labour
Climate in Lesotho', *LNDC Newsletter*, IV (1984).
MOLEFI, J., 'Existing Large Investments in Lesotho', *LNDC Newsletter*, IV
(1985).
MOLEFI, J., 'Upward Trend in Basotho Miners' Remittances from Gold
Mines', *LNDC Newsletter*, I (1987).
MOLEFI, J., 'Final Agreement Signed between LNDC and Shanghai
Corporation on Wool and Mohair Scouring Project', *LNDC Newsletter*,
IV (1987).
MOLEFI, J., '1987 Was a Year of Action for LNDC', *LNDC Newsletter*, I
(1988).
NEW YORK TIMES, 'Lesotho's Military Leader Ousted', 1 May 1991, p. 7.
THE SWAZI SUNDAY MIRROR, 'Swaziland Mechanised Farming Revives
Tinkhabi Project', 16 October 1988, p. 8.
THE SWAZI OBSERVER, 'Swaziland's Birth Rate "Highest in the World"',
24 February 1989, p. 1.
THE SWAZI OBSERVER, 'Tycoon Kirsh Under Fire From SFTU', 3 May
1989, p. 1.
THE TIMES OF SWAZILAND, 'E7 Civil Works on EEC Dams', 30
September 1988, p. 7.
THE TIMES OF SWAZILAND, 'Cotton's Best Season', 13 October 1988, p. 7.
THE TIMES OF SWAZILAND, 'Massive Rise in Local Sugar Sales', 16
November 1988, p. 7.
THE TIMES OF SWAZILAND, 'Tongaat-Hulett Earnings Are Up', 17
November 1988, p. 7.
THE TIMES OF SWAZILAND, '1988: A Record Year for Swazi Cotton', 22
November 1988, pp. 10–11.
THE TIMES OF SWAZILAND, '1988: A Record Year for Swazi Cotton', 22
November 1988, p. 11.
THE TIMES OF SWAZILAND, 'Where Tinkundla Needs Change', 7
February 1989. p. 8.
THE TIMES OF SWAZILAND, 'Zwane Pamphlets Probe', 11 March 1989,
p. 1.
THE TIMES OF SWAZILAND, 'Nine Thrown in Jail for 60 Days', 13 March
1989, p. 1.
THE TIMES OF SWAZILAND, 'Fear of the Death Threats', 14 March 1989,
p. 1.
THE TIMES OF SWAZILAND, 'Jail Bust "Tools Found"', 20 March 1989,
p. 1.

THE TIMES OF SWAZILAND, 'Truck Kills 11 Men', 25 March 1989, p. 1.
THE TIMES OF SWAZILAND, 'Cotton: What Collapse?', 12 April 1989, p. 7.
THE TIMES OF SWAZILAND, 'Harvest Joy for Hhohho', 27 April 1989, p. 1.
THE TIMES OF SWAZILAND, 'Citrus at Ubombo?', 8 May 1989, p.6.
THE TIMES OF SWAZILAND, 'Cotton Warning: No Polypropylene', 23 May 1989, p. 7.
THE TIMES OF SWAZILAND, 'Banks Strike is Off', 20 June 1989, p. 1.
THE TIMES OF SWAZILAND, 'Banks Crisis is Over', 27 July 1989, p. 1.
THE TIMES OF SWAZILAND, 'Kirsh Plans E 1 Billion Textile Plants', 4 August 1989, p. 1.
THE TIMES OF SWAZILAND, 'Cotton Heading for Another Record', 15 August 1989, p. 9.
THE TIMES OF SWAZILAND, 'Irrigation: Expansion Headache', 15 August 1989, p. 9.
WEEKLY MAIL, 'ANC Campaigns to Stop Debt Rescheduling', 21–27 July 1989, p. 15.
WEEKLY MAIL, 'South Africa and the Soviets: From Cold War to Hot Peace', 3–9 March 1989, p. 15.

REPORTS

ARMSTRONG, A., *A Sample Survey of Women in Wage Employment in Swaziland* (Kwaluseni: Social Science Research Unit, University of Swaziland, 1985).
CENTRAL STATISTICAL OFFICE, *Report on the 1986 Swaziland Population Census* (Mbabane: Apollo Printers, n.d.).
CHAMBER OF MINES OF SOUTH AFRICA, *The South African Mining Industry: Facts and Figures* (Johannesburg: Chamber of Mines of South Africa, 1988).
DURDLE, WAYNE, *Tibiyo Goat Project Reports* (Malkerns: Tibiyo Agricultural Projects, 1981–85).
DORAN, A AND WHELLER, G., *Swazi Textile Corporation (SWATEX) LTD Swaziland: Appraisal Report* (London: Commonwealth Development Corporation, 1984).
FOOD AND AGRICULTURE ORGANISATION, *Cotton Development in Swaziland* (Rome: Food and Agriculture Organisation, 1981).
GAY, JOHN, *Report on a Survey of Spinners and Spinning Cooperatives for CARE and Lesotho Handspun Mohair* (Maseru, Lesotho: CARE, 1985).
GAY, JUDITH, *Women and Development in Lesotho* (Maseru: USAID, 1982).
GOVERNMENT OF SWAZILAND, *Fourth National Development Plan 1983/84–1987/88* (Mbabane: Swaziland Printing and Publishing Company, 1983).
GOVERNMENT OF SWAZILAND, *The Regulations of Wages (Manufacturing and Processing Industry) Order*, Legal Notice No. 33 (Mbabane: Government Printing Office, 1988).

HUNTER, J. P., *The Economics of Wool and Mohair Production and Marketing in Lesotho*, ISAS Research Report No. 16 (Roma: Institute of Southern African Studies, 1987).

HUNTING TECHNICAL SERVICES LTD, *Review of Rural Development Areas: Interim Report* (Mbabane: Government of Swaziland, 1983).

LOUGHRAN, L. and ARGO, J., *Assessment of Handicraft Training Needs for Rural Women in Swaziland*, 1 (Mbabane: TransCentury Corporation, 1986).

MINISTRY OF AGRICULTURE, *Cotton Breeding in Swaziland* (Mbabane: Ministry of Agriculture, 1968).

NGUBANE, H, 'The Swazi Homestead' in F. de Vletter (ed.), *The Swazi Rural Homestead*, (Kwaluseni: Social Science Research Unit, University of Swaziland, 1983).

OLIVIER, J. W., Manager, The Employment Bureau of Africa Limited. Letter to Head of Research, Central Bank of Swaziland, 7 February 1989

ROSEN-PRINZ, B. and F. PRINZ, *Migrant Labour and Rural Homesteads: An Investigation into the Sociological Dimensions of the Migrant Labour System in Swaziland*, World Employment Programme Working Paper (Geneva: International Labour Organisation, 1978).

RUSSELL, M., 'The Production and Marketing of Swazi Women's Handicrafts', *Interim Report for ILO/DANIDA Project* (University of Swaziland: January–June, 1983).

RUSSELL, M., P. DLAMINI and F. SIMELANE, *Report on a Sample Survey of Women in Women in Development Project, Entfonjeni, Swaziland* (Kwaluseni: Social Science Research Unit, University of Swaziland for United Nations Children's Fund, 1984) p. 24.

RWOMIRE, A., *The Family Life Association of Swaziland: An Evaulation of Selected Programs* (Manzini: The Family Life Association, 1989).

SADCC, *SADCC Industrial Development Activity* (Dar es Salaam: SADCC Industry and Trade Coordination Unit, 1984).

SADCC, *Southern African Development Coordination Conference: A Handbook* (Gaberone: SADCC Secretariat. 1984).

SWAZILAND COTTON BOARD, *Annual Report and Accounts* (Manzini, Swaziland Cotton Board, 1988) p. 6.

TOMLINSON, F. R., *Summary of the Report of the Commission for the Socio-Economic Development of the Bantu Areas within the Union of South Africa* (Pretoria: The Government Printer, 1955) p. 35.

THESES AND DISSERTATIONS

ETTINGER, S. J., 'The Economics of the Customs Union between Botswana, Lesotho, Swaziland and South Africa' (unpublished Ph.D. dissertation, University of Michigan, 1974).

HARRIS, B. J., 'Nationalism and Development in Southern Africa: The Case of Lesotho' (unpublished Ph.D. dissertation, Brown University, 1982).

NICOL, M., 'A History of Garment and Tailoring Workers in Cape Town 1900–1939' (unpublished Ph.D. dissertation, University of Cape Town, 1984).

UNPUBLISHED PAPERS

HARRIS, B. J., 'Foreign Aid, Capital Investment and Migrant Labour' (paper presented at African Studies Association meeting, New Orleans, Louisiana, November 1985).
KLIEST, T. J., 'The Smallholder Cotton Sector in Swaziland', Research paper No. 2 (Kwaluseni: Social Science Research Unit, University of Swaziland, 1982).

Index